# CONSTRUCTIVIST STRATEGIES
## for
## Teaching
## English Language
## Learners

*For my mother, Gert Adelman, whose memory*
*guides my way, And for Joel McCullough, who walks beside me,*
*no matter how difficult the path may be.*

*—Sharon*


*For my mom, Jean Carter, whose desire to learn became my*
*desire and whose belief in me became my belief.*
*For Denise, whose wisdom, guidance, and compassion helped me*
*through many difficult times and whose influence*
*made me a stronger woman.*

*—Trina*

# CONSTRUCTIVIST STRATEGIES for Teaching English Language Learners



Sharon Adelman Reyes ❦ Trina Lynn Vallone

CORWIN PRESS
A SAGE Company
Thousand Oaks, CA 91320

KH

*For information:*

Corwin Press
A SAGE Company
2455 Teller Road
Thousand Oaks, California 91320
www.corwinpress.com

SAGE Ltd.
1 Oliver's Yard
55 City Road
London EC1Y 1SP
United Kingdom

SAGE India Pvt. Ltd.
B 1/I 1 Mohan Cooperative
    Industrial Area
Mathura Road, New Delhi 110 044
India

SAGE Asia-Pacific Pte. Ltd.
33 Pekin Street #02–01
Far East Square
Singapore 048763

Printed in the United States of America.

*Library of Congress Cataloging-in-Publication Data*

Reyes, Sharon Adelman.
Constructivist strategies for teaching English language learners/Sharon Adelman Reyes, Trina Lynn Vallone.
        p. cm.
Includes bibliographical references and index.
ISBN 978-1-4129-3686-6 (cloth)
ISBN 978-1-4129-3687-3 (pbk.)

    1. English language—Study and teaching—United States—Foreign speakers. 2. Second language acquisition—United States. 3. Limited English proficient students—Education—United States. 4. Constructivism (Education) I. Vallone, Trina Lynn. II. Title.

PE1128.A2R4725 2008
428.0071—dc22                                             2007033093

This book is printed on acid-free paper.

07  08  09  10  11  10  9  8  7  6  5  4  3  2  1

| | |
|---|---|
| *Acquisitions Editor:* | Rachel Livsey |
| *Managing Editor:* | Dan Alpert |
| *Editorial Assistants:* | Phyllis Cappello, Tatiana Richards |
| *Production Editor:* | Jenn Reese |
| *Copy Editor:* | Jane Haenel |
| *Typesetter:* | C&M Digitals (P) Ltd. |
| *Proofreader:* | Victoria Reed-Castro |
| *Indexer:* | Naomi Linzer |
| *Cover Designer:* | Tracy Miller |
| *Graphic Designer:* | Karine Hovsepian |

9/3/09

# Foreword

Sharon Adelman Reyes and Trina Lynn Vallone remind us in *Constructivist Strategies for Teaching English Language Learners* about what works in schooling, not just for English Language Learners (ELLs), but for all learners: Students will learn and progress academically when instruction connects with their prior knowledge, scaffolds meaning so that students can understand curriculum content, affirms their identities, and extends their knowledge of language far beyond everyday conversational fluency. When these conditions are in place, students engage with reading and writing and construct knowledge in ways that fuel sustained learning.

The authors contrast the critical constructivist approach they advocate on the basis of the research with the didactic approach that dominates curriculum and instruction for low-income students. American education has probably always been characterized by a pedagogical divide where low-income students receive instruction based on drill and practice while more affluent students are stimulated in the classroom to use their cognitive abilities to a much greater extent. However, the increase in standardized testing ushered in by the No Child Left Behind Act has dramatically increased the pedagogical divide as a result of the punitive sanctions imposed on schools that fail to demonstrate "adequate yearly progress." For a variety of reasons that have nothing to do with the quality of instruction, schools serving low-income students are much less likely to demonstrate adequate yearly progress than schools serving affluent students.

As one illustration of how far this legislation has drifted from its mantra of "scientifically based research," consider the fact that ELL students who have been in the United States for one year are required to take the same standardized tests as native speakers of English despite the fact that research from around the world has shown that at least five years is required for ELL students to catch up academically to native speakers (see Cummins, Brown, & Sayers, 2007). A major reason why five or more years is typically required is that ELL students are attempting to catch up to a moving target—native speakers who are continuing to expand their vocabulary knowledge and literacy skills. ELL student performance is interpreted as reflecting instructional effectiveness (or lack thereof), with background factors such as poverty and length of residence viewed as irrelevant. Thus, No Child Left Behind attributes the lower performance of ELL students who have been learning English for only one year to deficient instruction and penalizes teachers and schools for failing to do the impossible (raise ELL students' scores to grade level within one year of learning English). In the case of ELL students, and of low-income students in general No Child Left Behind represents an extremely efficient formula for demoralizing teachers and dissipating student effort.

In this context, *Constructivist Strategies for Teaching English Language Learners* represents a breath of fresh air. It highlights the limitations of teacher-centered didactic approaches that confine students to passive roles in the learning environment. These approaches are simply not consistent with the scientific evidence on how people learn. The National Research Council volume written by John Bransford, Ann Brown, and Rodney Cocking, *How People Learn* (2000), synthesized the research evidence on this topic in unequivocal terms: effective learning environments enable learners to build on their prior knowledge, develop deep understandings that promote the transfer of learning across contexts, and take ownership of the learning process through efficient use of a range of learning strategies. If new skills and information must be taught in a way that taps into students' prior knowledge, then one-size-fits-all didactic or scripted approaches that essentially ignore the diversity of student experience are unscientific, despite their protestations to the contrary.

The principles articulated by Bransford and his colleagues are entirely consistent with social constructivist approaches to learning and these principles provide the foundation for much of the classroom practice described and advocated in this volume. Reyes and Vallone, however, extend social constructivist approaches into the specific context of ELL instruction, thereby expanding the scope of this pedagogical orientation beyond the "generic" learner. The classroom visitations that we experience in this book bring home to us just how powerful constructivist approaches can be in engaging learners actively in knowledge building. Unfortunately, under No Child Left Behind, low-income students experience constructivist instruction far less frequently than their more affluent peers.

Clearly, the pedagogical divide reflects patterns of societal power relations. There is no way that Bill Gates, George Bush, or Bill and Hillary Clinton (or most of the readers of this volume) would have tolerated having their children in the scripted classroom environments that low-income children increasingly experience. So what relevance do societal power relations have for the ways in which teachers orchestrate their instruction? Reyes and Vallone are clear that effective instruction for low-income and

ELL students requires a *critical* constructivist, or transformative, approach. If learning is to be effective, and understanding deep rather than superficial, then literature, content textbooks, and media articles require not just literal comprehension, but critical analysis. Students need to learn how to read between the lines rather than just internalize the surface structure.

This orientation is crucial to the future of democracy. Critical literacy is all that stands between genuine democratic participation and an oligarchy of the rich and powerful. Money buys media, and media manufactures consent. Individuals without critical literacy have no defense or immunization against these increasingly subtle and pervasive forms of social propaganda. Thus, education for citizenship must teach students to "read" how language and other symbolic resources are employed in the service of power. This power can be either coercive or collaborative—coercive when it is used to the detriment of individuals groups, or countries, collaborative when it is used to increase the mutual power of partners or participants in a learning environment.

An obvious example is the extent to which ELL students' home languages are welcomed into the classroom and school as cognitive resources that contribute to students' learning. There is a clear rationale for encouraging newcomer ELL students to use their home languages. Students' prior knowledge is encoded in their home languages and therefore their home languages are clearly related to their learning of English and other academic content. Despite the obvious rationale for building on students' prior knowledge that is encoded in their home language, there are relatively few "mainstream" or ESL classrooms across North America where students are encouraged to use their home languages as tools for learning. Whether it is school policy or an individual decision on the part of teachers, this exclusionary orientation is clearly ideological rather than pedagogical. It reflects societal patterns of power relations that consign immigrant communities and children (and their languages and cultures) to inferior status. A teacher who pursues a transformative or critical constructivist path will likely challenge this exclusion of students' prior knowledge from the classroom both because it violates what we know from the cognitive psychology literature about how people learn and also because it reinforces societal patterns of coercive relations of power.

In societal contexts of coercive relations of power (which unfortunately characterize the vast majority of societies), the affirmation of ELL students' identity in the classroom inevitably entails a challenge by the teacher to coercive relations of power. Teachers and administrators who choose to take note of the scientific evidence about how people learn and are willing to challenge misconceptions and prejudice in the broader society will find in this book an inspiring vision and clear guidelines for implementing instruction that creates contexts of empowerment not just for students but also for educators.

—Jim Cummins

*Toronto, April 2007*

## REFERENCES

Bransford, J. D., Brown, A. L., & Cocking, R. R. (2000). *How people learn: Brain, mind, experience, and school.* Washington, DC: National Academy Press.

Cummins, J., Brown, K., & Sayers, D. (2007). *Literacy, technology, and diversity: Teaching for success in changing times.* Boston: Allyn & Bacon.

# Contents

Preface                                                     vii

About the Authors                                            xv

About the Contributor                                       xvi


**Chapter 1. Perspectives in Second Language**
**Acquisition and Learning**                                  1
    Language Acquisition                   2
    Language and Cognitive Development      5
    Language and Academic Content           7
    Language and Culture                    9

**Chapter 2. Program Models for Second Language Learners**   15
    Additive Versus Subtractive Program Models   16
    Mainstream With Modifications           17
    English as a Second Language (ESL)      17
    Transitional Program of Bilingual Instruction (TPI)   20
    Maintenance                             20
    Submersion                              20
    Submersion Versus Immersion             21
    Immersion                               21
    Structured English Immersion (SEI)      24
    Integrated                              24
    Enrichment                              25
    Newcomer Programs                       25
    Bilingual Whole Language and Beyond     26

**Chapter 3. Perspectives in Constructivism**               27
    Overview of Constructivist Perspectives   31
    Cognitive Constructivist Perspective    31
    Social Constructivist Perspective       33
    Guiding Principles for Constructivist Classrooms   36
    Concluding Thoughts                     38

**Chapter 4. Constructivist Practice for English Language Learners**  39
   Families and Communities  41
   Instructional Practice in Language Arts  42
   Instructional Practice in the Content Areas  53
   Assessment  58
   Summary of Suggested Practice for
      Constructivist Second Language Classrooms  61

**Chapter 5. Perspectives in Critical Pedagogy**  65
   Critical Pedagogy: A Different Perspective  66
   Critical Pedagogy: Guiding Principles  73
   Identity Formation in Critical Classrooms  79

**Chapter 6. Constructivist Classroom Connections:**
**The Great Second-Grade Bug Invasion**  81
   Guidelines for Practice  102

**Chapter 7. Constructivist Classroom Connections:**
**Intermediate Newcomers Meet the Universal Chicken**  107
   *Barbara Nykiel-Herbert*
   Guidelines for Practice  132

**Chapter 8. Critical Classroom Connections:**
**Eighth Graders Face a Fence on the Border**  135
   Concluding Thoughts  165

**Chapter 9. Toward Critical Constructivist Practice**
**With Second Language Learners**  167

**Appendix**  173

**Glossary**  177

**References**  181

**Index**  187

# Preface

## EDUCATIONAL EQUITY, DEMOCRACY, AND THE EDUCATION OF ENGLISH LANGUAGE LEARNERS

> Stepping out from the school building through the door that led to the mobile unit left an impression. The main building was warm and cheerful with students' work hung nicely on the walls and the smell of crayons drifting through the halls. Any student would feel safe and valued in this atmosphere. This stood in stark contrast to the mobile unit that housed the ESL and Bilingual students. This is the unit to which one was directed to work with the ESL and "non-language" learners. The unit was rusted on the outside and appeared to be in ill repair. The image of this mobile juxtaposed against the crisp, autumn sky will forever be etched in my memory. My first impression of this district's ESL/Bilingual program was a direct result of the environment in which the students spend their instructional time—**the mobile unit**.

These are the words a university student used to describe the school in which she completed her clinical hours. While the situation for many school districts is better than the one described above, for some the situation is far worse. Research indicates a severe shortage of teachers qualified to work with English Language Learners (ELLs). Although the population of bilingual students is growing exponentially, few teachers are available who possess the skills and preparation to teach them.

According to the U.S. Census Bureau (2003), the nation's foreign-born population accounts for 12 percent of the population. The number of children ages five to seventeen who spoke a language other than English at home more than doubled between 1979 and 2004 (U.S. Department of Education [NCES], 2007). This population trend is reflected in our schools and classrooms. Yet, the National Teacher Recruitment Clearing House (2003) reports a severe shortage of bilingual and ESL teachers throughout the nation. Seventy-three percent of students in need of bilingual and/or ESL services are not receiving them.

Given the growth of the student population for whom English is not a native language and the corresponding lack of qualified teachers, educators are in need of resources that can help bridge the gap. This book is designed to do just that. It is a hands-on guide that uses constructivist mainstream classroom curriculum as a starting point for practicing teachers. Monolingual teachers (as well as teachers who may be bilingual themselves but are not prepared to teach bilingually) are finding themselves unfortuitously placed in ESL or bilingual classrooms. Although they may be skilled teachers, they may not be prepared for teaching the students with whom they now share a classroom. This book addresses the needs of these teachers for methods and strategies based on both sound theory and best instructional practice. It uses constructivist mainstream classroom curriculum as a starting point and then adds modifications to make content more accessible to ELLs. It challenges teachers and students alike to become intellectually engaged in not only the classroom curriculum but also the world around them through attention to principles of critical pedagogy. The practices recommended in this book flow from the authors' premise that equity is the foundation upon which quality education for ELLs is based.

## SHARON'S DINNER STORY: AN IMAGINARY VIGNETTE

To understand just what is meant by equity, let's look in on Sharon's dinner meeting.

> Tom, Katie, and Bob are going to Sharon's house to discuss a school project. The meeting is set for the dinner hour. This poses a problem for Sharon, due to her lack of culinary skills. To solve her dilemma, Sharon orders a deluxe pizza divided into twelve large pieces. When the guests arrive and sit down around the dinner table, Katie declares that she is not hungry; she normally eats dinner at a much later hour. Still, who can resist a pizza? Katie slowly savors one piece while Tom, Bob, and Sharon each devour three large slices. With two pieces left on the table, all retire to the living room to discuss the business at hand. Several hours later, the guests return to the dining room, where Sharon has placed a fruit bowl for dessert. From the kitchen, where she is brewing coffee, Sharon hears a lively debate ensue. It appears that it is approaching Katie's customary dinner hour, and she is now hungry. As she lays claim to the remaining two pieces of pizza, Tom cautions her to wait. He tells her that everyone may want more pizza, and since there are four people and two slices, she may have one-half a slice, like everyone else. As what was initially a friendly debate becomes more heated, Sharon is summoned from the kitchen to intervene.

What should she do? If she wants to treat everyone equally she will bring in the pizza cutter and divide the remaining two slices. However, if she wants to be fair, she will give the two slices to Katie who never really had her dinner. The question is, what is more appropriate to the situation, equality or fairness, equality or equity? Surprisingly for Tom and Bob, equality is not always fair. But for Katie, who has historically been a late diner, fairness (equity) is more important if she wants to go to bed with a full stomach.

As frivolous as this imaginary vignette may be, it serves to illustrate a powerful educational concept: equality is not always fair. Equality of the moment may not translate to equality of outcomes. Equity, however, has equality of outcomes as a goal.

## LISA ENTERS FIRST GRADE

Let's apply the concept of equity to an educational context.

It is the first day of the school year, and Lisa is entering first grade along with twenty-six other students. Lisa, however, is the only learner entering the classroom with an exceptionality; she is learning disabled. Her IEP (Individual Educational Plan) calls for one hour per day of literacy development assistance from a certified special education teacher. This assistance may occur in the form of a pull-out or a push-in program, but the certified special education teacher must implement it. The school will consequently need to spend more money on the education of Lisa than on the other students in the class. If the school were to spend the same (equal) amounts on all twenty-seven children, Lisa would receive educational resources equal to the others and would not receive literacy assistance from a specialized teacher. Would this be fair? Of course not! Lisa needs the extra support that can be provided only by a certified specialist, and this support will require more resources. This is educational equity, for investing more in the education of Lisa will promote equality of educational outcomes; that is, all first graders will be ready for second grade next year.

What goals do the classroom and special education teachers have for Lisa? Is their primary concern Lisa's academic achievement, or are they more concerned with instilling in the rest of the class an appreciation of children with exceptionalities?

While the latter goal may be a fine one, the bottom line in education is the academic achievement of students, so we could reasonably expect that the first goal is primary. Furthermore, we might assume that Lisa's teachers believe that the other students will have more favorable opinions of Lisa if they see that she is able to participate fully in classroom activities.

This may seem like common sense. The reader may even wonder why we are bothering to make such an obvious point. We do so only for the purpose of analogy. We know there is a tremendous national achievement gap between African American and white students and between Latino and white students, yet many schools put forth their biggest efforts to respond to diversity by fostering cultural appreciation through activities such as hosting ethnic fairs and festivals. While we have nothing against such events, we suggest that investments of time and/or money are better spent addressing the achievement gap, or as Gloria Ladson-Billings (2006) has alternatively named it, the education debt. Just as it is more important for Lisa to have instructional support than for her classmates to appreciate her exceptionality, it is more important to students of color and ELLs to have a quality education than it is for others to appreciate their cultural heritage. Cultural appreciation does not necessarily imply quality academic education or educational equity. Culturally responsive pedagogy, "an approach based on using students' identities and backgrounds as meaningful sources of their education" (Nieto, 2004, p. 402), is more relevant to academic achievement and goes further in giving students the resources to enable their success. Furthermore, it provides firmer ground on which cultural appreciation can flourish.

## EDUCATIONAL EQUITY AND ENGLISH LANGUAGE LEARNERS

Due to the relationship between socioeconomic level, material resources, and immigrant status, significant numbers of students who live in educationally underserved communities are also struggling to learn the language of the majority culture. Such students face tremendous challenges in our schools. Although Latino children may form the largest numeric population of such students, they are by no means the only students in this situation. The National Clearinghouse for English Language Acquisition notes that U.S. students speak over 460 native languages, including Arabic, Armenian, Cantonese, French, Haitian Creole, Hindi, Hmong, Japanese, Khmer, Korean, Lao, Mandarin, Navajo, Polish, Portuguese, Punjabi, Russian, Serbo-Croatian, Tagalog, Urdu, and Vietnamese (Crawford, 2004). For these students, educational equity is a multifaceted issue, for it demands attention not only to the material and financial resources needed for a quality education but to the need for a strong second language pedagogy and curriculum as well. But exactly what does such a pedagogy and corresponding curriculum look like? We propose the following components as necessary for educational equity for ELLs:

- Access to oral (communicative) English language development
- Access to English language literacy and academic content
- Opportunities for cognitive development during academic instruction in English
- Access to literacy, academic content, and cognitive development in the native language
- Access to understanding and functioning in the new culture
- Maintenance of cultural and linguistic heritage

Students will be naturally propelled toward learning their second language in an English dominant society. The desire to communicate with others and the allure of the media may be even more powerful motivators than the school curriculum! However, whether ELLs acquire sufficient academic English and English literacy skills to compete with their English dominant peers is far from assured, nor are cognitive development and positive identity construction guaranteed.

When it is possible, native language instruction may play a pivotal role in the education of ELLs. Not only does it foster academic achievement and cognitive development, but it also uses the child's first language (L1) as a bridge to the second language (L2), and it may contribute to positive family dynamics and self-esteem (Wong Fillmore, 1991). Nonetheless, monolingual (English) teachers need not view their lack of bilingualism as an obstacle to providing their students with an equitable education. Constructivist pedagogy with modifications for language learning, coupled with a linguistically sensitive and culturally responsive approach that validates native language and culture, can provide a quality educational experience for their students.

But what exactly is constructivism? Constructivist learning theory focuses on the process of knowing and the nature of cognition. This contemporary view of learning postulates that people actively construct new knowledge in an effort to make sense of their surroundings. In this cognitive process, prior knowledge gained through both casual experience and formal instruction is built upon in an effort to achieve greater understanding. The focus in constructivist theory is on deep understanding as opposed to rote knowing and on the reflective transfer of knowledge to other subject matter and to life (Feuerstein, 1980). This emphasis on the prior knowledge of the learner is completely compatible with linguistic sensitivity and cultural responsiveness and thus can make an important contribution to educational equity for ELLs.

## DEMOCRACY AND EQUITY

We've spent time talking about equity. Now let's talk about another loaded word: democracy. In his 1916 seminal work *Democracy and Education: An Introduction to the Philosophy of Education,* Dewey wrote extensively about this concept in relation to education. Many of us (educators) believe that you cannot have a true democracy without an educated populace, hence that goal requires universal, compulsory, and free education. (We even go as far as to suggest that every citizen, no matter what they do in life, should have some type of postsecondary education.) Why? And just what is democracy? The *Merriam-Webster's* dictionary defines democracy as a "government by the people." How can "the people" govern with justice and fairness if they are not literate, critical thinkers who use reading, writing, and thought to reflect on and shape their world? We suggest that literacy and critical thought are the *basic skills* needed by *all* students, including ELLs.

*Is education necessary for democracy?* If literacy and critical thought are basic to meaningful democracy, and if these ought to be the basic skills learned by children and adolescents in schools, the relationship between democracy and education becomes clear. Universal, compulsory, free, and high-quality education is indeed necessary for a vibrant democracy.

*Is equity necessary for education to be democratic?* In other words, is equity necessary for education to support a government by the people, of *all* the people? We suggest that, without equity, education is not fair and therefore does not support a democracy.

*Can we have a healthy democracy, then, if we do not have educational equity?* If the response to this question is that without educational equity there is no true democracy, or that the democracy is then seriously flawed, the role of the educator becomes significant, and the role of the educator of ELLs becomes crucial.

In subsequent chapters, we will explore the role of reading, writing, and critical thinking in a democracy, literacy as empowerment, and the implications regarding teachers of ELLs. We will posit that reading, writing, and critical thinking are the cornerstones of democracy, that literacy is empowerment, and that all teachers should be critical literacy educators. We further propose that educational equity is fundamental to a vibrant democracy and that the role of the ELL educator is therefore foundational to the fabric of our society. As ELL educators ourselves, we do not take this charge lightly; hence, this book.

Our beliefs have been constructed out of our own educational experiences and have been reinforced through our own critical literacy development. Issues of democracy and equity have played themselves out in our own lives and have been instrumental in shaping our own educational philosophy and practice. Although our lives have taken different paths and thus have different contours, they have led us to the same place. We have become active advocates for educational equity for students who are ELLs.

Sharon taught elementary education in the public school system of a major Midwestern city for twelve years. Much of that time was spent working with ELLs. She left the classroom and spent four years as an elementary public school principal. Frustration with the lack of responsiveness to issues of educational equity led her to pursue a PhD in Curriculum Design with an emphasis on multicultural and bilingual education. She worked as an educational consultant as she completed her doctoral program and, as a single parent, continued to guide her own two children through public education, much of it in bilingual programs. She is currently an assistant professor at Loyola University Chicago, where she is developing and teaching programs that prepare educators to work with ELLs.

Trina taught a number of years in an elementary school before obtaining a Masters degree in Reading, as well as state certification as a Reading Specialist with a credential in ESL (English as a Second Language). She is presently a doctoral candidate in curriculum and instruction. Trina is currently an assistant professor and teaches at Trinity Christian College, a small liberal arts institution, where she instructs preservice teachers in the area of literacy, content area reading, general classroom methods, Foundations in ESL/Bilingual Education, and Cross Cultural Studies.

Just as this book was created through the authors' knowledge construction processes after many years of experience in a variety of different roles in the educational arena, so have you, the reader, brought your own unique life experiences with you to the printed page. We trust that you will, in good constructivist fashion, compare, contrast, interpret, and fuse your own lived experiences with those found in these pages. After all, this book is about *you* (the educator) and the important and critical difference *you* can make in the lives of your students and, consequently, in our world.

## ACKNOWLEDGMENTS

Our book reflects the contributions that many others have made to our lives and to our work.

Sharon acknowledges with gratitude Dr. Irma Olmedo, who mentored her through academia from her early days as a doctoral student to the present and who has become a dear friend, colleague, and role model. She acknowledges with appreciation Jim Crawford for his confidence in her ability to think and to write both critically and creatively. She thanks Dr. Priscilla Hartwig whose thoughtful commentary helped guide the early conception of this book but, more important, whose strength of character and unfailing integrity proved an unending inspiration as we forged ahead with our manuscript. Thanks, also, to Sharon's beloved family across the ocean, "Pepe" (José) Morejón Morejón, Mirta Jiménez Pacheco, and their lovely daughters Jeidy and Jeilyn, who welcomed her into their family and into their community and in so doing provided unending sustenance.

Trina sincerely thanks Rod Parker, whose patient editing, gentle encouragement, and steady confidence gave her the courage to write. She is also grateful to the people with whom she works each day. Dr. Hoekstra, without hesitation, gave her the time and the space to develop her ideas. She also thanks Angela Bowman, Lori Scrementi, Patricia Taliefero-Griffith, and John Hoogewerf, who gave her support and made her professional life an oasis as she worked on the manuscript. Last, she acknowledges her friends and her family who have stood beside her every step of the way.

This book might never have been imagined if it were not for Rachel Livsey, former acquisitions editor at Corwin Press. She devoted much time and energy to help conceptualize this book and provided the feedback necessary to carry it from book proposal to final manuscript. Dan Alpert carried on where Rachel left off. We feel privileged to have worked with such accomplished and visionary professionals and thank them both wholeheartedly for making this book a reality. For assistance in preparing the final draft, we thank Jennifer Mills. Special mention must be given to Tippi Price for her superb research skills.

Finally, we both wish to acknowledge that this book is part of a partnership between us, a partnership that started in 2002 when Trina enrolled in a graduate course that Sharon was teaching as part of a sequence leading to a state ESL credential. Little did we know at the time that over the years our relationship would grow into a collaborative authorship and a deep friendship—one of the wondrous and unexpected surprises that life has to offer when the human spirit is reciprocally nurtured.

The contributions of the following reviewers are gratefully acknowledged:

Thomas Farrell, Associate Professor, Department of Applied Linguistics, Brock University, St. Catharines, Ontario, Canada

Roberta Glaser, Assistant Superintendent, St. Johns Public Schools, St. Johns, MI

Janet Jones, Executive Director, Mead School District, Mead, WA

Bruce Marlowe, School of Education, Roger Williams University, Bristol, RI

Timothy Reagan, Visiting Professor of Education, Central Connecticut State University, New Britain, CT

# About the Authors

 **Sharon Adelman Reyes** holds a PhD in Curriculum Design from the University of Illinois at Chicago where she specialized in Multicultural and Bilingual Education. A recipient of the Kohl International Prize for Exemplary Teaching, she was an elementary school teacher for twelve years and an elementary school principal for four years prior to beginning her university career. She is currently an assistant professor at Loyola University Chicago, where she prepares future teachers of bilingual children and adolescents. Dr. Reyes has published in peer-reviewed journals in the field of Multicultural and Bilingual Education, has presented in her field locally, nationally, and internationally, and has served as an educational consultant in school districts throughout Illinois. Her current research agenda includes constructivist practice with English Language Learners (ELLs), bilingual/ bicultural identity construction in schooling, and the preparation of teachers and education leaders for diverse classrooms and educational contexts.

 **Trina Lynn Vallone** holds an MA in Reading and is a certified Reading Specialist with an ESL credential. She has spent several years researching multicultural education and language acquisition. Ms. Vallone has presented at conferences, where she has examined topics such as multi-cultural education, critical pedagogy, best practice for English Language Learners (ELLs), writers' workshops, content area reading, and working with struggling readers. Ms. Vallone taught primary-aged children before becoming an assistant professor at Trinity Christian College in Palos Heights, Illinois, where she teaches Methods of Teaching Reading, Foundations in ESL/Bilingual Education, Cross-Cultural Studies, and Reading in the Content Area. Currently, Trina is a doctoral candidate in Curriculum and Instruction at Aurora University in Aurora, Illinois.

# About the Contributor

 **Barbara Nykiel-Herbert,** a native of Poland, currently teaches linguistics at the English Department at Youngstown State University in Youngstown, Ohio. A former TESOL teacher and teacher-educator focused on language and literacy, as well as an author of children's books, she has worked in Poland, Ukraine, South Africa, Swaziland, Taiwan, and with refugee communities in the United States.

# 1 Perspectives in Second Language Acquisition and Learning

**Y**ou are about to embark on an intimate journey inside three classrooms where students are engaged in learning in their second language. You will be immersed in the world of each classroom through engaging narratives filled with authentic dialogue and rich description. Jill's primary-grade students explore the realm of insects with both scientific acuity and second-grade hilarity as they simultaneously learn a second language. Maria's intermediate students mix poignant stories of survival in the political struggles of their native land with stories of life in their new country as they learn to read and write in English. Monica prepares eighth-grade Latino students for the academic rigor of high school through a study of immigration that is close to their lived experiences and to their hearts. Although these three teachers are working in different content areas and with children of different grade levels, they all have in common a pedagogical and curricular approach based upon sound principles of second language acquisition and learning. The purpose of this chapter is to provide an understanding of these principles so that the strategies used by the three featured teachers are understood as they are revealed in the subsequent narratives and corresponding guidelines. To do so, we first turn to the literature on child second language acquisition.

## LANGUAGE ACQUISITION

Perez and Torres-Guzman (2002, p. 33) note that "language acquisition is one of the most important developmental tasks" faced by children. Virtually every child is successful in this endeavor when it comes to learning a first language, and when given the opportunity, most children can learn a second or even multiple languages. In fact, literature on child language acquisition that indicates children are able to become not only bilingual but also multilingual is virtually uncontested (Andersson, 1977; Hakuta, 1986). There is less agreement, however, over the optimal age at which to learn a second language, the amount of time it takes to become orally and academically proficient in a second language, and the instructional approaches and models that best support second language development.

Although it is generally agreed that children who acquire a second language at an early age have a greater likelihood of achieving native-like pronunciation, evidence indicates that fluency can occur with children beginning at any age, provided cognitive development continues in the first language. Children between the ages of eight and twelve are, in fact, said to have the edge over younger learners (ages four through seven) in second language learning due to their more advanced cognitive structures (Collier, 1989). Yet, some crucial factors that apply to younger learners could possibly counteract this advantage for the older learner: motivation; a school learning environment more likely to promote active, communicative involvement (Reyes, 1998); and lack of the language inhibition that becomes more prevalent as children reach adolescence. Jill's second-grade learners illustrate these points. They exhibit little, if any, inhibitions in speaking in their second language, perhaps because they are more interested in butterfly eggs than they are in the subjunctive tense. Jill focuses their attention on insects, not on grammar. Bugs, after all, are of inherent interest to many seven- and eight-year-olds.

Age is not the only factor that can impact language learning. Proficiency in the first language and cognitive development are also significant (Collier, 1989). Research indicates that it is crucial for children to develop cognitively through their first language until the age when first language development is more or less complete, usually at age twelve. Because in the United States academic instruction is given predominantly in English, student academic success is dependent upon the ability to communicate in that language, both verbally and in written form. As children advance through the grade levels, academic content becomes less context embedded and more context reduced (Cummins, 1994); that is, the content becomes less dependent on contextual clues and hands-on activities. There is less likelihood that teachers will bring bugs into the classroom for hands-on inquiry. Thus, English Language Learners (ELLs) are at a tremendous disadvantage. Often their lack of experience with the English language is misinterpreted as lack of academic ability, hence issues of language learning and acquisition become intertwined with issues of cognition and academic achievement. A child with an earlier base in a context-embedded school and second language experiences may well be at an advantage in our current educational framework. We suggest that such an educational base can be provided through a constructivist learning environment when the appropriate learning modifications are made. Insect study is only one small example of how this can be accomplished.

Just as lack of experience with the English language can be misinterpreted as lack of academic ability, so, too, can communicative levels of oral English be misinterpreted as representing equivalent levels of academic English. Cummins (1994) suggests that the Basic Interpersonal Communicative Skills (BICS) needed for everyday communication are quite different from the Cognitive/Academic Language Proficiency (CALP) needed to excel in school (Cummins, 1981). In Jill's second-grade classroom, we can see BICS at work, whereas in Monica's eighth-grade classroom the focus is on CALP. The majority of Monica's students are fluent speakers of English, yet their academic skills in English are still immature. This may result because Spanish is the language of the home or because it is the first language (L1) of the parents. Either way, instructional considerations are merited. Monica provides supports to her students as they acquire academic English, such as modeling and peer editing. She understands that, while BICS can develop quickly, students may need between five and nine years to reach a level of CALP equivalent to that of their peers for whom English is a native language. This is significant in terms of school expectations for student learning. When educators do not understand the length of time needed for students to acquire CALP, they may assume, in error, that children are not advancing at developmentally appropriate rates. Unfortunately, inappropriate student placement may be the result of inappropriate educator expectations. Developmental program models for ELLs serve to ensure that education is equitable because they allow sufficient time for second language proficiency to develop before students are expected to function predominately in English.

Two other concepts remain central to a discussion of second language development in children. The first is the difference between simultaneous and sequential bilingualism. Students who have been exposed to two or more languages before the age of three are considered simultaneous bilinguals; those who have been introduced to a second language after the age of three are considered sequential bilinguals (McLaughlin, Blanchard, & Osani, 1995). Jill's two-way bilingual classroom is composed of a mix of

4 ● Constructivist Strategies for Teaching English Language Learners

simultaneous bilinguals, Spanish sequential bilinguals, and English sequential bilinguals. The second distinction is between second language acquisition and second language learning. The use of a second language in a natural environment without formal instruction is considered second language acquisition, whereas "the process of formal language education where one aspect of the grammar is introduced at a time, and systematic feedback with error correction is provided" is considered second language learning (Diaz, 1983, p. 29).

Although the literature distinguishes between second language learning and second language acquisition, the distinction is not as clear in real classroom life, as we can see in the case of Jill's second-grade, two-way bilingual classroom, which integrates language and content learning. No formal language instruction is given on a regular basis; rather, students begin to use the second language (whether English or Spanish) in much the same way as they acquired their first language. For this reason, immersion programs tend to begin when children are quite young, preschool age if possible. Yet, these same children are involved in sequential bilingualism, and so at times they may require more formal language instruction to internalize more difficult linguistic concepts in their second language. Likewise, older children who are involved in formal language learning situations may have the opportunity to live abroad, where they can immerse themselves in their second language. Continuous exposure to the second language and its use for communicative purposes in authentic circumstances may imitate language acquisition. It may therefore be more helpful and practical to think of the difference between language acquisition and language learning as a continuum, with K–12 second language students falling somewhere between each of these extremes.

Constructivist practice for ELLs resonates with language development approaches that are focused on using language for meaningful purposes as opposed to more traditional methods of language learning that focus on grammar, language drills, and direct instruction. This will become increasingly clear when the reader encounters the classrooms of Jill and Maria, where second language development is promoted through methods and strategies that approximate first language acquisition. Here we will see classrooms in which all children are bilingual, whether simultaneous or sequential, and where language development occurs through natural means supplemented by occasional focused elements of more formal learning strategies. As would be expected, in both of these classrooms rates of second language acquisition differ for each student. Hakuta (1986) notes that some of the variables that determine how rapidly children acquire a second language are personality, social factors, and individual difference in verbal ability. Saville-Troike (1981) cites attitudinal factors and motivation as playing a major role in child second language learning. However, insufficient information exists for the creation of viable theories in at least two of these areas: motivation and personality (Van Groenou, 1993). All children are unique, and their life circumstances, though mediated by home, school, and society, are their own. Likewise, their roads to bilingualism are their own. The important point here is that they must be provided with an educational environment conducive to developing bilingualism. In the upcoming chapters, Jill, Maria, and Monica model how this can be done.

## LANGUAGE AND COGNITIVE DEVELOPMENT

Research indicates that there is no significant evidence of adverse effects on the speech and language development of children taught in bilingual classrooms. In fact, education for ELLs that incorporates native language instruction has been found to be advantageous to academic achievement (Rolstad, Mahoney, & Glass, 2005; Slavin & Cheung, 2005). Benefits to bilinguals include enhanced cognitive skills, superior developmental patterns, an ability to employ necessary cognitive and social strategies, the use of situational clues to understand what is happening, enhanced abilities in divergent thinking, an ability to think flexibly and abstractly about language (metalinguistic awareness), the enjoyment of linguistic possibilities, the early emergence of the idea that there is more than one way of saying the same thing, and the transfer of skills and knowledge from one language to the other (Van Groenou, 1993). In fact, a case can be made for a positive relationship among academic, cognitive, linguistic, and metalinguistic abilities. The active use (as opposed to passive exposure) of two different language systems causes children to compare and contrast aspects of the two languages and to put cognitive effort into separating them, thus strengthening cognitive as well as linguistic and metalinguistic ability. In the classrooms of Jill, Maria, and Monica, we see bilingual students who are simultaneously and actively engaged in both learning content and developing language. These students appear to be enjoying and benefiting from the learning environment in these second language classrooms. These portraits are not of ELLs on the verge of educational failure! We suggest that the evident joy in learning is due, at least in part, to the constructivist second language environment in which it occurs and to the high value placed upon bilingualism. Jill and Monica are able to model fully fluent bilingualism. Maria is able to model respect for bilingualism.

Second language acquisition research has suggested that the role of the first language (L1) is crucial to the development of proficiency in the second (L2) (Collier, 1989). This finding underpins one of two arguments central to advocacy for bilingual education. According to Cummins's (1978) interdependence hypothesis, the development of the learner's L1 will have a direct impact on future acquisition of the learner's L2 and, further, will make possible the transfer of knowledge across the learner's two languages. In the United States, there is no question of the dominance of English. Native speakers of English usually have numerous opportunities to develop their L1 proficiency. This is not the case for ELLs. Immigrant languages have been wiped out in the United States at a faster rate than anywhere else on earth (Hakuta, 1986). We can no longer depend on the home to be a site of ongoing development in the native language. Parents may mistakenly believe it is better to communicate with their children in the language in which they are least proficient. They may not understand that the greatest linguistic gift they can give to their children is the gift of fully developed language proficiency, that the language itself does not matter. It is the *development of a primary language,* whatever that language may be, that is most important.

The second set of conditions necessary for the linguistic, metalinguistic, academic, and cognitive advantages of bilingualism to accrue is based on Cummins's (1987) threshold hypothesis. This theory states that a learner needs to attain a high level of native language proficiency to achieve a high level of proficiency in a second language and, furthermore, that the attainment of high levels of bilingual language proficiency in turn paves the way for maximum academic and cognitive benefit. Although here we can see the importance of first language development in the home through conversational (communicative) skills, according to this theory academic language skills must also be developed for maximum benefits to accrue (Lindholm, 1992). This distinction is similar to the one made by Cummins (1994) regarding BICS and CALP. Thus, respect for the native language of the learner optimally needs to be coupled with continuing opportunities for academic language development in that same language. Yet we know that schools often do not provide this opportunity, sometimes due to philosophy and sometimes due to a lack of resources. When this happens, teachers are left to address the gap. In upcoming chapters, we will illustrate how mainstream teachers can address this challenge.

Evidence supporting the hypothesis that children who are learning two languages often demonstrate academic, cognitive, and metalinguistic gains that exceed those of their monolingual peers is both massive and impressive. This mounting pool of evidence is relatively recent and has its origins in the growth of French/English bilingual immersion programs in Quebec, Canada, in the 1960s. English dominant parents wanted to offer their children the possibility of becoming French/English bilinguals in a linguistic environment more natural and effective than that provided by traditional foreign language instruction. The English dominant children were enrolled in a program in which a teacher who was a native French speaker taught the academic content almost exclusively in French. The children developed native-like literacy and linguistic abilities in French with no loss to their native language development. As bilingual immersion programs spread across nations and involved more languages and more children from middle-class backgrounds, research results showing the academic, cognitive, and metalinguistic gains made by program participants continued to mount. This was in stark contrast to past research that may have been seriously flawed and did not control for variables such as class and home educational background. What is important here is that the tide had turned. No longer was bilingualism viewed almost exclusively as a handicap. The way had been paved for research that examined the benefits brought about by bilingualism. Fortunately, although limited, this trend continues. Recent research postulates that bilingualism can even counter some of the cognitive effects of aging (Bialystok & Freedman, 2007). It would be wonderful if we could visit students from the classrooms of Jill, Maria, and Monica sixty years in the future to test this hypothesis. Unfortunately, we will have to leave this to future researchers; perhaps some of the students in your classrooms!

## LANGUAGE AND ACADEMIC CONTENT

The current trend in second language education is based on integrating content and second language instruction. This way of teaching is commonly used for the instruction of both majority and minority language learners in two-way bilingual immersion (also referred to as TWI and sometimes as dual language) programs and for minority language learners in other types of second language classrooms. Language development through content parallels first language acquisition processes and has the added advantage of eliminating the need for a separate realm of instruction devoted exclusively to learning a second language. This principle places linguistics (language acquisition/learning theory) in the background and content in the foreground. The teachers' work, therefore, centers largely on curriculum. Curriculum, however, must be conducive for language development to occur during content instruction in a second language. There are certain guidelines that successful second language teachers seem to follow, and these are illuminated in the classrooms of Jill, Maria, and Monica. If these classrooms seem familiar to the reader who is not an experienced second language teacher, there is a reason. The same guidelines used by outstanding second language educators are often those used by mainstream teachers engaging in constructivist practice.

For example, think about how a young child might learn to tie her own shoes. The parent first demonstrates this skill while explaining what he is doing. The explanation is given in the language shared by parent and child, a language the child is still in the process of developing. The child is not concentrating on learning language, however; she is concentrating on learning how to tie her shoes. She is receiving *comprehensible input* from her parent, that is, language specifically adapted and modified to maximize understanding (Lessow-Hurley, 2005). Because the parent understands that the child will need some time to master both shoe-tying and linguistic skill, he is patient and supportive, thus lowering the child's *affective filter* (linguistic self-consciousness). In effect, at least three things come together to facilitate the child's shoe-tying ability: a context-embedded demonstration, appropriate linguistic support, and a stress-free learning environment.

This type of life-learning readily transfers to classroom contexts. Jill fills her classroom with insects for context-embedded instruction. She modifies her speech so that second language learners receive comprehensible input. She fills her classroom with patience, kindness, and laughter to lower the affective filter. The integration of life-learning with (native) language learning that occurs in home contexts parallels the integration of language learning with content learning in second language classrooms. However, to simultaneously accommodate the needs of both mainstream students and ELLs, instructional techniques must be modified to maximize the accessibility of the curriculum for ELLs. When modifications are made to constructivist practice, the learning experience can be powerful. Second language teachers know that instructional practice must be modified for second language learners when they are engaged in content learning in their L2. Mainstream teachers are familiar with scaffolding (providing supports to the learner until they are no longer needed). The distance between mainstream and second language teachers is not insurmountable; constructivist practice unites both through the medium of curriculum.

Language learning is about curriculum; after all, it is curriculum that drives second language acquisition. Just as Cummins (1978) hypothesizes that knowledge transfers across languages, Bransford and colleagues (2000) hypothesize that knowledge transfers across contexts and that the expert is able to reconstruct this knowledge in different settings. In Jill's classroom, knowledge gained about insect reproduction transfers across languages. The Spanish-language-based unit on insects does not need to be repeated in English; the students naturally transfer that knowledge on their own. Similarly, the scientific process that Jill's students have used to come to conclusions about insect behavior can be recycled and used in other scientific contexts, for example, in a study of the life cycle of frogs. We strive to encourage mainstream educators to transfer their knowledge of constructivist practice and reconstruct it in the service of ELLs.

*Sheltered instruction* and *scaffolding* are two modifications that can be used when teaching content in a second language. Sheltered instruction uses comprehensible input and context-embedded instruction within a social, communicative context to provide access to both the core curriculum and to the English language (Lessow-Hurley, 2005). In other words, it is instruction in a second language that maximizes communicative opportunities and thus provides access to classroom curriculum. Scaffolding provides support to students through modeling, feedback, instruction, and questioning. It is based on the premise that, whatever the learner is able to do with assistance today, the learner can do alone tomorrow. Scaffolding is based upon what Vygotsky (1978) has named the "zone of proximal development" (ZPD) and defined as "the distance between the actual developmental level as determined by independent problem solving and the level of potential development as determined through problem solving under guidance or in collaboration with more capable peers" (p. 86). Specific sheltered strategies that teachers can successfully use, such as the modification and support of "teacher talk," as well as examples of scaffolding instruction will be provided in the upcoming chapter on constructivist practice and will be illustrated in the classrooms of Jill, Maria, and Monica. Because these teachers have facilitated the development of learning communities, the children in their classrooms have lowered their affective filters and are able to move from comprehensible input to output in their second language. In other words, sheltering and scaffolding have provided comprehensible input, and the teacher has provided a safe environment so that students are well equipped to speak freely in their second language without fear of errors.

## LANGUAGE AND CULTURE

According to Diller and Moule (2005), "identity refers to the stable inner sense of who a person is, which is formed by the successful integration of various experiences of the self into a coherent self-image. *Ethnic identity* refers to that part of personal identity that contributes to the person's self-image as an ethnic-group member" (p. 120). Culture is a marker of ethnicity, and language is often associated with both. Language can be the key to open up culture, and, as Bialystok and Hakuta (1994) point out, "Few of us . . . learn a second language as an end in itself. . . . Mostly we learn second languages to gain access, through verbal interaction, to cultural dealings with people who lay claim to that language" (p. 161).

Just as children are not born with a particular language, Ovando, Collier, and Combs (2006) note that "children are not born with a culture, they learn it" (p. 194). Some studies suggest that by the age of six children have already begun to develop cultural identities (Hamers & Blanc, 1992). Human beings, it seems, are uniquely programmed to acquire culture. The specific parameters of the culture they acquire appear to be set by the cultural environment in which they are raised. The bilingual child, however, does not develop two separate cultural identities; rather, the cultures represented are merged into one unique identity. The relationship between bilingualism and cultural identity is circular. Bilingualism affects cultural identity, which in turn affects further bilingual development (Hamers & Blanc, 1992). As previously noted, bilingual students may develop a heightened metalinguistic awareness (the thought process regarding language and linguistic principles). Conversely, based on our fieldwork, we postulate that students who must negotiate two cultures may develop a "metacultural awareness," a heightened awareness of one's own culture in relation to the culture of others. Thus, language and culture may exert their influences in similar and often interconnected ways.

Many theorists believe that issues of children's self-identity are directly related to the development of ethnic attitudes, which are usually set by the fourth grade (Katz, 1982). Recent studies have found positive associations between ethnic identity and self-esteem in minority youth. In addition, many theorists believe that social and psychological well-being is predicated on ethnic identity and that ethnic identity formation takes time and consolidates with age. Self-confidence and self-esteem are expected to increase as one moves from an unexamined identity to searching for identity achievement (Dinkha, 2000).

Although the home environment is the primary source of cultural identity in children, the school can play an important secondary role. Research has not borne out the idea that parents are their children's primary socializers; the roles of peers and school are also significant in areas such as the formation of "racial" attitudes (Katz, 1982). Ocampo, Knight, and Bernal (1997) suggest that ethnic self-identification may be affected by the way young children are socialized both within and outside of families. They postulate that the development of ethnic identity could be better understood if increased attention was given to socialization theory. All of this research points to the importance of school experiences in shaping cultural attitudes and, hence, identity. For the bicultural child who may one day face conflicting messages regarding culture and ethnicity and the related issue of "race," an early and firm foundation in biculturalism may be one prerequisite for a positive identity in adult life.

Cavallaro (2005) discusses the connections between language and ethnic group affiliation at length. Based upon an extensive review of salient research, he notes that language is central to the maintenance of ethnic/cultural heritage and identity at both the individual and group levels. Language is the carrier of culture; thus, losing one's language is the equivalent of living outside of one's culture. Ethnic identity and heritage language facility are strongly related (Baker, 2001; Cho, 2000); heritage language development often has a positive impact on identity formation (Cho, Cho, & Tse, 1997; Feuerverger, 1991; Tse, 1997). In Jill's classroom, we can see the development of a heritage language where it might otherwise be lost. For Maria's students, loss of the heritage language is less of an issue; here acquisition of both communicative and academic English paves the way for bilingualism, biliteracy, and perhaps bilingual/bicultural identity construction. The majority of Monica's students are already fluent bilinguals. The challenge for them is attaining higher levels of academic English and then using this ability to construct identity and to make sense of the world.

For students such as those in Monica's classroom, there is more to identity construction than the development of ethnic identity. Hawkins (2005) notes the value to children of acquiring identities as learners within schools. We suggest that the development of ethnic identity and academic identity may be linked and that it is important for educational programs to maximize the possibility for bilingual children to construct identities as learners that are parallel to their ethnic identities. McKay and Wong's (1996) study of four Chinese American secondary school students offers insight into the interplay between identity construction and academic achievement. Identity construction is named as the mediating factor in the students' differing levels of academic achievement and second language (English) learning.

Identity construction is inherent to childhood and adolescence, and schools are primary sites for that ongoing process. When the school context highlights a motivating and stimulating learning climate, such as illustrated in the classrooms of Jill, Maria, and Monica, positive student interpretations of a bilingual/bicultural environment may result. This outlook could pave the way for the development of positive attitudes toward bilingualism and biculturalism that may, in turn, provide the foundation for healthy, school-supported identity construction. We advocate further exploration of this supposition.

It is important to note that identity construction is ongoing and occurs in multiple ways. Bilingual programs that emphasize native (or heritage) language and culture encourage positive associations with the minority language and culture and may contribute to healthy identity formation. Pedagogy that is both constructivist and linguistically sensitive and culturally relevant inherently pushes this agenda by valuing and validating prior knowledge and family, home, and community experience and by providing opportunities for authentic language learning/acquisition through a content-based language curriculum. Furthermore, as we will see in upcoming chapters, a critical pedagogical approach to curriculum promotes healthy identity construction through social action. When students view themselves as actively shaping their own lives rather than passively accepting the status quo, they are empowered. When they feel they have a stake in what happens in their families and communities, they are connected. It is easy to imagine how such attributes could contribute to healthy identity in youth.

Whenever possible, literacy and content instruction in the native language should be provided to ELLs. As previously noted, a plethora of research studies has shown that such learning experiences foster academic and cognitive development and function as a bridge from the first to the second language in literacy development. In addition, Wong Fillmore (1991) suggests that first language loss in children may contribute to a deterioration of family relationships because parents and children may no longer share a common primary means of communication. During a discussion in one of Sharon's classes, this topic was a potent one with the students who were concurrently involved in clinical experiences in ELL contexts. It was noted that the use of multiple languages within one family unit could easily exert an influence upon family relationships. When Sharon challenged the students to come up with a term to describe this phenomenon, one student, Katie Fiorelli, came up with "interlinguistic familial relationships." It was easy for the class members to see, based upon their ongoing clinical experiences, how continued development in the native language could positively impact family dynamics and how the lack of a shared family language could negatively impact these crucial relationships.

Culturally responsive pedagogy utilizes students' identities and backgrounds and is therefore consonant with constructivist principles that validate the prior knowledge and cultural backgrounds of the learner. We suggest that culturally responsive pedagogy can be thought of as a type of cultural constructivism. Promoting native language and culture is thus compatible with constructivist education and may encourage healthy identity construction and the development of positive self-esteem. Yet, the majority of teachers of ELLs are not fluent in the language of their students. Although this may pose a significant challenge, it is one that can be successfully addressed. Educators who teach in the English language may be linguistically sensitive whether or not they speak the native language or languages of their students. Monolingualism need not imply linguistic insensitivity. There are many ways to validate and foster native language and culture as well as to encourage identity construction. Maria models many of these strategies. Although she herself is bilingual, she does not speak the native languages of her students. This does not prevent her from empowering her students as they acquire English language literacy.

Each educational context is unique. There is no formula for linguistic sensitivity. We believe that teaching is just as much an art as it is a science, and we encourage educators to invent their own unique ways of demonstrating linguistic sensitivity and culturally responsive pedagogy. We offer the following suggestions merely as a starting point from which your own reflections and pedagogy can evolve.

- Have books available for use in the students' native language(s)
- Invite bilingual parents, community members, and/or older students into the classroom to read to/with students
- Invite bilingual parents, community members, and/or older students into the classroom to share knowledge with students
- Send notices and newsletters home in the native languages of the students
- Employ teaching assistants who speak and are literate in the native language(s) of the students
- Incorporate the students' cultural heritage in classroom activities
- Be aware of diverse learning and communication styles
- Seek to enrich your own cultural and linguistic knowledge through research and "teacher radar" (Nieto, 2004); when you realize you don't understand a student response or interaction, do the research necessary to get up to speed
- Utilize the "funds of knowledge" represented by family members of the students in your classroom (Moll, Amanti, Neff, & Gonzalez, 1992); tap into the rich knowledge available in the students' homes and communities by bringing it into the classroom

As demographics in the United States continue to change, issues of ethnic identity continue to surface (Tomlinson-Clarke, 2001). School is one of the primary socialization vehicles of childhood and adolescence and as such may well be one of the sites where issues of identity closely linked to ethnicity are most salient. Our schools do more than teach academics. As socializing agents of students, schools have the opportunity to profoundly influence identity construction through their pedagogical and curricular stance and their ability to provide services and to forge alliances with parents, families, and communities. Conversely, lack of sensitivity in these areas can create additional stressors for children and adolescents as they seek to develop constructs about self and society that inform diversity. The search for identity is universal. The challenge for educators and for parents is to provide support systems that respect diversity and are available to all children and adolescents yet are responsive to individual circumstance.

# 2 Program Models for Second Language Learners

**W**ith the growing numbers of ELLs in our schools come a plethora of programs developed to meet the rising challenge posed by changing classroom demographics. Some of these programs have been developed through a long tradition of second language research and corresponding practice; others have been thrown together without sufficient reflection and expertise to be truly successful. Some of these models are conducive to constructivist practice, and others are less so. We encourage educators to shape quality programs for ELLs in their schools with local context and resources in mind. Of course, a program model, no matter how carefully articulated, is only as good as the pedagogy practiced and the curriculum implemented within the school in general and the classroom in particular.

Although constructivist practice can be implemented in most classrooms, certain educational programs for ELLs are more conducive to constructivism than are others. Immersion models, for example, are intricately tied into pedagogy and curriculum that is inherently constructivist, and the roles of teachers and students in such programs also parallel such roles in constructivist practice.

## ADDITIVE VERSUS SUBTRACTIVE PROGRAM MODELS

The distinction between additive and subtractive (Cummins, 1981) program models for ELLs is significant here because constructivist theory and practice stress the importance of prior knowledge and respect the background of the students, including native language and culture. Additive bilingual models strive not only to maintain but also to develop the first language while the second language is being added. Subtractive bilingual models are concerned only with the development of the second language (English in the United States); in essence they strive to replace the first language with the second, at least in the academic realm. Programs that are subtractive in nature (due to limitations of resources as opposed to philosophical stance) can still be linguistically sensitive and culturally responsive, however. The accompanying chart (see Table 2.1) has been titled Models of Educational Programs for Bilingual Students because English-only program models by definition are monolingual. Often such programs are incorrectly classified as bilingual program models. In essence, English-only programs are subtractive in nature because they strive to replace the students' native language with a new language. By contrast, programs that strive to maintain the students' native language and add a second language (English) are by nature additive. We have chosen to use the additive/subtractive distinction as the primary means of classification by program model. The additive/subtractive distinction does not seem sufficient, however. There is wide variation in subtractive models. Therefore we have applied an additional criterion: whether the model is linguistically sensitive and culturally responsive. We have noted in Figure 2.1 which models have the potential to be, or by their nature are, linguistically sensitive and culturally responsive. We suggest that these are the models in which constructivist practice for ELLs can best occur.

Although additive models may be preferred, they are not always realistic. Resources and context may not support their development. A sufficient number of qualified bilingual teachers may not be available, or there may be a multitude of languages represented in the student population of ELLs, with only minimal representation from each linguistic group. However, educators (both monolingual and bilingual) working within subtractive models may well be linguistically sensitive and culturally responsive and as such have a significant role to fulfill in the education of their linguistic minority students.

Numerous models of educational programs for bilingual students have been developed, and ways of organizing such programs have been devised by researchers and educators. Unfortunately, many organizational designs and charts can prove more confusing than helpful, because "no size fits all" in quality educational programs. Context and available resources are strong determinants of program design, and many programs contain features of more than one model. The following discussion and accompanying figure is presented in an attempt to present an easily understandable method of classifying educational programs for ELLs that can be adapted to suit new program models as they are developed by practitioners. It contains examples of currently existing programs as well as hypothetical programs that may (or could) exist if existing components were placed together. In that sense, this chart and accompanying narrative is meant to be a summary not only of what is but also of what could be, or perhaps of what already exists but has not been written about. This discussion, then, is just as much about envisioning a brighter future as it is about informing our knowledge of current program models. This is done in the hopes of empowering educators to tap their own creativity and ingenuity in adapting existing programs and creating new ones to serve the needs of their students and constituent communities, keeping in mind the limitations of their current resources.

## MAINSTREAM WITH MODIFICATIONS

Fortunately, few educators today would support a submersion experience for ELLs. To deny that such situations exist, however, would fly in the face of reality. What, then, can a teacher do if placed in a submersion educational context? The first step toward pedagogical and curricular change would be to modify the curriculum to support the educational growth of ELLs in a manner consistent with constructivist practice. A second step would be to add modifications such as sheltering and scaffolding. Within almost any mainstream classroom, teachers can rethink their pedagogy and curriculum to accommodate ELLs while providing an enriching curriculum for all students. Linguistically sensitive and culturally responsive teachers can use the social integration of students inherent in a mainstream classroom for the benefit of ELLs. Because curricular modification happens in the classroom, no change is needed in school structure. The addition of a pull-out program for native language literacy and content instruction could combine with a modified constructivist classroom curriculum to maximize linguistic, academic, and cognitive student development. It would, however, require some modification of classroom structure.

## ENGLISH AS A SECOND LANGUAGE (ESL)

Because they support language and academics in the majority language only, ESL contexts are by nature subtractive. They may be structurally

**Table 2.1**    Models of Educational Programs for Bilingual Students

| Subtractive | Additive |
| --- | --- |
| Submersion | |
| Mainstream with modifications in L2 | Mainstream with modifications in L2 and with maintenance (pull-out) in L1 |
| | Enrichment (religious and private schools; foreign language models) |
| ESL (pull-out and push-in; language arts only and integrated content/language) | |
| Transitional bilingual | Transitional bilingual with extended native language maintenance component |
| English immersion | English immersion with native language maintenance component |
| | One-way bilingual immersion |
| | Two-way bilingual immersion |
| Integrated | Integrated with two-way bilingual immersion component |
| | Bilingual whole language & multiage bilingual whole language |

designed as either pull-out or push-in models, and on a curricular level they may strive to teach only English language arts or to integrate language and content. Pull-out models are the most traditional and involve an ESL specialist working with ELLs in a location apart from the rest of the students. In push-in models, however, the ESL specialist comes into the mainstream classroom and either provides support to ELLs or teams with the classroom teacher in providing instruction to the class. In push-in programs, the ESL specialist has the additional role of contributing to the pedagogical knowledge and strategies that the classroom teacher uses as a basis for working with ELLs.

Just as pull-out programs are the more traditional structural organization, so, too, is teaching English Language Arts the more traditional instructional mode used with ELLs. More recently, emphasis has been placed on the integration of language and content. Although the integration of language and content can be accomplished in both pull-out and push-in models, teaching English Language Arts only is usually accomplished in a pull-out model. We suggest, however, that such an approach does not maximize the time devoted to academic achievement, nor does it sufficiently tap the linguistic benefits available from interactions with peers through the social context of learning.

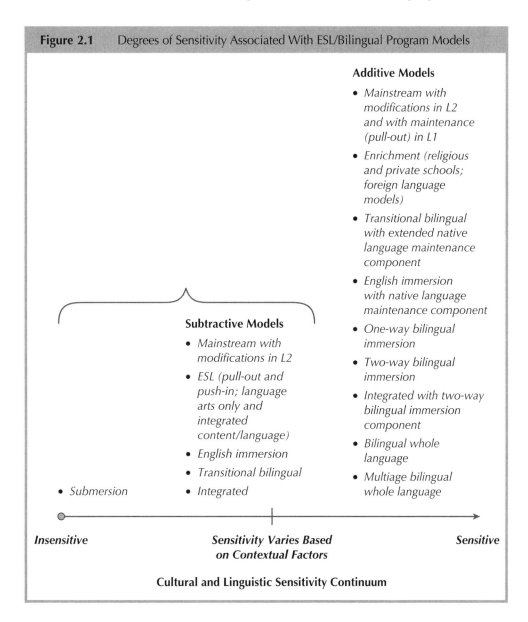

**Figure 2.1**    Degrees of Sensitivity Associated With ESL/Bilingual Program Models

Although subtractive in nature, ESL programs have tremendous potential for being linguistically sensitive and culturally responsive. Some schools and districts that understand the importance of native language instruction do not have a student population of any one language group sufficient to support a bilingual program. Sometimes teachers of the minority language are not available. In these cases, a strong ESL program that seeks to validate the linguistic and cultural heritage of the students may be the best option for the instruction of ELLs. In a school or district that has selected an ESL program over a bilingual program for ideological reasons, linguistically sensitive and culturally responsive pedagogy becomes much less of a possibility. Even in these situations, however, the mainstream teacher who is tuned in to issues surrounding the education of language minority students has the potential to create an instructional oasis for ELLs through a constructivist curriculum with modifications.

## TRANSITIONAL PROGRAM OF BILINGUAL INSTRUCTION (TPI)

Transitional programs of bilingual instruction (also referred to as TPI) are the most common models for the bilingual instruction of ELLs. In such programs, students get support in native language literacy and content in decreasing amounts of time as part of a transitional process to an English-only curriculum. This process is usually complete in three years, and this forms the basic criticism of transitional programs. Research has consistently shown that ELLs need from five to nine years in bilingual programs to be able to negotiate the English mainstream curriculum on par with their English dominant peers (Cummins, 1981). Thus, ELLs who enter mainstream classrooms after completing TPI are often at a severe disadvantage academically, and educators may blame the learner rather than the program model for the academic weakness that results.

## MAINTENANCE

Schools cognizant of the deficiencies of TPI can compensate by adding a native language maintenance component to their program. In this model, students can continue to develop both academically and cognitively in the native language through pull-out programs that pick up when the three years of enrollment in TPI classrooms end. Schools may choose to offer additional support in academic English as well.

Transitional models are subtractive because their goal is the transition to an English-only curriculum in as short a time as possible. However, when a native language maintenance component is added, such programs may become additive.

## SUBMERSION

Although we have included it in Figure 2.1, submersion is not really a program model but, rather, the lack of a model for students who are ELLs. In submersion classrooms, ELLs are treated in the same manner as English dominant students; no supports or accommodations are provided in their learning experience. If you hear someone declare that his or her grandparents were immigrants and did just fine in U.S. schools without any special supports, you are listening to a submersion supporter. Beware of the fallacies inherent in this argument! If you were to talk to these same grandparents, you might find that life was difficult and that they made the transition to an English dominant environment with considerable hardship. In addition, it is essential to consider historical context. Our grandparents did not need to prepare for a society in which education was a prerequisite for the use of technological resources or for advancement in almost every aspect of life. Furthermore, in a democratic society the inadequacies of the past should not be used to argue for inadequacies in the present. Human history should be moving forward, with each generation improving on the conditions of the one prior. Why should education be an exception to this goal? Do those who argue for retaining antiquated models of education for ELLs also advocate stopping advances in technology?

## SUBMERSION VERSUS IMMERSION

It is essential to note the differences between submersion and immersion (a model that will be discussed in detail in upcoming sections). In both submersion and immersion classrooms, the learner is exposed to a learning environment that is dominantly or completely in the second language. There are two essential differences between these approaches, however. In submersion, no supports are provided to the learner. The immersion environment is filled with educational supports; language is sheltered, and learning is context embedded and rich in scaffolds and hands-on learning opportunities. Furthermore, philosophical and curricular tenets require the teacher to be linguistically and culturally sensitive. In a submersion environment, on the other hand, teachers and administrators are not required to make any linguistic or cultural accommodations for the learners. Students are on their own to negotiate an educational environment in their L2. Submersion is therefore not only subtractive but also linguistically insensitive and culturally nonresponsive.

## IMMERSION

Much confusion exists with regard to the word immersion because so many variations exist. What all immersion programs have in common, however, is that they strive to replicate acquisition of the second language in much the same manner as the first language was acquired. Thus, language is not explicitly taught; rather, the primary instructional means used is context-embedded content area instruction in a second language. All immersion programs highlight the integration of language and content. This makes sense when one thinks about how each of us acquired our first language. Our parents and/or primary caregivers did not give us formal instruction in our native language. They instead gave us a type of informal instruction on life through the means of language rich in comprehensible input. The literature refers to this specialized, sheltered language as "motherese," "child-directed speech," or "caretaker speech" (Lessow-Hurley, 2005).

In the most popular model of immersion programs, referred to as either two-way bilingual immersion (TWI) or dual language programs[1], language minority and language majority students become bilingual in classrooms together as language is learned through content, with the majority of the curriculum presented in the minority (target) language. Corresponding program goals are threefold: that all children become bilingual and biliterate, that they achieve academically at or above grade level norms, and that they develop positive cross-cultural attitudes (Christian, Montone, Lindholm, & Carranza, 1997). Current research (Christian, Genesee, Lindholm-Leary, & Howard, 2004; Howard, Sugarman, & Christian, 2003) suggests that all three goals are being met. Because all children are expected to maintain their native language and culture while adding a second language, two-way bilingual immersion programs are by nature additive (Cummins, 2000).

The social context of learning is emphasized through the inclusion of a mixed linguistic minority, linguistic majority, and bilingual peer group. The rich resources that children of differing language backgrounds can give each other is one of the foundational pillars upon which TWI programs are based. Such programs are referred to as "two-way" because of this bilingual peer group. However, a bilingual peer group is not always possible. For example, for some indigenous languages there is not a sufficient population of children who are native speakers of the minority language to support a two-way program. These contexts are ripe for the creation of one-way bilingual immersion programs that often have as their goals the linguistic and cultural revitalization of endangered languages. Today, one-way programs exist in the United States in languages such as Hawaiian, Yup'ik, and Navajo. Revitalization through bilingual education efforts exists throughout the world. The Maori immersion programs in

---

1. There is some confusion in the literature because the term "dual language programs" is sometimes used as a generic term for any type of bilingual program.

New Zealand are only one example of this growing worldwide trend. However, all one-way programs are not based on linguistic and cultural revitalization. It is possible to have programs composed primarily of English dominant speakers who receive their comprehensible input in the L2 primarily through the classroom teacher. We suggest, however, that whenever possible a mixed peer group can provide the most potent second language learning experience.

It is important to note that, with the exception of structured English immersion (explained later in this chapter), all immersion programs are additive and use natural approaches replicating first language acquisition through the integration of language and content instruction. Comprehensible input along with the appropriate modifications for second language learners are inherent in the curriculum, as is an inherent focus on the relationship between language and culture and the accompanying bicultural curriculum. All of this drives an inherently constructivist curriculum, although it has not yet been labeled as such in the literature. However, while an individual teacher may choose to engage in constructivist practice, it is not possible to have an immersion classroom outside a schoolwide program; one-way, two-way, and similar models must be implemented collectively across the school curriculum.

Fundamental to immersion education is the integration of language and content learning; language is learned through content, with the majority of the curriculum presented in the target (minority) language. Children are expected to become bilingual naturally as they are immersed in context-embedded learning environments in their second language. The necessity for a context-rich, hands-on, discovery-based curriculum drives instruction. Students who are receiving input in their second language need to depend on a host of contextual clues to maximize understanding. This pushes not only a type of sheltered instruction but also a constructivist pedagogical approach. Without such an approach, such programs might well be doomed to failure. We have noted that parents with children in immersion programs who move out of state often try to locate immersion schools for their children in the new locale. They feel that not only will their children continue to become bilingual but they will also continue to have authentic and engaging learning experiences. Although they may not be consciously aware of the educational principles guiding their beliefs, they have inherently come to see the strong connection between natural methods of second language learning and constructivist curriculum and pedagogy. In other words, the language learning theory behind immersion education drives an inherently constructivist curriculum, although it has not yet been labeled as such in the literature.

## STRUCTURED ENGLISH IMMERSION (SEI)

Another immersion model that highlights an entire peer group dominant in one language is called structured English immersion, also known as SEI. In this case, the peer group is composed entirely of speakers with dominance in a minority language (or languages), and the goal is to achieve fluency in English. Considerable controversy surrounds such models because of their subtractive nature, as opposed to other immersion models. SEI is, in essence, an ESL program that instructs through the integration of language and content. Ovando et al. (2006) note that the highly structured nature of the original instructional design runs counter to natural language acquisition processes, which are not sequential but complex. Yet, just as ESL programs may be the best option for ELLs in specific contexts, so, too, is there a place for a variation of SEI. When instruction occurs in a manner that is respectful of natural language acquisition processes and is linguistically sensitive and culturally responsive, quality programs can emerge. The further introduction of a native language maintenance component can bring such programs out of a subtractive paradigm. Of course, one could argue that, with all of these modifications, calling such a program SEI would be a misnomer! However, our purpose here is to encourage the emergence of new instructional models for ELLs by the creative restructuring of local resources within local contexts. In our efforts to create viable program options for our students, program labels should not restrict us.

Many variations of immersion models already exist. In addition to the ones we have discussed, programs are in existence that highlight the acquisition of heritage languages that are not endangered (such as French in Louisiana), as well as programs that have trilingualism as a goal (for example, English, French, and Hebrew). Some schools offer partial immersion programs, and others offer late start immersion. Given the seemingly limitless possibilities, why not reinvent English immersion programs?

## INTEGRATED

A common criticism leveled against bilingual education is that it segregates ELLs from the mainstream. TWI programs have successfully met the challenge of integration of ELLs and mainstream students. Unfortunately, despite their growing popularity, TWI programs are still few and far between in terms of access to the general student population. Therefore, integrated instructional models have been developed that offer ELLs bilingual opportunities without sacrificing the benefits of educational interactions with mainstream students. Although still in their infancy, evidence points to the effectiveness of integrated programs in accomplishing this goal (Brisk, 1998; de Jong, 2006). In such programs, ELLs continue to receive their primary instruction within bilingual class-rooms but come together with mainstream classes for some content area instruction, usually science, social studies, or math. The partnered bilin-gual and mainstream teachers plan and implement instruction together. Although the majority of content is presented in English, students are allowed to use both languages during instruction, and some instruction in the minority language may be included. ELLs receive linguistic bene-fits from interactions with native speakers of English, and English speak-ers may pick up some elements of the minority language. Although integrated instruction involves more complex instructional planning, requires some schoolwide organizational changes, and presents some pedagogical and curricular challenges, it holds promise of addressing the isolation that some students (and teachers) experience within bilingual programs. When combined with an immersion component for main-stream students and extended over time, it can be additive for children from both linguistic backgrounds.

## ENRICHMENT

Enrichment models of bilingual instruction are usually designed for children from a linguistic majority background. They are by nature addi-tive, and they assign value to bilingualism in English dominant students. For this same reason, the terms linguistic sensitivity and culturally rele-vant pedagogy are largely irrelevant. Schools that highlight enrichment models may be religious or secular and may involve traditional foreign language instruction for part of the day or immersion education for the entire day. There is much variation in enrichment models, including the development of private immersion preschools and even day schools in a host of different languages, from French to Japanese. Most frequently, however, enrichment bilingual education takes place within religious con-texts, such as instruction in Hebrew or Yiddish within Jewish religious schooling (Lessow-Hurley, 2005).

## NEWCOMER PROGRAMS

A word about newcomer programs is warranted in our discussion. Such programs have, for the most part, been designed with newly arrived immi-grant students at the secondary education level in mind. Such programs may take any number of forms, including the creation of schools that serve newcomers exclusively for several years only. Program goals include over-coming the trauma of relocation, learning English, adapting to U.S. school-ing and society in general, and successful transitioning to mainstream schools (Lessow-Hurley, 2005). However, because newcomer programs are generally reserved for secondary level students, we have limited our discussion of such models and, for the same reason, have not included them in Figure 2.1 or Table 2.1.

## BILINGUAL WHOLE LANGUAGE AND BEYOND

Whitmore and Crowell (1994) describe life in a "bilingual whole language community." Their portrait of life in Crowell's third-grade classroom, known as "the Sunshine Room," helps us envision what more bilingual classrooms might be like. The emphasis here is not necessarily on bilin-gualism but on learning and living joyfully using the rich resources (lin-guistic and otherwise) that bilingual students represent and bring with them to a classroom community. The Sunshine Room reminds us that there is much we have yet to invent and reinvent in the way of educating bilingual children. In fact, we have witnessed in our travels multiage/TWI/whole language classrooms that have not yet been described in the literature. We suspect that, wherever linguistically sensitive and culturally responsive teachers are allowed to practice teaching as both an art and a science, inspirational classrooms and models of educating ELLs come into being and flourish.

With the exception of submersion, which in reality is not a model but the lack thereof, all program designs have the potential to be linguistically sensitive and culturally responsive. This potential exists because you, the teacher, remain in a pivotal role in the educational process. You can choose to make a stand for educational equity in your own classroom. If you are fortunate enough to be able to design a program for your ELLs, you will want to consider educational philosophy as well as the local context and available resources (see Chapter 7). Remember, the program components described in this chapter are much like pieces to a puzzle; they need to be arranged and rearranged according to both local context and availability. Yet a program model is only a framework. It is what happens *within* a model—pedagogy and curriculum—that lies at the heart of education. Best practice can occur within multiple program models within multiple contexts. In upcoming chapters, you will see best practice come to life in three different classrooms and three different contexts. You will also see how students' native language and culture are validated even when the teacher is not conversant in the languages of her students.

# 3 Perspectives in Constructivism

The National Research Council (2005) in its treatise on *How People Learn: Brain, Mind, Experience, School* discusses constructivism as part of the "new science of learning" (p. 10). Like many educators, we were exposed to constructivist methodology during teacher preparation or through professional development, but we have continued to grow in our knowledge of this sophisticated learning theory. Constructivists draw from two theoretical perspectives: cognitive constructivism and social constructivism, both of which suggest people actively *construct* knowledge in an effort to achieve greater understanding.

An essential component of both perspectives is the idea that learners *construct* knowledge using their prior experiences as a foundation. Knight (2002) suggests that "a constructivist's view [is], . . . in essence, [that] we construct knowledge based on what we already know, and each idea we learn facilitates our ongoing intellectual development" (p. 3). Comparing a constructivist classroom with a didactic classroom will make it easier to understand.

For the sake of illustration, the first teacher we will describe teaches from a traditional perspective. Teaching from a philosophical stance that views students as blank slates, or tabula rasa, she approaches her lesson by seriously undertaking to *explicitly teach* her students the predetermined curriculum. If we were to visit her fifth-period American History class, we would see her teaching a lesson on the cold war era. She would have prepared for class by reviewing state standards, putting her lecture notes on a PowerPoint slide, and creating a corresponding worksheet on which students can take notes. As demonstrated in her preparation for class, this dedicated teacher spends an inordinate amount of time planning and grading and doing the myriad things that good teachers often do.

To begin class, the teacher stands at the podium and welcomes her students, expressing genuine interest in their lives. Once class begins, she reviews what students learned the previous day; she then cues the projector and starts the PowerPoint presentation. The teacher does not want to simply *give* the students a copy of the PowerPoint printout because she thinks they will then not be engaged in the lesson. Additionally, when she prepared her district lesson plan, she listed a note-taking worksheet as a modification for ELLs. Consequently, when going over terms students need to know for the upcoming test, she instructs students to find a pencil and paper and take notes on the corresponding worksheet. During the course of the lesson, one student raises her hand to ask a question about Ronald Reagan; she respectfully tells the student to stay focused on the lecture, because it will eventually address her question. It is quiet in this classroom, except for her lecture, and students have been "on task" from the beginning of class when they were asked to answer questions about the information they had previously been taught. For homework, our teacher hands out a worksheet meant to be used with the textbook; she assigns the textbook reading and reminds her students that she will be collecting the worksheet, so they should put their best effort into completing it. The dismissal bell rings just as she hands out the last sheet. She wishes the students a good day and resets the projector for the next class.

If we look closely at our hypothetical teacher, we see that she prepares quite well for class and delivers content that is necessary for students to know to be prepared for the state exam. We know that, in addition to meticulously preparing for instruction, she integrates multimedia and technological tools and cares about her students. We would find her teaching "didactic" (or direct) (Smerdon, Burkam, & Lee, 1999). Smerdon and colleagues state that didactic teachers

> often instruct the entire class as a unit, write notes on the chalkboard [in our case PowerPoint], and pass out worksheets for students to complete. In [these] classrooms, knowledge is presented as fact, students' prior knowledge experiences are not seen as important, and students typically are not free to experiment with different methods to solve problems. . . . In these traditional classrooms, it is teachers who are active; they convey facts and inculcate knowledge. (p. 6)

As this teacher reflected after instruction, she believed the lesson went well because she covered all the material from the textbook and the students were engaged, as evidenced by their note taking. Also in her postinstructional reflection, she noted that the next time she taught this content she might include some visual and auditory components to the PowerPoint so she could reach more learning modalities.

A constructivist teacher would approach the same material in a much different way. Let us take a look at this type of classroom.

As she welcomes the students, the constructivist teacher is curious to see what she will be learning with her students. She is cognizant of the fact that she has students from many different cultures in her class who will likely bring a variety of experiences and perspectives related to the cold war, which is her content. She is just as excited to share information as to learn from her students. To prepare for class, she thoroughly reviews the content as well as the state learning standards so she has an idea of the information with which students will need to be familiar to do well on the high-stakes tests in her district. Although she is aware of these predetermined objectives, she also knows the students will have an integral part in how the lesson flows and how the content will unfold.

To begin the lesson, she asks the students what they know about the cold war. When no one replies after a minute or two, she asks if they can infer anything from the title *the cold war*. Isabella responds by asking if it had anything to do with the Cuban Missile Crisis that she had heard her parents—first generation immigrants—talk about. Although not a direct answer to her question, the teacher realizes Isabella has a connection to the content, which resonates with her unique experiences. "Well," the teacher replies, "I guess you might say that was one of the events that led up to the cold war." During the course of classroom discussion, Isabella explained that her parents were small children in Cuba when the Cuban Missile Crisis occurred. In this rich and social classroom environment, discussion continues as the students examine the political climate in both Cuba and the United States during the time period leading up to the cold war.

At one point during her lesson, the teacher asks the students to work in groups, consult a variety of sources, and write a list of events they feel were significant factors leading up to the cold war. She explains that she wants them to find several different sources, and as a class they brainstorm a list of ways they might find information. The list includes their textbooks, the classroom library, and the Internet. Knowing her ultimate goal is for her students to write a research paper, she asks each group to keep index cards on which they are to write what they consider to be significant quotes. Taking this opportunity to discuss what is reliable and unreliable information, she encourages students to share criteria they have used in the past to evaluate sources from the Internet.

As the groups begin their tasks, the teacher walks around and guides discussions as the students struggle to understand the material they are reading. In an effort to help them learn, she asks her students thoughtful questions and facilitates their discussions such that they gain a better understanding of content. To conclude the class, she asks each group to lead a discussion about one of the events they have listed. As the students share, she compiles a class list, a combination of the ideas students formed in their groups. The teacher asks the students to go beyond the list and write a list of principles for foreign policy. Together they carefully construct the list. Finally, she asks the students to read the list chorally and to write it in their notebooks. The bell rings, and the teacher dismisses the class as the students are still in discussion about whether one country has the right to colonize another. Students' idiosyncratic responses reflect the various cultural backgrounds from which they come.

As this teacher reflected on her lesson, she knew it had gone in a direction other than what she had anticipated. She found herself enriched by the contributions of Isabella, who gave the class a unique perspective of the events that unfolded. She believed the students were gaining an understanding of foreign policy and would be well prepared to write the research paper when she assigned it. Last, she knew the students would be able to meet the state learning standards when her unit was finished. A Venn diagram (Figure 3.1) will help us note the differences and similarities between the constructivist and the didactic teachers.

Certainly both teachers have planned well for their lessons, are experts on their content, and have the academic growth of their students as their goal. As we saw, however, the way in which they approach teaching is

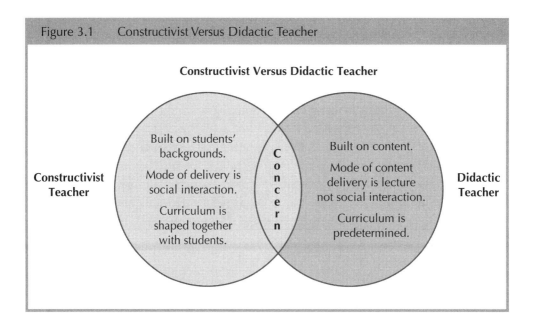

Figure 3.1    Constructivist Versus Didactic Teacher

**Constructivist Versus Didactic Teacher**

**Constructivist Teacher**

Built on students' backgrounds.

Mode of delivery is social interaction.

Curriculum is shaped together with students.

Concern

Built on content.

Mode of content delivery is lecture not social interaction.

Curriculum is predetermined.

**Didactic Teacher**

quite different. We see the constructivist teacher relying much more on the students' backgrounds and social interaction than does the didactic teacher. As we continue to examine the foundational beliefs of constructivism, our hope is that you clearly see the principles guiding teachers who practice from this perspective and the benefits of constructivist methods for ELLs.

## OVERVIEW OF CONSTRUCTIVIST PERSPECTIVES

Constructivism can be thought of as a "theory of knowing" (Fosnot, 1996, p. 15) because it examines the way in which we know and learn. As we examine factors related to the construction of knowledge, we find two focal points: that of *cognitive constructivism* and that of *social constructivism.* Cognitive constructivists focus on the *cognitive* processes associated with constructing knowledge as individuals make sense of new information with which they are confronted. Social constructivists concern themselves with the *social* and *cultural* processes at work (Windschitl, 2002).

While there is a different focus in each of these perspectives, they are not mutually exclusive. Windschitl (2002) explains, "some scholars have proposed a useful synthesis of cognitive and social constructivist perspectives, claiming that knowledge is personally constructed and socially mediated" (p. 137). There is thus an advantage in considering both perspectives when we teach. In this section, we will present the cognitive as well as the social constructivist perspectives, draw conclusions, and present a list of guiding principles for constructivist classrooms. In the next chapter, we take theory into the classroom and suggest a variety of constructivist strategies beneficial for all students, but especially for ELLs.

## COGNITIVE CONSTRUCTIVIST PERSPECTIVE

Central to a cognitive constructivist point of view is the idea that all learning is born out of what we already know. According to Knight (2002), Piaget, known as the father of constructivism, "suggested that we construct new knowledge when we experience new information that is incongruent with our prior knowledge" (p. 3). Thus, the learners' backgrounds are of utmost importance. When we can make sense of such knowledge, we are in a state of *equilibrium* regarding that knowledge. According to von Glasersfeld (1989), this is the time when our perception of the world makes sense and where "conceptual conflicts or contradictions" are not "brought to the surface" (p. 4). Many of us are familiar with this cognitive state; it occurs when things are what we expect them to be.

Equilibrium is achieved through a process of assimilation and accommodation to our existing schema (the clusters of information stored in the brain). Essentially, we all have existing schema (or ideas), which represent our knowledge structures. For example, each of us has schema (or ideas) that represent what we know regarding our families, language, culture, mathematics, history, and so on. When we are presented with new information, we assimilate it into our existing schema, and, if it does not fit with our preexisting knowledge structures, we accommodate or change our schematic representations. When we form new cognitive structures, which are representative of our new ideas, our schema has been changed, and learning has occurred.

Von Glasersfeld (1989) gives the example of a baby and a rattle that is helpful in understanding these concepts. He explains that, because a baby has learned that when you shake a pretty thing it makes noise, the baby will form a schematic representation of the event—when you pick up something that looks like a rattle, it makes noise. When the baby is in another situation, for example, at dinner, and picks up a spoon, the baby may think the spoon is a rattle until it is shaken. At that time, because there is no noise, "perturbation, or disappointment" occurs (von Glasersfeld, 1989, p. 5). Von Glasersfeld claims that this disappointment "is one of the conditions that set the stage for cognitive change" (p. 5).

Perturbation, thought to be part of the cognitive constructivist model, is also referred to as disequilibrium, which happens when things are not what we expect. Disequilibrium, Knight (2002) implies, is when new learning takes place. For this reason, it is important that, as students learn, they struggle to make sense out of new information. Constructivist practice allows the learner to be confronted with and to solve difficult problems. In this paradigm, however, it is important that the challenges with which students struggle as they seek to construct new knowledge is in their zone of proximal development (ZPD) and that scaffolds are provided as a way of support. The ZPD and scaffolding will be further explained later in this chapter.

Disequilibrium is analogous to a snow globe. When the snow is settled and we can clearly see the village, it represents equilibrium. Then someone picks up the globe and shakes it; we see the beautiful snowflakes floating in the water, *but we can no longer clearly see the village.* This represents cognitive dissonance, which occurs when we are presented with information that does not resonate with our background knowledge. We are in effect *shaken up* as we experience this delicious disequilibrium. Finally, the snow softly falls once again to the bottom of the globe, and as it does, we are transported once again to the tiny snow-covered village, which we again see clearly. This analogy, of course, relates to the state of equilibrium experienced once we have new cognitive structures in place representing our new learning.

Note, however, that the scene is a little different than it was before the snow globe was shaken because the snow has fallen in a different way, in different places. This difference is significant in that it represents new understandings that we realize as we move from one cognitive state to another. As we reorder our knowledge, we are "involved in the process of inventing or at least reinventing," which requires "the reorganization of old 'data' and the building of new models for that learner" (Fosnot, 1996, p. 18). When we look at *constructivism* in this way, the term itself seems perfectly appropriate.

## SOCIAL CONSTRUCTIVIST PERSPECTIVE

The focus of cognitive constructivism is on how *individuals* learn; constructivists who emphasize *social* processes view knowledge as having both individual and social components and hold that there is no meaningful way in which these components can be viewed separately (Fosnot, 1996). This idea is based on the work of Lev Vygotsky, whose belief in the social mediation of knowledge is succinctly summarized by Wink and Putney (2002, p. 28):

> Vygotsky's social/cultural/historical perspective was evident in his conviction that all learning was first accomplished through the language that flows between individuals. Language and action, for Vygotsky, were tools of mediation for learning. Speaking reorganizes our thinking, and our languages come to us as a cultural heritage through our interactions with others.

Once again, we see the usefulness of a social constructivist approach when teaching ELLs, for both language and content are learned through social mediation. Significantly, it is *through* the process of socially *constructing* content knowledge that ELLs also learn language.

The notion that meaning is negotiated in social and cultural environments through language flows from a social constructivist perspective and has significant implications for the instruction of ELLs. This is different but not completely inconsistent with the cognitive constructivists' view of meaning. The cognitive constructivist would claim that, while language plays a role in negotiating meaning, the construction of knowledge is largely an individual endeavor that occurs during specific stages of cognitive development and as we move from disequilibrium to assimilation and accommodation. If we understand that meaning is socially negotiated, and if we understand that learning takes place within the context of one's cultural background, we are obligated to advocate for students to have access to native language support while learning specific content. To disallow students their native language becomes an issue of equity and hegemony in the school environment. Wink and Putney (2002) posit, "All who are aware of the importance of primary language and academic success will understand that, whenever possible, students must be engaged in building on previously acquired knowledge through their primary language in order to continue to improve in their newly acquired language" (p. 79).

Language use in a classroom may also impact students' perceptions of significance and power. Hruska (2000) points out that "identities are socially produced. People implicate their relationships and identities to each other and position each other through language. Positioning can affect not only the construction of identities but also who has access to which discourses" (p. 11). Once again, we see the equitable foundation evident in constructivist classrooms, particularly when students' cultural backgrounds are built upon and access to native language is allowed. Hruska conceptualizes the debate in bilingual education as a sociopolitical one. "It is about power relations. These power relations, their underlying ideologies, and related educational practices, shape the meaning of bilingualism in a specific context" (p. 11).

The ZPD and scaffolding are generally understood to be integral components of social constructivism. The ZPD refers to the distance between what a student knows and what she can learn with the help of a knowledgeable adult; it is within this zone that optimal and/or proximal development takes place. Implicit in the ZPD is the importance of social interaction as the process by which students learn. As teachers facilitate discussion, they use scaffolding techniques to provide temporary support for constructing meaningful knowledge structures among their students. Scaffolding refers to temporary support given to students by more knowledgeable persons, most probably teachers, until they can be independent with a learning task. There are two significant notions being implied as we discuss the role of the adult in a constructivist paradigm. First, we emphasize, once again, the importance of social interaction as students learn; teachers and students talk together, and everyone supports each other in the process. Second, the adult needs to have an excellent grasp of the content being covered and must develop skills in processing content as she simultaneously provides scaffolds students need as they construct new knowledge.

Another important consideration regarding the ZPD is that the learning task should not be too difficult or too easy for the learner. This is a conundrum for teachers because it is often a challenge to find the place where students will best thrive. Each student has a different ZPD, and a number of assessments are required to determine just what it is. *Informal reading inventories* can be useful assessment tools in this regard. These types of reading inventories are designed for classroom teachers to use informally, and they are particularly helpful because the teacher sits down with the student, listens to him read, marks and analyzes his miscues, asks a series of questions, and determines his independent, instructional, and frustration reading levels. As the teacher spends time with the student, she begins to get an understanding of his background knowledge and how that is affecting his ability to meaningfully process reading texts. Additionally, the informal reading inventory gives the teacher a sense of the student's instructional level—the level at which a student can be successful with the help of an instructor—*or the student's ZPD*. Although an informal reading inventory is only one small piece of an overall diagnostic reading assessment, it does give classroom teachers a gauge, particularly in finding appropriate leveled texts. It can prove to be a valuable assessment.

One last story will illustrate the ideas we have discussed in this section. Trina's nephew, Collin, has always been a curious child. When Collin was about four years old, he developed a love for Legos; he enjoyed *constructing* complicated and sophisticated models. According to his dad, Tony (T. Russell, personal communication, September 25, 2006), Collin would envision something and begin putting pieces together. In this way, Collin tapped into his background and prior knowledge about what he wanted to build as well as the way in which he might assemble the intricate pieces. As he worked, he would look puzzled and would try different combinations of the pieces, turning one this way and then the next, struggling to find the perfect fit. Collin was experiencing disequilibrium, assimilation, and accommodation. Seeing him work, Tony would join him on the floor and scaffold Collin's learning; Collin would ask him questions such as, "How should I try this one?" to which Tony might reply, "Would this work better?" Together they would work and talk, trying to solve the problem of the Lego puzzle. The ZPD was evident because the task was challenging for Collin, but he could complete it with the help of his father who was socially facilitating his impending success. Finally, Collin and Tony would complete the model, most likely a Star Wars space station, and would proudly display it to the members of the family who would praise the work they had done. Just as Tony is rewarded by working with his son, we are fortunate as teachers to guide *our* students to representations of what we learn together.

# GUIDING PRINCIPLES FOR CONSTRUCTIVIST CLASSROOMS

## Principle #1—New Learning Builds on Prior Knowledge

Both cognitive and social constructivists believe that new learning is built on prior knowledge. If we look back to the two teachers from the beginning of our chapter, we can see that the didactic teacher did not consider the students' prior knowledge as she taught her lesson on the cold war. This behavior is representative of a transmission model, or paradigm, of teaching, which assumes students are empty vessels into which teachers pour content knowledge. Conversely, constructivists believe that "learning occurs because each of us uniquely creates or builds our own knowledge. . . . We construct knowledge based on what we already know, and each idea we learn facilitates our ongoing intellectual development" (Knight, 2002, p. 2). The significance of this principle takes on new dimensions when you work with ELLs. Teachers must respect the cultural backgrounds of students because it is through tapping into that background that we help students learn. An implication of bringing students' background into the classroom is that the curriculum is not predetermined; it is likely that students' backgrounds will shape the curriculum in the way that the constructivist teacher's students did in the beginning of our chapter.

## Principle #2—Learning Is Mediated Through Social Interaction

Both culture and language play a part in how students learn. DeKock, Sleegers, and Voeten (2004) suggest that, although knowledge is individually constructed, it is mediated through social interaction and in culturally situated contexts. Social interaction provides necessary scaffolds for students as they process content. When the constructivist teacher at the beginning of the chapter put students together to compile lists and do research, she provided a supportive environment (or scaffold) for students as they worked cooperatively in groups. It is important that groups and social activities are *purposefully* planned and that they include *challenging* work for students to complete. The groups should not be competitive. Alfie Kohn (2004) cautions us not to "combine collaboration and competition, for example, by putting students into groups but then setting the groups against one another. The reason for cooperative learning, students infer, is to defeat another bunch of students learning together. Cooperation becomes merely instrumental, the goal being to triumph over others" (p. 162). Students should feel safe in cooperative groups, and not fear making their team lose by taking necessary risks that will be needed to learn together.

The social and cultural components of constructivism provide two more reasons why this methodology is appropriate for ELLs. It is exciting to examine how it meets their specific needs because of the central role of language. As students discuss and share their experiences, they are encouraged to relate to their culture, and as they learn through dialogue and discussion, ELLs are positioned to learn both content and language.

## Principle #3—Problem Solving Is Part of Learning

This principle relates to disequilibrium and the ZPD. Students must struggle appropriately with content, because if it is too easy or too difficult, they will lack the context in which new cognitive structures can be formed. DeKock and colleagues (2004) suggest that "most constructivists . . . argue that the most important goals of learning in the school context are problem-solving, reasoning, and critical thinking skills—the active and reflective use of knowledge, and self regulation skills" (p. 146).

If we compare, once again, the two teachers from the beginning of the chapter, we see clearly how the didactic teacher primarily *delivered* content—she did not ask questions, she did not challenge students, nor did she challenge students to solve problems. The constructivist teacher, on the other hand, asked the students to brainstorm, to research, and to answer questions about foreign policy and colonization. She asked her students to solve problems, while providing the support they needed. These methods are integral to constructivist practice.

## Principle #4—Learning Is a Process, and Teachers Are Facilitators of That Process

Learning is a process. As we have noted in this chapter, we construct knowledge through a process that includes disequilibrium, assimilation, accommodation, and equilibrium through the use of language and culture. While some may describe the didactic teacher we discussed earlier as a transmitter of knowledge, the fact remains that her students still engaged in a process of learning. Although she did not elicit discussion or ask students to solve problems, they processed information individually and, in doing so, tapped into their own background knowledge; they likely found themselves experiencing disequilibrium, assimilation, and accommodation. What was missing was the intentional facilitation of knowledge by the teacher, who might have implemented strategies based upon the principles we have discussed. Rather than facilitate, the didactic teacher lectured and gave students the material they needed to know.

For the reasons previously discussed, this approach comes with unique consequences for ELLs, who may feel that their culture is invisible in the classroom curriculum.

## CONCLUDING THOUGHTS

This chapter has explained two perspectives in constructivism, giving you the basic framework necessary for understanding this sophisticated learning theory. We have also attempted to provide a rationale for practicing constructivist methodology with ELLs. The next chapter describes some practical, constructivist strategies that can be used in your classrooms.

# 4 Constructivist Practice for English Language Learners

Constructivist practice can be powerful for ELLs. Second language teachers know that instructional practice must be modified for second language learners when they are engaged in content learning in their L2. The distance between mainstream and second language teachers is not that large; language learning is about curriculum, and, after all, it is curriculum that drives second language acquisition. Just as Cummins (1978) posits that knowledge transfers across languages, Bransford and colleagues (2000) hypothesize that knowledge transfers across contexts and that the expert is able to reconstruct this knowledge in different settings. We encourage mainstream educators to transfer their knowledge of constructivist practice and reconstruct it in the service of ELLs.

The integration of second language learning with content learning makes it possible for constructivist teachers to simultaneously accommodate the needs of both mainstream students and ELLs because constructivist second language classrooms integrate language, content, and process. For ELLs who are learning in their L2, however, modifications are needed to maximize educational success. *Sheltered instruction* is a modification that can be used when teaching the core curriculum through the majority language, in this case English (Peregoy & Boyle, 2005). Sheltered instruction provides access to both the core curriculum and English language development and offers opportunities for social integration. According to Lessow-Hurley (2005), "teachers use strategies to encourage English acquisition through comprehensible input [modification of speech to maximize understanding] and contextualization" (p. 84). Specific sheltered strategies that teachers can successfully use, such as the modification and support of "teacher talk," will be described in subsequent sections.

Although many educators do not describe themselves as constructivist, in essence they teach in a manner consistent with constructivist pedagogy. This holds true for ESL and second language educators as well; after all, it is not how you label yourself but what you actually *do* that matters. In this book, we are applying constructivist pedagogy to bilingual education. This connection already exists; we are merely pointing it out. Good bilingual and ESL teachers who are constructivist in approach make modifications as a matter of course when they are teaching students in their second language. However, mainstream constructivist teachers may not be adept at making the modifications necessary to ensure the academic success of ELLs. Furthermore, while constructivist practice is often discussed in the professional literature, it is not as frequently implemented in practice. Through viewing the classrooms of Jill and Maria and analyzing the curriculum, pedagogy, and interactions within, we will attempt to address that gap.

Nowhere is the connection between constructivist practice and bilingual education clearer than in the case of TWI pedagogy. As pointed out earlier, two-way pedagogy drives an inherently constructivist curriculum; thus not only are language and content integrated, content and process are integrated, and this occurs within an environment that actively promotes peer social interaction as part of the learning process. In essence, there is a triangular relationship between content, language, and process, and it is all mediated by social interaction. This goes counter to the grain of traditional Western pedagogy in which elements of an education are separated out, "taught" separately, and then put back together, counter to the intuitive processes of life learning. Instead, immersion students learn language, content, and process (investigation, critique, questioning, discovery, the scientific method) simultaneously, as in life. As you will soon discover in our visit to the classroom of Jill Sontag, such a curriculum facilitates active engagement in the learning process.

It is quite possible to simultaneously meet the instructional needs of ELLs and mainstream students. As noted earlier, modifications made for the benefit of ELLs can enhance the educational experience of mainstream students because the *intent of such modification is to make the curriculum more accessible.* While the original intent may be to make the curriculum more accessible for ELLs, the net effect of such modifications is to make the curriculum more accessible to *all* students. In addition, when a second language is developed and reinforced through content, the mainstream teacher can integrate second language instruction into the content curriculum.

Whereas constructivist practice is best practice for ELLs who are simultaneously learning both language and content, constructivist practice in the native language is also advantageous. Group work, thematic instruction, and authentic assessment can and should take place in both English and the native language whenever possible. Finally, many of the constructivist educational activities that are used for second language instruction and development are just plain fun!

## FAMILIES AND COMMUNITIES

To tap the rich resources offered by family and community, we must look beyond the stereotypical view of the "deficit" backgrounds of our ELLs. When we do so, we may find what Moll and colleagues (1992) have termed "funds of knowledge" communities that offer knowledge and skills in disciplines such as medicine and agriculture. We can begin in our classrooms by viewing our students' backgrounds as strengths, as Monica does in the eighth-grade unit on immigration. This approach is advocated by Zentella (2005) who points out that, although teachers and Latino parents see a shared responsibility in the education of children, "neither fully realizes what is expected of them" (p. 176). According to Zentella, understanding the concepts of *respeto* (respect), *educación* (education), and *confianza* (trust) are essential to bridging this gap. She tells us that in partnering with our students' families *"con respeto"* (with respect) we need to first see what is there, to look beyond stereotypes and labels so that we can see the rich language and literacy practices embedded in our students' families and communities. *Confianza* can be built by ensuring that the informal conversations and formal communications we have with parents regarding the education of their children are two-way, that we provide for appropriate translation but that we also truly engage in communication. In the critical constructivist practice advocated in this book, this communication means that we engage in dialogue not only with our students but also with their families.

We can begin with an understanding of how education is understood within the context of our students' cultural backgrounds.

For Latinos, *educación* is linked with a good upbringing and based on *respeto* as the foundation for learning. Moral and academic aspects are fused in *educación,* not just the formal schooling stressed in "education." Rooted in an agrarian model of human development that arose in societies requiring collective work and the supervision of elders, aspects of the traditional model help Latinos adapt to difficult new circumstances that threaten the cohesion of the family in the United States (Reese et al., 1994).

—Ana Celia Zentella (2005, p. 178)

Different cultures and communities may have differing understandings of the term "education." If we find ourselves working with children and youth with whom we share little cultural knowledge, we can turn on our "teacher radar" (Nieto, 2004) and begin the research we need to do to access this information. "Research" need not imply formal academic study. We can begin by simply asking a more knowledgeable colleague or a bilingual parent for insight, comparing this new information with our classroom observations, and then making appropriate curricular and instructional modifications.

## INSTRUCTIONAL PRACTICE IN LANGUAGE ARTS

Just as there are foundational principles for guiding instructional practice with ELLs in the content area, so, too, can we highlight such principles for ELLs in the language arts. These principles are similarly informed by the combination of language acquisition research and constructivist theory. First and foremost, we return to the concept of transfer. Just as content knowledge transfers from the L1 to the L2, so, too, do literacy concepts. For ELLs who are already literate at the appropriate developmental level in their L1, the native language serves as a springboard to literacy in the L2. These students already understand letter/sound relationships, and that meaning comes from the printed page and must be negotiated with the knowledge of the reader. They have already developed meanings and strategies that transfer over to literacy in the L2. For younger and more immature literacy learners, use of an emergent literacy perspective can be effective in promoting L2 literacy due to its emphasis on immersing students in meaningful, functional uses of reading and writing. Books and other sources of information with strategies for teaching the language arts abound and are readily available in print or electronically. The remainder of this chapter suggests a variety of classroom strategies that emphasize constructivism.

*Reading aloud* to students accomplishes a variety of purposes and allows them to hear fluent reading with proper intonation and inflection in the L2. To modify this practice for ELLs, teachers may do the following:

1. Select books to read aloud that reflect the cultures represented in their classrooms. This familiarity allows students to build upon their backgrounds.

2. Ask students what they already know about topics that arise.

3. Read with inflection, gestures, humor, and drama; act out scenes in the book.

4. Develop vocabulary and understanding within the context of rich and wonderful stories as they (teachers) facilitate discussion and questions.

5. Guide students in using graphophonic, semantic, and syntactic cueing systems within the context of rich children's literature.

The *language experience approach* is useful when modified for ELLs. In this approach, the class discusses a common experience they have shared as the teacher writes what the students dictate. For instance, in the younger grades, the teacher might schedule a class fieldtrip that reinforces content, and then asks the children to write a story with him after returning to class. He might ask, "How should we begin our story?" When the children reply, the teacher writes exactly what they say on a chart or on the board. Composing together, the teacher takes the opportunity to think out loud about their writing. For example, he might say, "We want this sentence to show that we are excited. How do we accomplish this?" We suggest that, if the students offer a grammatically incorrect response, the teacher may want to model his thinking in making the *written* correction. After the story has been written, the teacher might ask the students to read it together chorally. There are also many extension activities that can be done with the story, for example, teaching sight words, noting word families, and checking for comprehension. Of course, much is dependent on the story itself, but it is safe to assume that the activity will be rich with meaningful opportunities for teaching. The teacher might also make a collection of stories that can be published in the school library and used in the years to come.

With older students, teachers can make a point of writing responses (which have been elicited from students) on the board. An example of this activity might be reading a book with the students and then making a Venn diagram on the board comparing two characters from the story, again modeling thinking in making written corrections. As the teacher asks specific questions of the students, he writes exactly what they say on the board. This approach can easily be modified for use in other content areas as well.

The connection between the language experience approach and constructivism is seen through an emphasis on students' individual backgrounds as they interact with the story, through the social interaction involved, and through scaffolding and problem solving about appropriate syntax and semantics. The method is powerful for ELLs because of the shared experience; in this way, the teacher provides a common starting place from which all students may springboard. It allows students to integrate reflections of their own culture, and it reinforces the connection between print and meaning. This latter aspect is particularly helpful as we seek to make complicated content comprehensible. In this regard, the teacher may also modify the approach by drawing pictures to represent content and/or meaning.

*Teaching word families* becomes a constructivist strategy when it is done using whole selections of children's literature rather than worksheets and contrived texts. For example, a teacher might use the book *Click Clack Moo Cows That Type* (Cronin, 2000) to teach the /oo/ sound. She could begin the lesson by doing a picture walk-through of the text, asking questions and building on answers from the students. Continuing with the read aloud, she could direct the students' thinking by making use of the Directed Reading Thinking Activity (DRTA). Roe, Smith, and Burns (2005) describe the DRTA as a strategy in which the teacher reads a text and asks students to predict upcoming events as she reads. Proceeding through the story, the teacher directs the students to check their predictions. This strategy builds essential metacognitive skills as it builds on the background and ideas of the students. To modify the activity for ELLs, a teacher could have her students act out the story. To incorporate word families after the story has been read, the teacher could ask her students, "What sound do you hear in moo?" Next, she might ask the class to make a list of words that have that same sound. To extend this activity, she might ask the class to work with magnetic letters on the board, practicing phonemic awareness as she changes the /m/ in moo to b, z, c, and so on and elicits from them the beginning, medial, and ending sounds in the words. Last, the teacher might guide the students to write a letter that follows the same format as the letter the animals in the book wrote. To further modify this activity for ELLs, she could give them a letter-writing scaffold where parts of the letter have already been written.

*Wordless books* are wonderful because they can be used to generate thoughts for speaking, reading, and writing. An excellent example of a wordless book is *Tuesday*, by David Wiesner (1991), in which there are few words but rather spectacularly mysterious pictures that tell the story of a frog invasion of a town. To teach this lesson as a constructivist, the teacher might put students into cooperative groups to write a story that supports the pictures. Of course, before putting students into groups, she would have shown the pictures in the story, asked questions, and modeled writing a similar story with the students. More ideas for wordless books are given in the visual arts section of this chapter.

The use of *literature circles* is compatible with a constructivist approach, for students are encouraged to draw from their prior knowledge in making meaning as they work through chapter books or novels *together.* If you have ever been part of a book club, then you have a good understanding of literature circles. If a teacher decides to implement literature circles, he or she will form temporary groups consisting of four to six students each. Each group chooses the book with which it would like to work. This is an important point, because this choice allows students to interact with literature in which they are interested and that probably is closely related to their experiences. As students work on a novel, they are each assigned roles to assume in their literature circles. Daniels's exhaustive work on literature circles suggests that, every time the students' circles meet, the individuals are responsible for presenting information to the group as delineated by their roles. Roles for consideration can include the following (Daniels, 2002):

- *Illustrator*—The illustrator draws a response to the text, which shows how the reader pictures the text.
- *Vocabulary Enricher*—This student selects challenging vocabulary words to present to the group.
- *Literary Luminary*—This student selects a passage that he likes and presents it to the group.
- *Researcher*—This student researches the historical time period, cultures, and other aspects of the setting in which the book takes place.
- *Connector*—This student finds a way to connect the book to her life and the lives of the students.
- *Travel Tracer*—This student keeps track of the settings in the story.
- *Summarizer*—This student summarizes the reading that was assigned.
- *Discussion Director*—This student comes with questions that will evoke meaningful discussion.

Literature circles are ideal for ELLs because they are social learning activities that can easily be differentiated by assigning an appropriate role for each student. In this way, the ZPD is considered. Additionally, literature circles allow the background of students to come to the fore as they interact with a text; scaffolding is an integral piece of the literature circle approach and is seen in the roles as well as in the discussion. Finally, there is social interaction and problem solving in the circles as students work through the novel.

*Listening and speaking* are foundational to successful second language acquisition for ELLs, and constructivist teachers can tap into a multitude of creative arts–based activities to this end. Many of these activities segue naturally into reading and writing activities. We suggest movement (for example, play-party songs such as "Little Sally Walker" from the African American tradition, creative movement, and pantomime), the dramatic arts (such as storytelling, creative drama, choral reading, and readers' theater), music and rhythm (songs, jazz chants, rap, and play-party songs), visual arts (drawing, painting, arts and crafts projects), games (show and tell, board games), and jokes and riddles.

There are also a plethora of *technological tools* that can assist with second language acquisition. Software packages are exhaustive in supplementing curriculum in areas such as vocabulary and writing; many also have voice capabilities. While we list a few resources here, we do so with the caveat that each must be examined as it relates to your particular classroom and students. Additionally, we suggest technology be used *within the context* of a balanced program.

Sources for interactive software include:

- http://www.meritsoftware.com
- http://teacher.scholastic.com/products/zipzoom/index.htm
- http://www.pearsondigital.com/ellis/teacher
- http://www.clarity.com.hk/program/index.htm

*Creative movement* activities can be particularly useful with students in the early stages of second language learning. Comprehensible input can be maximized when stories are enacted through pantomime. Roles need not be assigned; in the early grades, all of the students can enact all of the roles as the teacher speaks or reads. This strategy not only eliminates competition for choice parts but eliminates self-consciousness. If all of the students are actively involved, there is no one left to stare! Songs and poems also offer opportunities for students to respond to comprehensible input through movement, as well as provide built-in scaffolds for speaking. Children who are afraid to find their own words in a second language may appreciate the structure afforded by refrains and simple poems. Similarly, repetitive or significant lines in stories can be verbalized along with the teacher as the children pantomime them. Because first language literacy is enhanced through artistic literary endeavors, all students can benefit from these practices.

The *dramatic arts*, including storytelling, choral reading, readers' theater, and creative drama, offer limitless possibilities for facilitating language arts development with ELLs. *Storytelling* can take many forms, from the purely verbal and anecdotal to the formal written genre. Likewise, *choral reading* can be as simple as an entire class reading of a short poem or as intricate as a scripted production with separate choreographed voices.

*Reader's theater* is a specific genre of theater meant to illuminate literature rather than stage a production. Lines are not memorized but read, with the script in full view. Props, costumes, and scenery are often only suggestive or symbolic. Choreography and staging are purposefully minimal to illuminate and give voice to the written word. Increasingly commercial scripts are available for use in elementary and secondary school classrooms, but virtually any work of literature can be converted into a reader's theater script. For all these reasons, reader's theater lends itself easily to the classroom while providing a scaffold to literary language for second language learners, for scripts are predominantly in the present tense and are thus easier for linguistic negotiation.

*Children's drama* is an art form in its own right, with the goal of the educational development of children rather than the creation of future career artists. It consists of two component parts: children's theater and creative drama. While children's theater typically focuses on *product*, creative drama focuses on *process*. With the latter, the teacher is less concerned with a final theatrical production than with the learning possibilities that the *process* of engaging children and youth in drama opens up. Creative drama has the potential to impact not only content area growth (as discussed in the upcoming section on social studies) but also the affective, cognitive, and developmental growth of children. To this end, it utilizes informal and engaging techniques such as role-playing, theater games, and improvisation and thus provides an excellent vehicle for lowering the affective filter and providing comprehensible second language input in mainstream classrooms where children from linguistic minority and linguistic majority backgrounds are integrated. Successful drama activities can segue into writing if students decide to create scripts out of material originally created from improvisations. Again, because of the more limited use of tense in dramatic scripts, such writing is inherently sheltered from more advanced grammatical structure.

The inherent motivational quality of *music* as well as its link to memory makes it an ideal medium for oral second language development. In fact, a recent study (Wong, Skoe, Russo, Dees, & Kraus, 2007) suggests that "experience with music at a young age in effect can 'fine-tune' the brain's auditory system" by enhancing "the brainstem's sensitivity to speech sounds," and the study advocates experiences with music as beneficial for all children. Action songs are pure linguistic scaffolds already commonplace in primary grade classrooms. Play-party songs (games with accompanying songs and motions) from African American traditions similarly embed language learning in engaging and enjoyable activities. Jazz chants are also easily adapted to second language acquisition. For older learners, the contemporary genre of rap can provide the same function.

The *visual arts*, from drawing and painting to arts and crafts projects, are also inherently motivational and natural scaffolds for language learning. Students in beginning stages of second language acquisition can use the visual arts as an alternative to verbal response. For more advanced second language learners, visual art forms can be a trigger to verbal response. Wordless books offer an excellent example of this principle. Teachers can use the pictures, created specifically to elicit a response, to motivate children to speak in their second language. In a mainstream classroom, the creation of a wordless book could become an alternative to a written story for a child in the early stages of English language acquisition. Book covers are themselves a visual genre, which are often readily available, beautifully illustrated, and easy to incorporate in classrooms. As visual literacy continues to be an area all students are required to develop, the importance of visual activities in the classroom gains importance.

Visual arts can also be used with the *Picture-Word Inductive Model*. This approach as described by Joyce, Weil, and Calhoun (2004) is a way to integrate fine arts, literacy, and culture. For example, a teacher could bring in a painting (by a well-known artist) that reflects the cultures of students in her classroom. As Joyce and colleagues explain, "[The teacher] asks the student to study the picture and take turns identifying items and actions. . . . As each item is named, [she] . . . draws a line from the word to a place on the background paper where she prints it, spells it, and then has the students spell it and say it" (p. 77).

The teacher talks about the picture, especially noting the cultural connections, the colors, relative elements of art, and so on. Explaining what inference is, she will ask her students appropriate inference questions. Next she will ask students to think about the objects, people, and actions they have identified and labeled and will make a list of those items. According to Joyce and colleagues (2004), students then put the words on cards and work with the cards until they are familiar with them. The teacher then guides students in putting the words into categories according to similar characteristics. With ELLs this is a meaningful way to teach vocabulary and expose them to rich and beautiful pieces of art, which can help them feel their culture is valued. Eventually, the teacher will work at making sentences with the words the students have listed and categorized. An extension activity might have students write about the personal meaning they derive from the pictures.

There is no limit to the language learning possibilities offered by *games*. Like arts-based activities, they tend to engage students immediately. Games may be effectively used to scaffold not only language learning (for example, show and tell, and jokes and riddles) but also academic content (for example, board games such as Bingo). Board games may be purchased or teacher created to fit specific curricular needs.

*Writing* can be engaging as well. Students can have immediate success with structured poetry before moving on to less structured forms. Process writing can take the fear out of writing due to its inherent scaffolding process and is thus well suited for ELLs. Wordless books are a powerful learning tool that can trigger discussion in the L2, leading to response activities in drama, music, visual art, movement, and writing. Technology, in its many forms, can provide unending support to L2 language arts development, as can educational excursions and field trips.

Perhaps the best-known form of *structured poetry* used in classrooms is the Haiku. It is based upon a syllabic pattern expressed in three lines expressing a single idea. The first line contains five syllables, the second contains seven syllables, and the third line contains five syllables. For example:

Flowers are blooming

Yellow, red, orange, purple

The earth comes to life

The Haikon is a pictorial representation of the Haiku. The Haiku above could be converted into a Haikon by drawing the outline of a flower and writing the lines in the poem around its shape. The Tanka adds two more lines to the Haiku, each containing seven syllables. For example:

Flowers are blooming

Yellow, red, orange, purple

The earth comes to life

In colors that invite me

To go into the garden

While the Terquin uses structure, it does not require a rigid syllabi formula. It contains three lines on a single subject and offers the opportunity for even the beginning ELL to be a successful poet. The first line contains a one-word noun. The second line describes the noun with two or three words, and the third line is either a synonym of the noun or describes a feeling about it. For example:

Soccer

Kicking, running, punting

Happiness

The Cinquain also uses structure without a rigid syllabic formula but is a bit more sophisticated. The first line is a noun. The second line uses two words to describe the noun. The third line contains three action verbs that describe the noun, while the fourth line contains four words that describe feelings about the noun. The fifth and final line is one word that is synonymous with the noun used in the first line. For example:

Dog

Warm, furry

Bark, jump, run

Care, share, sad, happy

Friend

The Diamante combines grammatical structure with pictorial form in seven lines. It splits thematically in the fourth line so that the first half of the poem is conceptually the opposite of the second half of the poem. It is graphically represented in a diamond shape. For example:

Day

warm, bright

running, jumping, playing

school, park, sofa, bed

sleeping, snoring, dreaming

cool, dark

night

As illustrated above, the first line is one word, a noun, and the last line is its opposite. The second and sixth lines contain two adjectives that describe the respective nouns. The third and fifth lines contain three action verbs each, and the fourth (middle) line is split with two nouns relating to each opposing concept.

These structured poetic forms can be successful with ELLs because they are literary scaffolds. Rhyming verse may present a particular challenge for ELLs with limited English vocabulary, and free verse may prove too intimidating. Structured poetry, however, offers creative success while reinforcing aspects of English vocabulary and grammar. A multitude of structured poetic forms exist and are easily obtainable through texts or over the Internet. Teachers can engage the class in the structured form most generally suited to their English proficiency level or can offer choice in poetic form. Publishing student work in a poetry anthology can offer further incentive for writing, as can illustration and choral reading.

*Literature-based instruction* is another effective approach for ELLs. With literature-based instruction, rich children's literature is the basis for reading instruction. Teachers use trade books (generally defined as books for sale to the general public) as a springboard for language arts development. This strategy is powerful because it allows for context-embedded instruction; using whole books also encourages diverse representations of literature. Teachable moments will naturally emerge from the wonderful writing of authors who have skillfully mastered their craft. Within a literature-based framework, teachers may easily integrate other content areas and write thematic units, which are thought to be particularly useful for ELLs. Figure 4.1 shows a semantic map that was developed for a thematic unit on *Charlotte's Web* (White, 1952).

A *dialogue journal* is a strategy that allows scaffolding and peer interaction. A dialogue journal occurs when two people engage in writing back and forth to each other. For example, the teacher might read a short poem and give the first prompt for the dialogue journal, such as, "Write a question about the poem for your journal partner." The first partner writes the question, which is then given to the second partner, who responds and then writes a question for the original partner. The journal goes back and forth for two or three exchanges.

*Process writing* is particularly useful with ELLs because it consists of a series of scaffolds, each one leading seamlessly to the next, with significant peer support. The sequential stages in the writing process are prewriting (brainstorming and other strategies), drafting, revising, editing, and publishing. In process writing, students are encouraged to write from experience, thus validating prior knowledge and life experience. Cooperative assistance is provided in the form of peer input (ideas, suggestions, critique, feedback) during each phase of the process. Editing is not attempted until the revision process is complete so that students can focus on creativity and meaning. Just as sheltering is a language scaffold, process writing is a literacy scaffold. While mainstream students may not need scaffolding for oral language development to the same extent as ELLs, our experiences have convinced us that virtually all students need scaffolding with writing. In this sense, process writing may be one of the most powerful means by which the needs of both mainstream and ELL student populations can be met.

**Figure 4.1**    Thematic Content Planning With *Charlotte's Web*

### Fine Arts

- **Visual** Bring in a picture or painting of a farm and a city. (This also relates to the social studies activities.) Use the Picture-Word Induction Model (see text) to label the objects.

- **Creative Movement** Have students pantomime actions of the various animals. Have students select **music** they think represents the animals.

### Science

- Since *Charlotte's Web* takes place in a farm setting, integrate science content by studying **plants** and how they grow.

- Integrate science content that examines **classification** groups of animals.

**Charlotte's Web
Integration of
Content**

### Social Studies

- Since *Charlotte's Web* is a story, which connects to **communities,** integrate a study of different **roles** one might have in a community.

- Compare and contrast a **rural** and an **urban** community. Allow students to share information about the communities in which they have lived.

### Language Arts

- Have students adapt a portion of the book to a **reader's theater** script and then rehearse and perform it for their peers and/or for other classrooms. (This also relates to the fine arts activities.)

- Include spelling words from other content areas. For example: **Science:** plant, seed, grow, water, animal, etc. **Social Studies:** farm, city, farmer, etc. **Fine Arts:** Use words elicited from the students in the Picture-Word Induction Model for spelling words and to brainstorm ideas for writing.

*Note:* When planning thematic units for ELLs, it is important to overlap as much as possible because repeated exposure to vocabulary and content reinforces internalization of material.

# INSTRUCTIONAL PRACTICE
# IN THE CONTENT AREAS

Constructivist teachers can implement specific instructional strategies and learning activities to engage *all* students in content learning; however, as in the language arts, it is necessary to use sheltering and scaffolding as modifications to the curriculum. Peregoy and Boyle (2005) note that there are specific ways to do so. They highlight the importance of nonverbal activities for both teachers and students. Teachers can support their talk through nonverbal means such as visuals and hands-on experience. Students can contribute to classroom and cooperative group activities through nonverbal means until they are ready to begin speaking with more confidence in their second language. To get students to the *output* or speaking stage, they will need to receive continual *comprehensible input.* This can be done through modification of teacher talk, and Peregoy and Boyle (2005) note multiple ways of doing so, including adjusting rate of speech, phrasing and rephrasing, vocabulary, pauses, sentence expansion, gesture, facial expression, and dramatic expression.

*Think Pair Share* is an effective content area strategy. When explaining difficult concepts, stop and simply ask students to pair together and explain what they are learning in their own words. After a few minutes, the teacher can elicit responses from the students. This simple strategy can be an immense help to students as they encounter more difficult content.

*Modeling* and *think-alouds* are extremely beneficial for ELLs. Essentially, these strategies involve demonstrating and allowing students to have access to the teacher's thought processes. An especially powerful example of modeling and think-alouds emerged as Sharon supervised the clinical experiences of students working with ELLs. One of her students, Jayne Hutchins, reflected on her experience: "The first lesson I taught ... was with three groups of four students each. I taught one group at a time a math lesson on addition." Jayne writes that the activity was not a success. She was equally unsuccessful with the second group. Then she had an epiphany. She realized that she needed

> to somehow get them thinking about what they were doing and how they would come up with the answers in their brains so that they could better understand the math actually being taught. That was when it hit me. . . . I changed the way I spoke, and instead of saying "let's say I was to pick a five. What number would I have to add to equal seven?" I said "Hmmm I want to add two numbers that equal seven when added together. Hmmm I think that if

I choose a five I am going to need what number? Hmmm let me see five plus what equals seven. Oh, five plus two equals seven." This group had a much easier time understanding my directions and doing the activity because they knew how to go through the steps of the activity in their heads. They were also much more engaged and interested in learning because what I was saying made sense.

This strategy can be effective with all content areas.

Content area instruction with ELLs in their second language, informed by both language acquisition research and constructivist theory, integrates comprehensible input and social interaction with opportunities for functional, meaningful communication. It does so through sheltered instruction and scaffolding in combination with instructional strategies such as *cooperative group work, thematic instruction, problem-solving activities, project-oriented learning,* and *authentic assessment.* Constructivist practice maximizes the supplementary support offered by cultural institutions such as museums and arts organizations as well as maximizing the rich resources offered by communities and families.

A cooperative learning strategy students enjoy is called *jigsaw,* and it works nicely with many content areas. The teacher breaks the class up into groups. For the purpose of easy math, let us assume there are three groups of three students each. Using science as our content area, we would assign Group I to become an expert on mammals, Group II to become an expert on reptiles, and Group III to become an expert on birds. To become experts, the teacher guides the students to various resources, gives them a way to organize the information they find by way of a scaffold, and guides them on how they will present information in their new groups. Once all the groups are ready, the whole class comes together and forms new groups, which we will refer to as *sharing groups*; the sharing groups consist of one person from each expert group. The job is for the expert to teach the new group about his or her area. Figure 4.2 will help you understand this strategy; it reflects the final groups on presentation day.

In the content areas of math, science, and social studies, *vocabulary building activities* are foundational, for understanding content area vocabulary is the key to opening the content itself. Of course, written and visual context clues are foundational in promoting vocabulary development, as is exposure to new words as modeled repeatedly in the teacher's speech. For ELLs, however, this is only a starting point. Vocabulary development must not be taken for granted. Cognates, words that have similar sound and meaning in multiple languages, provide an easy entry to new vocabulary. Tapping a common Latin root and exploring word families can be especially useful in teaching science vocabulary. In math, where one word

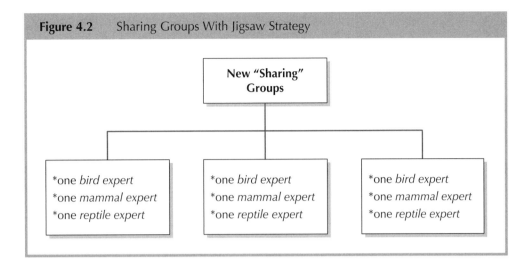

**Figure 4.2** Sharing Groups With Jigsaw Strategy

New "Sharing" Groups

*one *bird expert*
*one *mammal expert*
*one *reptile expert*

*one *bird expert*
*one *mammal expert*
*one *reptile expert*

*one *bird expert*
*one *mammal expert*
*one *reptile expert*

can signal an entire mathematical process, teaching specific math synonyms can be crucial. For example, as Peregoy and Boyle (2005) point out, the words *add, plus, combine,* and *sum* all signal addition. Graphic organizers may be particularly helpful in social studies because they can succinctly illuminate with specific words the relationships between people and society that are so fundamental to the discipline. Jesness (2004) suggests strategies such as using word blocks (root words, prefixes and suffixes), explanation of idioms, and dictionaries (picture, bilingual, and electronic).

Embedding content area studies in real life experiences is especially important for ELLs, because not only does it develop vocabulary but it also helps bridge the gap between content and language through comprehensible experiences. *We suggest that comprehensible experience in the content area is parallel to comprehensible input in the language arts.* Further, we suggest that such experiences can lower the affective filter by getting students actively involved in learning activities.

Particularly in math and science, the use of manipulative and concrete objects can assist in teaching content through a second language. This technique is especially apparent in Jill's classroom, as she guides her students through a thematic unit on bugs. In addition, the process-oriented inquiry approach that she utilizes for bug study gives the students access to not only science content but also science process. In an inquiry-oriented approach to science, students are able to define problems, state hypotheses, gather data, record observations, draw conclusions, and summarize findings, like "real" scientists. Doing so in either pairs or in small groups taps into the social context of learning and maximizes opportunities for peer-supported second language learning. All of these elements come together to provide a rich opportunity for the integration of language, content, and process.

*Problem solving* activities can be assigned in pairs or small groups for math as well as social studies and science activities. For example, working on story problems in a group can be helpful. The teacher may give the students a piece of butcher paper, go over the story problem criteria, and have the students write the word problem and draw different possibilities. Project-oriented learning activities work well in all content areas. Taking advantage of cultural institutions need not be restricted to the social studies curriculum. Museums that highlight science, technology, and the environment are good examples of cultural institutions that provide unending resources for the study of math and science.

The social studies curriculum offers infinite possibilities for bridging the gap between content and language through comprehensible experiences that connect to the students' lives and thus inherently lower the affective filter. *Oral histories*, for example, allow students to make connections between their own lives and the broader discipline of history. Olmedo (1993, 2006) has written extensively about the possibilities inherent in this genre. She notes that not only can it strengthen both oral and written language development but that engaging students in oral history projects with members of their own families and communities holds other pedagogical benefits: building on prior knowledge, broadening the knowledge base by engaging with families and communities, and structuring project-oriented experiences within cooperative groups. An additional benefit may be the enhancement of student self-concept, which we have referred to earlier as identity construction. Olmedo sees this enrichment occurring when we validate the life experiences of ELLs as they "see that their families have something worth sharing with mainstream culture" (p. 8). In the context of mainstream classrooms, we may also validate the life experiences of English dominant students with a second language heritage. We note the strong connections to constructivist theory embedded in the practice Olmedo suggests.

Olmedo offers guidelines for oral history projects. She suggests starting out by targeting social studies concepts and then preparing interview guides with the following basic categories from which questions may flow: grandparents, childhood, the migration experience, and life in the new land. (For the complete listing of sample questions, see Appendix.) If necessary, these guides can be translated into the native languages of the interviewees, thus offering bilingual students an important role and allowing ELLs less fluent in their second language with opportunities to contribute to the group. After the interview guides are prepared, students will need practice asking questions with the use of a tape recorder, an exercise that can be achieved in cooperative groups. When the students feel more comfortable with this skill, and to model by example, a guest can be invited into the classroom for a group interview. The subsequent session can be discussed and transcribed collectively by the entire class. At this point, students should be ready to work in smaller groups. They can select interviewees, divide responsibilities for the project, interview their guest, and create the final transcription. When complete, full class follow-up activities may include selecting themes illuminated by the various guests as well as comparing and contrasting the interviewees' experiences.

Many of the creative arts can be useful in social studies. Through the use of dramatic play, for example, classrooms might have any number of centers that develop written and spoken languages. Play grocery stores, carpentry shops, hospitals, and libraries lend themselves well to developing emergent literacy skills and can teach content at the same time.

History may seem an intimidating subject to some students, yet stories are uniquely and fundamentally part of the human experience. Storytelling is embedded in many cultures just as the word story is embedded in the word history. (Many feminists point out the gender bias inherent in this word, a point that can be legitimately discussed with students.) Yet, as Olmedo points out, "much of history is written from the point of view of the winners rather than the losers. It is not surprising that the experiences of many of the ethnic groups in our classrooms are not found in many textbooks. However, such experience can be documented from the raw, historical material offered by students and families" (p. 8). Thus, not only can oral history projects engage and empower students, they can provide teachers with access to fascinating and important information that might otherwise remain invisible.

Urban areas usually offer a wealth of options for exploring the social landscape of specific locales, the nation, and the world through museums and other cultural institutions. Museums often host specific programs for groups of school children and youth, as well as offering continuing opportunities for teachers. In addition to permanent collections that are connected in a variety of ways to the discipline of social studies, special exhibitions can generate learning possibilities enhanced by the excitement of leaving the classroom walls. Field trips to museums and cultural institutions can be extended through inquiry-based projects or response activities through the creative arts. The dramatic arts can enhance the social studies curriculum in multiple ways such as role-playing, reenactments, simulation, and improvisation.

## ASSESSMENT

"As educators, we are constantly challenged to make informed decisions about our students; to do so, we plan, gather, and analyze information from multiple sources over time so that the results are meaningful to teaching and learning" (Gottlieb, 2006, p. 1). So begins the text *Assessing English Language Learners.* To the experienced teacher, these words hardly seem frightening. Yet many educators cringe at the word "assessment."

To explain this attitude, we return to our example of the child learning to tie her shoes. The young learner in our example is engaged in an authentic learning experience. Her parent is watching her attempt to tie her shoe while offering support and guidance on the road to independent action. Thus, teaching and assessment are seamlessly interwoven. The parent is not thinking of "assessing" the child but rather of guiding the child. Imagine the response if the child were to be graded on a shoe-tying rubric or if her abilities were to be compared by percentile and stanine to other children of her age! We can speculate that any of these scenarios might serve to raise the affective filter of both the child and the parent to the point that it might actually interfere with the learning process. Yet, this is what we do continuously in schools throughout the nation. It is small wonder that so many educators fear assessment, for it has been redefined to mystify rather than illuminate instruction. We believe that it is this artificial separation of instruction and assessment that causes assessment to drive curriculum and that makes educators fear assessment.

A tremendous emphasis is currently placed on formal, norm-referenced standardized tests. Due to the necessity for students to have mastered academic language to be successful on such high-stakes tests, they pose significant challenges for ELLs (Reiss, 2008). One issue involves distinguishing and separating what is being assessed. When assessing ELLs, one must realize the difference between language proficiency and mastery of content. Gottlieb (2006) agrees. She writes, "In the assessment framework for English language learners, we first differentiate language proficiency from academic achievement" (p. 23). Traditional assessments, as described by Mueller (2006), tend to measure both one's ability to understand academic language and one's ability to understand content. However, the most obvious issue with standardized tests for ELLs is the absurdity of being academically ranked after taking a high-stakes test in a language in which the learner may not be proficient.

Because this book is about *constructivist* practice, we have chosen to focus our discussion on *classroom* assessment; specifically, we will look carefully at authentic assessment and its link to constructivist practice. If we allow ourselves the freedom to define assessment in authentic terms, it need not be so frightening. Assessment in constructivist practice is based upon "procedures for evaluating student achievement or performance using activities that represent classroom goals, curricula, and instruction or real-life performance" (O'Malley & Valdez Pierce, 1996, p. 237). It should be observation based, be continuous over time, and utilize a variety of techniques to supply the teacher with multiple sources of data on student development. For ELLs, authentic assessment is based upon activities that reflect educational equity; that is, activities that foreground the linguistic and cultural backgrounds of students.

Also termed performance assessment or alternative assessment, authentic assessment is characterized by having students "perform real-world tasks that demonstrate meaningful application of essential knowledge and skills" (Mueller, 2006). Authentic assessment is formative and is done simultaneously with classroom instruction; it informs the instructional decisions teachers make. The essence of formative assessment is realized in its Latin root *assidere,* which means *to sit beside.* The example given earlier in the chapter of a child learning how to tie her shoe is a beautiful illustration of assessment because it shows the idea of *joining together* in the learning process, with the adult coming *alongside* the child to see if she is learning. The goal is learning, not evaluation. This kind of assessment is practiced in hundreds of classrooms every day by highly skilled teachers and can be accomplished through such simple techniques as teacher observation and discussion. It "allow(s) one to determine the degree to which students know or are able to do a given learning task, and . . . [identify] the part of the task that the student does not know or is unable to do" (Carleton College, Science Education Resource Center, 2006).

In both purpose and application, formative assessment is separate and distinct from evaluation. Evaluation, a summative assessment, is used to determine what students know *after* presentation of content; for example, following an entire instructional unit. This difference is significant, especially for those who view learning as a continuing process. With summative evaluation, a grade is usually attached, and the goal is to place a value judgment on the degree to which students have mastered content. Formative assessment, rather, involves many different measures, the purpose of which is to feed data back into the instructional loop (see Figure 4.3). Constructivist learning theory is thus at the core of formative authentic assessment, as demonstrated by its fluid nature, determined by the *students'* understanding at any given time. The ZPD is integral, as are the background and thoughts of the students.

Herrera, Murry, and Morales Cabral (2007) illuminate the constructivist nature of authentic assessment when they note, "Successful classroom instruction focuses on the *construction* of meaning and helps students develop lasting connections between new learning and existing knowledge. Ultimately, this type of instruction depends on the effective preassessment of students' content-area knowledge, skills, and capacities" (p. 62). Just as preassessment helps teachers in planning curriculum, postassessment helps teachers ascertain the effectiveness of the curriculum. Constructivist teachers recognize that student difficulty on postinstructional assessments may signal that either preassessment techniques or classroom curriculum need to be refined. We thus suggest that authentic assessment may function not just as assessment of the students but also as assessment of our own effectiveness as educators.

Other types of assessment are appropriate for constructivist second language classrooms. Diagnostic assessment, for example, can be an important tool in customizing instruction to individual student need. We have limited our discussion, however, to the type of assessment most easily integrated into the constructivist second language classroom and that used in the three different contexts described by our featured teachers.

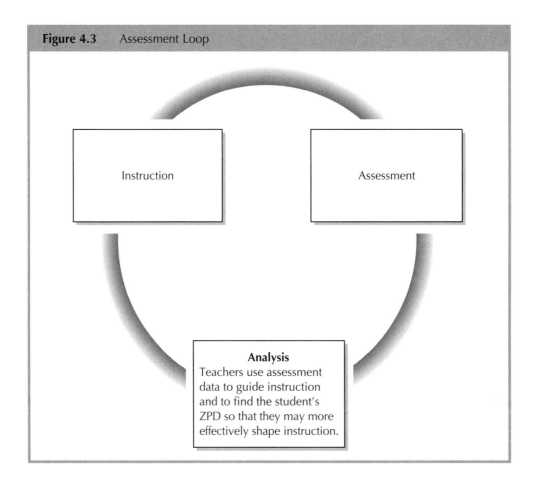

**Figure 4.3**      Assessment Loop

Instruction

Assessment

**Analysis**
Teachers use assessment data to guide instruction and to find the student's ZPD so that they may more effectively shape instruction.

When Jill converses with her students about butterfly eggs, she is assessing the second language proficiency of her Spanish language learners. Maria is able to access second language literacy over time as she reviews her students' original compositions in English. Final questions on index cards provide Monica with artifacts that she can use to evaluate progress in the development of academic thought. All of these assessments are embedded in instructional practice. They illustrate the concept of assessment as feedback into instruction, but they are only three small illustrations of many possibilities. Other ways of assessing students through authentic means include checklists, running records, educational games, student self-assessment reports, and student-teacher conferences such as those used in reading and writing workshops.

However, the most natural means of assessment are ongoing teacher observation and the review of student artifacts. Something as simple as a smile can give a type of data unobtainable by a standardized test score. Reviewing student work over time, ranging from daily assignments to artifacts that culminate project-oriented and theme-based learning, makes up assessment that is part of normal instructional planning. Students can self-select the work that they feel is most significant in portfolios, teachers can request that specific assignments be included, or a combination of both methods of selection may be used. Whatever way is chosen, an excellent record of student development over time results. Most important, however, is eliminating the cultural bias inherent in other forms of assessment, for when assessment is used to rank and sort students, educational inequity usually results. The fact that we live in an educational environment that mandates a tremendous amount of standardized testing only serves to emphasize the need for teachers to implement authentic assessment. It may be one of the most important means that we currently possess of leveling the playing field for linguistic minority students.

## SUMMARY OF SUGGESTED PRACTICE FOR CONSTRUCTIVIST SECOND LANGUAGE CLASSROOMS

A summary of recommended activities for engaging second language learners in constructivist language arts and content area instruction is provided here, but this list is by no means meant to be exhaustive. Consistent with constructivist practice, we encourage you to borrow from other educators and other disciplines, and to revise, create, and re-create activities that will enhance student learning in a manner that keeps it comprehensible for ELLs.

- Use students as language models for peers
- Contextualize instruction to promote language acquisition
- Use music to reinforce memory
- Maximize the social context of language acquisition
- Teach language through content
- Model incessantly
- Use humor to motivate language acquisition
- Scaffold instruction in L2
- Shelter teacher talk in L2 through hands-on experience and visual aids
- Modify teacher talk in L2
- Teach and reinforce L2 vocabulary
- Use concrete objects such as manipulatives
- Embed instruction in real life experiences; facilitate context-embedded learning
- Use problem solving activities
- Use cooperative group work
- Have students work in pairs
- Choose curricular topics of inherent interest to students
- Link content areas thematically; utilize thematic units
- Engage students in scientific study through scientific methods
- Use a process-oriented inquiry approach
- Use project-based learning
- Utilize cultural institutions
- Utilize community resources
- Utilize family resources
- Use educational drama techniques such as role-playing, reenactments, simulations, and improvisation
- Promote critical thinking and critique
- Encourage students to ask their own questions and find their own answers
- Use silence as a learning tool
- Use the creative arts frequently
- Seize the moment: utilize authentic learning opportunities and do not be a slave to the lesson plan
- Maximize the social context of learning
- Choose multidimensional assessment
- Use oral histories
- Consider literature circles
- Try readers' theater
- Use jigsaw activities
- Employ the language experience approach

- Exercise Think Pair Share
- Apply the Picture-Word Induction Model
- Use authentic, formative assessment

And remember, making the curriculum accessible for ELLs can make the curriculum accessible for everyone!

# 5 Perspectives in Critical Pedagogy

**I**n Chapter 8, we take you into a *critical* classroom in a major Midwestern city. As you will see, the students are lively and curious as they engage in meaningful dialogue within the critical framework their teacher has chosen for teaching a unit on immigration. An introduction to critical theory will be necessary to fully appreciate the dynamics at work in this classroom; the goal of this chapter is to give the background you will need to make the journey.

The first time Trina ever heard of critical pedagogy was in a graduate-level class that examined theoretical foundations in bilingual and ESL education. Unfortunately, it is possible—and some would say probable—that one might obtain a teaching certificate and never be exposed to this idea. Reasons for this are many: critical pedagogy is not a list of things to do in teaching, for it is not a teaching *method*. Rather, as the name implies, it is an art of teaching, or a way of teaching, in which the world is viewed through a critical lens.

When one examines the works of scholars in this field such as McLaren, Giroux, Marcedo, and Freire himself, you find a labyrinth of language difficult for both graduate and postgraduate students to navigate. Ironically, this pedagogy of (and for) oppressed people is posited by scholars who have chosen a linguistic style not easily understood by laywomen and men. Critical scholars have been criticized for this inaccessibility. Whatever your opinion of the scholarly discourse, one might argue with some validity that the complex essence of "the literature" is part of the reason preservice teachers often are not exposed to critical pedagogy.

Another reason critical pedagogy is not be widely known by teachers is because of the standards-based educational environment in which teachers currently find themselves. Objectives are already defined, and finding a way of teaching that encourages students to critically examine their reality can be a challenge. Given the complexity of these issues, *our* hope is to show one way in one classroom where principles of critical pedagogy are being followed. Our hope is that this example will inform your practice. The ways in which you might apply what you learn will be as varied as the districts, principals, and students with whom you work.

One cannot examine critical pedagogy without a discussion of Paulo Freire who wrote *Pedagogy of the Oppressed*, originally published in 1970. Freire was a literacy educator in Brazil who taught colonized peasants how to read with phenomenal success. Germane to his pedagogy was bringing his students (peasants) to a place where they understood their oppressed position and how their own literacy was essential for freedom. Rooted in Marxist ideology, Freire believed that education (at its worst) could be used to transmit knowledge working to favor the best interest of the *oppressor*; for him, education thus meant transmitting content that reinforced a subservient class of peasants living in poverty. Freire saw this practice as unacceptable, so he taught the peasants in a way described as critical pedagogy.

You may be wondering what in the world such a radical-sounding philosophy has to do with you. Certainly terms such as *oppressed*, *oppressor*, and *Marxism* will seem far removed from your classroom. Yet, a book on teaching students for whom English is not a native language cannot be complete without examining ways in which language and power are related and negotiated in classrooms and society.

## CRITICAL PEDAGOGY: A DIFFERENT PERSPECTIVE

Perhaps a good way to gain an understanding of critical pedagogy is to relate it to an ordinary experience. As is often the case, Trina one day found herself working in the local bookstore's coffee shop. Whether reading articles, grading papers, visiting with a friend, or writing, a bookstore with a coffee shop is an inviting place for people to think, to design, to talk, to grow, and to learn. That day, she savored the aroma of the "beach blend" she was slowly nurturing as she thoughtfully engaged in the writing process—wishing perhaps to be on the beach listening to the waves lap the shore and enjoying the blend of the day in the atmosphere for which it was intended. Instead, she set her screensaver on the beach scene and continued her cognitive pursuits.

Feeling the need for a distraction, Trina embarked upon a journey and meandered into the education section of the bookstore, where she found herself immersed in a section with as many titles as flavors of coffee in the café: *Daily Warm-Ups: Reading Grade Six, Core Knowledge Sequence: Content Guidelines for Grades K-8, The Social Studies Teacher's Book of Lists* (2nd edition), *The Weekly Curriculum: 52 Complete Preschool Themes*, and *Laura's List: The First Lady's List of 57 Great Books for Families and Children*. A close examination of two titles is particularly useful for our discussion on critical pedagogy. The first is *Core Knowledge Sequence: Content Guidelines for Grades K-8* published by the Core Knowledge Foundation. As she leafed through the book, Trina saw what the authors considered to be essential content explicitly presented. This content included phonemic awareness, decoding/encoding, suggested stories to use in class, and sayings and phrases students should know—sayings such as "A dog is man's best friend; A place for everything and everything in its place; and Where there's a will there's a way" (1999, p. 10).

For social studies, there was a list of American presidents students should know, including "George Washington the 'Father of His Country,' Thomas Jefferson, . . . Abraham Lincoln." Symbols and places determined to be essential included "the American flag, the Statue of Liberty, Mount Rushmore, and the White House" (p. 13). The authors asserted that a *core knowledge sequence* reflected such things as "elements of art, living things and their environment, elements of music, the America Revolution, America becomes a world power, decline of European colonialism, civil rights, algebra, civics, the constitution [etc.]."

The introduction to the book stated:

The Sequence [of core knowledge posited by the authors] represents a first and ongoing attempt to state specifically a core knowledge that children should learn in American schools. It should be emphasized that the Core Knowledge Sequence is not a list of facts to be memorized. Rather, it is a guide to coherent content from grade to grade. . . . [To derive the Core Knowledge Sequence], first, we analyzed the many reports issued by the state departments of education and by professional organizations—such as the National Council of Teachers of Mathematics and the American Association for the Advancement of Science—which recommended general outcomes for elementary and secondary education. We also tabulated the knowledge and skills specified in the successful educational systems of several other countries including, France, Japan, Sweden, and West Germany. In addition, we formed an advisory board on multiculturalism that proposed a core knowledge of diverse cultural traditions that American children should share as part of their school-based common culture. (p. 1)

A second title worth inspection is *The Social Studies Teacher's Book of Lists* (2nd edition). This book included lists in the areas of U.S. history, world history, American government, consumer economics, sociology, psychology, and geography (Partin, 2003, pp. ix–xxi). Trina asked one of her cohorts at the bookstore to randomly select a page in the book. Admittedly the young man looked at her strangely, but he selected two pages. Listed below is a portion of the content from those two pages:

### List 94—Fads and Fancies of the 1970s

| | |
|---|---|
| Afro (Haircut) | Maxi-skirt |
| backgammon | mechanics' jump suits |
| Ben Franklin glasses | mood rings |
| beanbag chairs | mutton-chop sideburns |
| bell-bottom pants | peace symbol |
| bib overalls | pet rocks |
| biorhythms | string bikinis |
| Cbs | puka shell necklaces |
| chokers | punk fashions |
| clacker balls | roller disco |
| cybernetics | skate parks |

The second list (remember that the pages were "randomly" selected!) was as follows:

### List 95—Movies of Ronald Reagan

| | |
|---|---|
| *Accidents Will Happen* | *Knute Rockne—All American* |
| *An Angel From Texas* | *The Last Outpost* |
| *The Angels Wash Their Faces* | *Law and Order* |
| *The Bad Man* | *Louisa* |
| *Bedtime for Bonzo* | *Love Is on the Air* |
| *Boy Meets Girl* | *Million Dollar Baby* |

| | |
|---|---|
| *Brother Rat* | *Murder in the Air* |
| *Brother Rat and a Baby* | *Naughty But Nice* |
| *Cattle Queen of Montana* | *Nine Lives Are Not Enough* |
| *Code of the Secret Service* | *Night Unto Night* |
| *Cowboy From Brooklyn* | *Prisoner of War* |

The book's introduction explained that the National Council for the Social Studies "has established ten interdisciplinary thematic standards that encompass the subject areas of social studies" and that the lists included in the book will "enhance those themes" (Partin, 2003, p. iii).

There are similarities between the *Core Knowledge Sequence: Content Guidelines for Grades K-8* and *The Social Studies Teacher's Book of Lists* (2nd edition). Both texts stimulate the reader to ask the same types of questions. For example, who decided what core knowledge is? Why did these guidelines for content include phonemic awareness and decoding? Who selected the sayings included in the core knowledge sequence? Why were those particular ones included? When examining the book of lists, you probably wondered, Why was this compilation of lists selected as the one you should use? How was it decided what content was included in the book of lists? How was it, for example, that a list of movies starring Ronald Reagan was selected?

Certainly, both authors relied on organizations in relevant fields to write their books. Someone (or perhaps an organization or state board of education or even a national council in some content area) decided what was important for children to know, and it is likely they did so without knowing the children. In fact, it is a reasonable assumption to make that the authors did not know the ethnic, racial, and socioeconomic backgrounds of the children in the classrooms where teachers would be using their materials. As we think about these issues, we must ask an essential question: Who *should* decide the content we teach? Should they be legislators, business executives, publishers, educational researchers, brain researchers, social researchers, professional educators? Your answer to this question indicates your theoretical proclivity regarding curriculum and instruction.

To further clarify, consider the work of E. D. Hirsh, a well-known writer in the field of education. Having particular concern for the quality of education, Hirsh wrote a book titled *Cultural Literacy: What Every American Needs to Know*. Believing that educators are not producing students who are culturally literate, he put forth a list of "geographic names, historical events, famous people, scientific terms, and patriotic lore that he believes represent the contents of the national culture—what every literate American should know" (Andre & Velasquez, 1998, p. 1). By definition, Hirsh views a *literate* student as someone knowledgeable and competent about culture. What is significant is his assertion that cultural competence, as well as literacy, requires familiarity with "one's own national culture" (Andre & Velasquez, 1998, p. 1). For our purposes, that requirement means that the children we serve, whose native culture is other than mainstream, must learn content to bring them to a level of competency regarding culture in the United States.

Those who believe that students cannot learn meaningfully outside of their own lived experience have criticized Hirsh for his position (Andre & Velasquez, 1998). Filling students' minds with content determined important by others, it has been argued, is not reflective of the pluralistic society in which we live. To be relevant, and consequently effective, for our students, we need to allow them access to curriculum closely mirroring *their* culture. *Critical philosophy and constructivist methodology allow us to do so.*

Hirsh's ideas of cultural competence and objective content knowledge are framed within a culture that continues to grow in linguistic, cultural, racial, and socioeconomic diversity. It is within this diverse context that we must ask and reflect on the significant questions asked by Andre and Velasquez (1998): "Whose form of knowledge, culture, vision, history and authority will prevail as the national culture? Is it [cultural competence] an attempt to force on all citizens the values implicit in the culture of the dominant social class?" Further contemplating these issues, Andre and Velasquez question whether the benchmarks in such a curriculum would be written by anyone unlike Hirsh himself who is "white, middle-class [and] male" (p. 2).

An experience Trina once had with a student may help illustrate an important point as we look again at who decides what we teach—an essential theoretical question for curriculum writing. Part of Trina's teaching responsibilities includes teaching in an adult studies program. It is an accelerated program in which students obtain a teaching certificate. As with most educators, Trina's is a rewarding career in which she gets to know students quite well and is able to see them fulfill their dreams. One student she will never forget is Robert. He was about twenty-four years old when he began his coursework, and when he came in for his initial interview, she knew he was someone unique. Robert came in late one night after he got off work. He was still dressed in his work clothes, dirty jeans with holes in the knees, a well-worn T-shirt, and work boots worthy of pouring concrete—which was his current occupation—in the hot sun, and he sported a golden tan. When Trina asked Robert why he wanted to teach, he talked about how he knew it was time for a change. With his face lit up like a young child at his own birthday party, he told her he looked forward to getting back in school and learning. Getting back to school and learning!! How refreshing. Robert was a natural intellectual, always absorbing, always questioning.

Robert was in Trina's class for two separate courses, and she grew to appreciate his unique approach. He was the kind of student who thought at an analytical level—one of those students you know can write better than you do (she always encouraged him to publish)—a philosopher searching for conceptual frameworks on which to hang his newfound methodological knowledge. Robert was also sensitive to diversity. He believed that all students could learn and saw what he perceived to be systematic inequities in schools (particularly in funding structures).

When it came time for Robert's student teaching internship, he requested an urban school; it was one of those schools theorized about in class—high poverty level and high numbers of African American and Latino students. He told Trina that his friends and some family members had asked him about that choice. Why would he want to go into *that* school? Why choose a school where he would be sure to encounter difficult circumstances? He did it, he said, because he believed he could help students in the school learn, and that prospect excited him.

Robert was in Trina's Senior Seminar class where students debriefed about student teaching, among other things. Every Monday she asked Robert how he was doing, and often he would have a frustration to share. Along with the normal issues associated with an internship, which we once described as analogous to cooking in someone else's kitchen, Robert was faced with issues unique to the urban setting in which he was completing his student teaching internship; for example, there were not enough books, students were not motivated, and test scores had plummeted. He came each week looking for ways to solve problems and continued researching for answers.

One Monday, Robert looked particularly discouraged, so Trina asked him how things were going. Not that she would necessarily have answers for Robert, but together they usually brainstormed solutions for the problems he was experiencing. Robert looked at Trina and said something almost incomprehensible about the novel the students were being made to read. With further probing, she discovered that the test scores had been low, so someone, somewhere, decided that *The Red Badge of Courage* should be a mandated part of the curriculum. Presumably, reading this book would automatically result in higher test scores.

This choice was especially troubling for Robert, as he knew many of his students were already unmotivated and disinterested. Robert had particular issues with the book because it was "Victorian, baroque—hard to get through" (R. Andujar, personal conversation, August 5, 2006). Robert also questioned whether a significant number of his students would engage with this literature, which, in his opinion, did not reflect the non-linear, episodic traditions of storytelling in their culture and with which they were familiar. Citing *Their Eyes Are Watching God* (the story of a black woman and the struggles she faces with marriage as she seeks to find her own identity) as an example of the type of literature appreciated by several of his students, he struggled with the rationale of assigning this particular novel.

For the purposes of this book, Robert graciously allowed us to share some of the raw and edgy reflective journals he kept during his student teaching internship. We are thankful for Robert's candor and willingness to share what were his deepest thoughts and, at times, first gut-wrenching reactions as he negotiated one of the hardest processes a new teacher must undergo—student teaching. As you read the passage, pay close attention to the way in which he describes his students. Ask yourself, What is important to these students? What would be effective curriculum for them?

> This class is definitely the neediest and the most at risk. Half the students do not come regularly and out of those who do, only about a quarter read outside of the classroom. Even though there are no foreseeable disciplinary problems, this class is definitely wanting in motivation. . . . The lesson introduces one of the main themes of *The Red Badge of Courage*—courage. It encourages students to reevaluate their concept of courage. . . . The students do not see the importance of English and do not fully understand the consequences of academic failure. I grew up more privileged than them, and I still saw school as more or less pointless. For students of poverty connecting the present to the future and thinking about consequences is extremely difficult. The culture of poverty does not promote these skills and couched with the fact of their adolescence, they are extremely hard to reach. I tell them how American Lit relates to the real world, why it's important, why they need to be successful in school. They might snicker, their eyes might glaze over, they might laugh, a few might look embarrassed. I don't know how to reach them. (R. Andujar, personal journal, February 6, 2006)

Robert was faced with issues essentially the same as those raised earlier by Andre and Velasquez (1998) as they critiqued the idea of Hirsh's cultural competence. Why, for example, was it decided that *this* novel was important for Robert's students to read? *Was* this the appropriate book for them? *Why* was it selected? Was it an *equitable* choice? These are significant questions to examine, and they provide a good framework for processing the philosophical principles in which critical pedagogy are rooted.

As you prepare to read the next section in which these principles are presented, consider, for a moment, the following quotation from Macedo in the foreword of Freire's (1998) *Pedagogy of Freedom: Ethics, Democracy and Civic Courage*: "If . . . 'at risk' students are denied the opportunity to study and critically understand their reality, including their language, culture, gender, ethnicity, and class position, for all practical purposes the 'at risk' students will continue to experience a colonial experience" (p. xxvii). Macedo (as cited by Freire) shows us a picture of colonization in (and possibly through) education. In some ways, Andre and Velasquez (1998), who imply that a predetermined, objective curriculum is inequitable and unjust in our pluralistic society, echo Macedo. At the heart of these issues is power, and, certainly, as teachers of ELLs, we need to carefully examine the ways in which power is negotiated through the use of curriculum, language, and culture both inside and outside our classrooms.

In the next section, we present some guiding principles of critical pedagogy. You may feel as though you have traveled back in time to your first class in education, during which you looked at philosophies and pioneers in the field. It is doubtful, however, that you discussed at any length this philosophy; the reasons for that omission, we hope, you will surmise.

## CRITICAL PEDAGOGY: GUIDING PRINCIPLES

As stated earlier in this chapter, critical pedagogy is not a list of steps for successful instruction. Because it stands in stark contrast to prescriptive methodologies and curriculum, we hesitate to present a "list" of anything associated with it. Admittedly, doing so is a reductionist approach and may border on standardizing what is, by definition, fluid—intended to be shaped by teachers and learners together during instruction. Having made that statement, we attempt to present guiding principles here that communicate the fundamental essence of this complicated and sophisticated pedagogy.

### Principle #1—Critical pedagogy is not prescriptive: Teaching and learning emerge as students and teachers position themselves in the world

Wink (2000) describes critical pedagogy as a way of knowing wherein students not only read the word but also the world. In a critical model, then, students are encouraged to examine *their lived experiences in relation to the content with which they are interacting.* As students engage in learning about American literature, for example, they will ask questions such as, Am I reflected in this literature? Why or why not? One could argue, in the case of Robert's class, that, if it was a critical classroom, the students would have reflected not only on the story but on why it was selected for *them.* They might have engaged in discussion that would have led them to conclude that it was not an equitable choice; rather, it put them at a distinct disadvantage because their culture was not reflected in it and, overall, the readability of the text was much too difficult.

Freire and Macedo (1987) describe reading the world as closely examining power structures and our roles within them. Wink (2000) further describes critical literacy as recognizing "that reading does not take place in a vacuum; it includes the entire social, cultural, political, and historical context" (p. 57). Given this criteria, another way students might have positioned themselves in Robert's classroom would have been to look carefully not only at the issues of the Civil War as they read the story but to extend their view through a critical lens and examine examples of systemic racism in our world today and how it affects *them.*

Teaching and learning are fluid in these kinds of classrooms, and boundaries are blurred as both teachers and students negotiate their identities relative to their own experiences in the broader society. Giroux (1988) asserts that, when preparing students to evaluate and think critically about issues, we must look beyond curriculum as just the facts; rather, we must provide a broader context that gives students the framework for critical examination in their own world:

> If students are not taught to look at curricula knowledge, the facts, within a wider context of learning, . . . the relationship between theory and "facts" is often ignored, thus making it all too difficult for students to develop a conceptual apparatus for investigating the ideological and epistemological nature of what constitutes a "fact" in the first place. . . . [This is] not only boring for most students but also, most importantly, mystifying. Rather than develop an active critical thinker, such a pedagogy produces students who are either a fraud or unable to think critically. (p. 61)

### Principle #2—Teachers do not lecture: They are facilitators who instruct through dialogue

Do you remember a class wherein the teacher stood up and lectured? You might have had difficulty staying awake as your head bobbled back and forth . . . back and forth. Perhaps you looked up at the round, black and white clock on the wall—the one with the *huge* numbers. You watched as the second hand slowly made its way around to the twelve again . . . and again . . . and wished the minutes away; the time seemed to drag like it did on the road trips you took with your family when you were young. Only this time, you think better of asking the professor, "Are we there yet?"

As the class progressed, you might have begun thinking about going to the computer lab to print out a paper for your next class, or about the thank-you card you had to buy, or about which classes you needed to take next semester, or when you were going to send in the paperwork to renew your teaching credentials. Since not all people are auditory learners, we are sure many of you can relate to the lecture-based classroom scenario just described. Such a learning environment is quite objectionable for a critical classroom.

*Dialogue is an essential component of a critical classroom.* As students and teachers discuss issues and ask critical questions, both learn together. In contrasting critical pedagogy to alternative methods, Freire (1970) described the "banking education" where teachers "deposit" information into the heads of students. In his discussion, he listed *non-dialogical* characteristics of a transmission model, some of which include the following (p. 73):

- The teacher teaches, and the students are taught
- The teacher knows everything, and the students know nothing
- The teachers thinks, and the students are thought about
- The teacher talks, and the students listen—meekly
- The teacher disciplines, and the students are disciplined
- The teacher chooses and enforces his choice, and the students comply
- The teacher chooses the program content, and the students (who were not consulted) adapt to it [think of Robert's classroom]
- The teacher is the subject of the learning process, while the pupils are the mere objects

An important distinction regarding dialogue is that it is *more than discussion.* Freire saw it as teaching rather than mere facilitation. In a conversation with Macedo in which he sought to answer his critics, Freire emphasized that teaching takes place *through* dialogue. One could argue that this position is inconsistent because he criticized education in which ideologies are perpetuated. Yet, when pressed, he indicated that, regarding the peasants with whom he worked, he was not *imposing* his views but rather was giving alternatives (Freire & Macedo, 1995). What we can learn from Freire as he talked with Macedo is that dialogue is purposeful in critical classrooms; it must be open and truthful, difficult and revealing; it must *teach*. This kind of teaching takes a lot of skill and practice; it can be difficult to guide conversations and build on the experiences and discussions of your students. If you are used to a transmission model, it can feel frightening as you relinquish some of the teacher control to which you have become accustomed. As you will see in Monica's classroom, however, the results of such pedagogy may result in a higher level of student engagement and create classrooms where, through dialogue, we model the kind of critical reflection needed for CALP with ELLs.

Dignity and respect must be paramount in a critical classroom. Freire talked in detail about the kind of environment in which students will participate in difficult dialogue. He passionately stated (1970) that, for students to engage in dialogue, "humility, intense faith in humankind, love, trust, and hope" (p. 88) must be present. We equate this atmosphere with a safe learning environment, and it is just as important in our classrooms today as it was in the past for Freire in Brazil. It is only in an accepting and affirming environment that students feel valued and respected as they share their beliefs, ideas, and concerns and take the risks necessary to learn. As you read about Monica's classroom in Chapter 8, pay close attention to how the teacher affirms each student—creating a wonderful learning environment. In a critical classroom, this affirmation is essential as teachers seek to have meaningful discussions with their students. The affective filter must be such that students are comfortable doing the difficult work of critical reflection.

## Principle #3—Critical pedagogy does not ignore the white elephant in the room: It names problems and develops critical consciousness

Most of us have been in a situation wherein there was a problem that no one was addressing. A humorous example can be seen in a clip from the *Oprah Winfrey Show*. Jaime Kennedy, who has a show similar to *Candid Camera*, was featured as a special guest, and in a segment on *Oprah Winfrey* he plays a prank on a woman who thinks she has won a makeover. Jamie Kennedy assumes the role of an eccentric hairdresser who is going to make this lady over into a beautiful woman. In a hilarious scene, he expresses his beauty philosophy for this unsuspecting client. She sits quietly as he works his magic on her, fixing her hair in the wildest ways and dancing a magic dance (in which he circles around her and chants) in preparation for the great beauty transformation. He acts in ways obviously outside the norm, yet none of his assistants seem to be bothered. People pass by and seemingly ignore his outrageous behavior, as his client waits—making very curious facial expressions as she obviously questions his ability. She never voices her concerns, however. She ignores the *white elephant* of his strange behavior, just as everyone else does. It isn't until she looks in the mirror that she begins to express her concerns.

In critical classrooms, white elephants are not ignored. Instead, they are named and somehow represented. *Codification* is the process during which students represent their reality, and it occurs simultaneously with dialogue. Freire used codification to help his students read the word and their world by representing thought and language with pictures, or even writings in the sand. One codification, for example, depicted words of a popular song; his students used the codification as a basis for discussion about the possibility of learning to read in order to understand the words. The codifications were not to inform students about culture but rather to discuss it and their roles in it (Fink, 1999).

If we think back to the *Oprah Winfrey* example, we realize that codification took place when the unsuspecting woman looked at herself in the mirror; she began to realize the problem with her makeover. Interestingly enough, it is when students see their own "reflection" in society's mirror that they, too, begin the process of codification.

Codification and *problem posing* are closely related. Whereas codification names reality, problem posing critically examines it. Wink (2000) suggests that problem posing is more than problem solving:

> It brings interactive participation and critical inquiry into the existing curriculum and expands it to reflect the curriculum of the students' lives. The learning is not just grounded in the prepared syllabus, the established, prescribed curriculum. Problem posing opens the door to ask questions and seek answers not only of the visible curriculum, but also of the hidden curriculum. (p. 60)

An important point is that, as students codify and problem pose through dialogue, they develop *conscientization* or critical consciousness. This process is what leads to the next, and final, principle.

## Principle #4—Critical pedagogy does not maintain the status quo: It is essentially transformative

As discussed earlier in this chapter, critical pedagogy is rooted in radical political traditions. Focusing on liberation and transformation, critical pedagogy has historically examined oppression and unequal power structures, specifically looking at ways in which hegemonies are maintained (Darder, Baltodano, & Torres, 2003). Hegemonies are subtle forms of oppression in which those who are oppressed accept their oppression. We argue that standardized tests, which are the gatekeepers to college and on which not all cultures are reflected, are hegemonies.

To understand this point, it might be helpful to review our earlier discussions about curriculum and who decides what is important for students to know. Rather than suggesting a list of movies made by Ronald Reagan as relevant curriculum or selecting curriculum material for urban students that is not written in a linguistic style accessible to them, and rather than saying, as Hirsh does, that there is *one essential* curriculum and all students should learn it, critical classrooms should:

> call upon teachers to recognize how schools have historically embraced theories and practices that function to unite knowledge and power in ways that sustain asymmetrical relations of power under the guise of a political view of education—views that are intimately linked to ideologies shaped by power, politics, history, culture, and economics. (Darder et al., 2003, p. 7)

Perhaps no other principle is more pertinent for teachers of students whose native language is not English; often it is we who are the students' and families' advocates. In a critical classroom, education seeks to prepare students so that they can critically examine policies and practices, literature and curriculum, rules and regulations—which affect *them*—to determine if they are equitable.

*Praxis* is the culmination of dialogue. It is transformation in action and comes about as students and teachers find ways to affect change as a result of their discovery. Essentially, it is the action that takes place as a result of reflection (Finn, 1999; Freire, 1970; Giroux, 1988; McLaren, 2003; Wink, 2000). Nieto (2004) explains that praxis is "the process of connecting reflection with action in the pursuit of knowledge and social change" (p. 384). Peter McLaren (2003) gives an example of praxis in the classroom as he writes about a classroom activity during which students investigated the kinds of jobs available in their communities. As a result of this study, students looked at the political agendas of those holding office.

It is important to note that the journey toward transformation should be based on *authentic* experiences of students. Activism for the sake of activism may be valuable, but praxis needs to be a result of students' critical exploration of issues that come from their own backgrounds and that affect their own realities. Freier's work in Brazil was purposeful in that it rooted instruction in the culture of the peasants with whom he worked. Authenticity is foundational as teachers teach from a critical perspective.

# IDENTITY FORMATION IN CRITICAL CLASSROOMS

Notable, yet not as significantly present in the literature, is the idea that students negotiate their identities as they participate in the dialogical and transformative structures in critical learning environments. Roles of teachers, in these classrooms, are not clearly defined. Critical classrooms are thus places where teachers and students renegotiate their identities during the process of classroom discussion. Bean and Thomas (2003) posit that they (students and teachers) "view . . . identity as open to creation and recreation rather than a fixed property that [they] were born with."

O'Brien (2001), citing Weedon, also suggests that classrooms can be thought of as places where the identities of students and teachers are fluid; they change as discourse takes place. It is likely that in a critical classroom in which dialogue is paramount and where students are not viewed as blank slates on which the teacher prescribes knowledge but rather as co-travelers on a journey toward personal reflection and societal transformation, identities evolve. More research is needed in this area, but as we continue on to Monica's classroom in Chapter 8 and encounter her wonderful bilingual students, we believe you will find many instances in which they connect with, examine, and change self-perceptions.

It is exciting to think about classrooms with ELLs that reflect the principles of critical pedagogy. This possibility is particularly significant for non-native-English speakers because they may have internalized the "negative opinions that mainstream groups hold about their culture and language. [This] . . . encourages the self-depreciation that contributes to their withdrawal and educational failure" (Espinoza-Herold, 2003, p. 20). Critical, bilingual classrooms will provide a safe learning environment where students can negotiate issues of language and culture so that they can examine their own reality and can place value on it. You will see this happen many times during the critical dialogue in Chapter 8. Without these kinds of classrooms, we run the risk that ELLs will be forced to "adopt a new identity, . . . a new way of life, . . . result[ing] in alienation from their cultural roots and language and the formation of a confused identity" (Espinoza-Herold, 2003, p. 6). What is exciting for us is that critical classrooms provide a catalyst for students to find value and dignity in all cultures and in all languages.

# 6 Constructivist Classroom Connections

## *The Great Second-Grade Bug Invasion*

Immersion education holds promise not only for the future of bilingual education but also for a better world, for it promotes a number of models that foster educational equity as well as bilingualism for all, intercultural appreciation, linguistic and cultural revitalization, and social justice. It can thus be consistent with constructivist or critical constructivist practice. Of course, as with all models of programs for ELLs, some models do a better job of meeting these goals than others, and models have the potential to be subverted for other than their original purposes.

The majority of immersion programs in the United States use Spanish as the target language (that is, as the minority language to be acquired). Immersion programs exist in many more languages, however—Japanese, German, Navajo, Yup'ik, and Hawaiian, to name only a few. Although many variations of immersion exist, the basic tenet of all immersion education is that second and subsequent languages are best internalized in a manner that simulates first language acquisition. Although immersion is sometimes equated with submersion, as noted in Chapter 2, no comparison could be farther from the truth. In first language acquisition, a child's linguistic environment is rich with supports, from "motherese" to language scaffolding, and with an inherent understanding of and respect for the developmental process of language acquisition. In submersion, the classroom environment provides no such supports, and student efforts to provide their own may be misunderstood. In immersion, a natural approach strives to replicate first language acquisition through content instruction in a second language. Furthermore, social context is of the utmost importance; in this case, it is accomplished by having a peer group composed in part of native speakers of the L2 of the learner.

Fundamental to immersion education is the integration of language and content learning; language is learned through content, with the majority of the curriculum presented in the minority (target) language. Children are expected to become bilingual naturally, as they are immersed in context-embedded learning environments in the target language. The necessity for a context-rich, hands-on, discovery learning–based curriculum drives instruction. As in constructivist classrooms, the immersion environment is stimulating and activity based and stresses experience, interaction, and dialogue (Morgan, 1982). Students who are receiving input in their second language need to depend on a plethora of contextual clues to maximize understanding. This need pushes not only a type of sheltered instruction but also a constructivist pedagogical approach. Without this approach, such programs might well be doomed to failure.

The roles of teachers and students in immersion classrooms are consistent with constructivist theory as well; teachers are facilitators of the learning process and learning environment, and students collaborate with peers to construct knowledge through daily interaction between speakers of the minority and majority languages. Children have the opportunity to develop both their native language and metalinguistic skills through not only teacher facilitation but through teaching their native language to others. At the same time, they are able to develop their second language skills by learning from both their peers and their teacher. In this manner, everyone in the classroom becomes both a teacher and a learner, a powerful and motivational force in the educational process and, again, a process in perfect sync with constructivist education.

Saville-Troike (1981) recognizes the important function of motivation in second language learning. She states that "every child learns a great deal of his language from his peer group, and one of his strongest motivations for learning language is his desire to communicate with them. . . . Children from diverse language backgrounds will readily learn to communicate with one another when they have both need and opportunity to do so" (p. 31).

In TWI programs, language minority and majority students become bilingual together. TWI programs can be successful for both language minority and majority children for a host of reasons. Speakers of the target language (in this case, Spanish) growing up in an English dominant society may not have had their native language skills sufficiently developed. In a two-way program, these skills can be strengthened and then used as a bridge to the second language. With a firm linguistic base in their first language, these children can more efficiently and successfully acquire English. Because speakers of the target language usually become orally proficient in English by the time any formal instruction in that language occurs, instructional lags are not significant.

For language majority (English dominant) children, the context-embedded environment of the two-way bilingual classroom, particularly in the early years, provides for successful experiences in the second language. The comprehension skills of these children develop rapidly in this natural language environment, thus permitting assimilation of educational information from the start. Yet, the influence of the dominant society facilitates the continuing development of their linguistic ability in English.

Immersion education mandates consistency across grade levels; it is dependent upon children starting as early as possible (indeed most quality immersion programs strive to include preschool programs) and exiting as late as possible (usually eighth grade, although some high school programs exist and certainly more are needed). Furthermore, in keeping with the collaborative nature of such programs, time must be incorporated into the teacher day for educators to plan collectively. Immersion must therefore be incorporated throughout a school program or within an entire school; it cannot exist isolated in individual classrooms but must be implemented collectively across school curriculum.

These principles are highlighted in the following narrative in which second-grade teacher, Jill Sontag, facilitates learning in a context-rich curricular environment throughout a thematic unit on insects. She does so within the context of a schoolwide, TWI program that most children begin attending in preschool or kindergarten. The peer group is a mix of English dominant, Spanish dominant, and (English/Spanish) bilingual children, and the target language is Spanish. This narrative thus focuses on the Spanish language acquisition of English dominant children.

By allowing opportunities for social interaction within this context-embedded classroom environment, Jill lays the foundation for authentic language learning situations to occur spontaneously. Note that these teaching strategies highlight not only immersion pedagogy but also constructivist practice with modifications for second language learning and can be applied to other educational models for second language learners that are compatible with constructivist pedagogy.

This chapter will conclude by listing the teaching strategies that have been highlighted in the narrative. These strategies are divided into three categories to coincide with the three goals of all TWI programs: bilingualism for children of all language backgrounds, high levels of academic achievement, and positive cross-cultural attitudes. Connections between immersion pedagogy and constructivist practice are highlighted.

> Two mixed gender lines formed in the small classroom entrance hallway. Jill told the children, in Spanish, that another change had occurred with the butterflies and cautioned them not to scream out their enthusiasm as they had on Wednesday, which had been a particularly loud day.
>
> > In two-way bilingual immersion classrooms, teachers adhere to a separation of language through the medium of content area instruction. Thus, in this second-grade classroom, the science curriculum is insect study and the linguistic medium of instruction for science is Spanish. By giving instructions in Spanish, Jill sets the tone for both linguistic and content learning. Here we see the integration of language and content instruction.
>
> Antwan peeked through the hallway and surveyed the room.
> "Look over there, look over there!" His announcement was loud, but he didn't scream. In his excitement, he paid no heed to his teacher's subtle request to communicate in his second language.
> Alicia spotted them next.
> "Butterflies!" Spanish dominant Alicia continued the student talk in English.
>
> > At this point, Jill is faced with a dilemma. She has signaled to the class that dialogue should be conducted in Spanish, yet student talk has ensued in English. To force the children to speak in Spanish during this moment of authentic engagement would be counterproductive; it could promote a negative attitude toward the target language and deter from engagement in the learning process.
>
> Jill stepped aside, and with quiet enthusiasm children flocked to the net cage at the side of the room. Five now empty brown chrysalises, cracked and dry like mealworm skins, hung from the top of the cage. Four speckled butterflies clung motionless to the net, and one rested on red paper petals surrounding a vial containing a liquid set inside a plastic cup. Their wings were a mix of black flecked with white and orange flecked with black, although only one displayed its colors with open wings. For ten minutes the children responded with excited gasps and initial observations.
> "Oh, butterflies!"
> "Come here. Two . . . three!"

"Ooooooooohhhhh!"
"Watch, watch. They think that paper is a flower!"
"ANDY, ANDY!"
"Ssssshhhh, ssssshhhh."
"Mueva, Jorge."
"Lookat this one Jonathon, lookat, lookat!"
"Lookat the color."
"Teacher, what about these colors?"
"Oh! Four!"
"One more, one more!"
"Lookit, lookit, he's trying to fly! He's trying to fly . . . the one."

> Again, despite Jill's linguistic cue, English dominates the content-related student talk. Yet, knowing that it is common to speak in one's dominant language in times of excitement and respecting her students' authentic enthusiasm and delight, she allows each child the right of self-expression.

Glenna remained near the front hallway deep in conversation with Amber. After a few minutes, she, too, joined the children clustered in front of the butterflies. They were huddled too tightly for her to get through. Josh gently parted the crowd. Ronald put his right arm over her shoulder and drew her in closer to the net. Ernest, imitating his teacher, walked over and teased the group, telling them to go to their tables: "¡Va a tu mesas!" His grammar may have been flawed, but his intent was clear, as he told his classmates to go back to their assigned tables.

> Although imitating his teacher for the sake of laughs, Ernest's remarks reflect the power of teacher modeling on second language learning and acquisition.

Glenna examined the butterflies and then walked toward her table. Damion, seated in his chair, tried to catch her attention.

"I have a flipper toy," he said, looking up at her with adoration.

"Soooooooo?" Glenna replied coolly, and walked away, deliberately avoiding a conversation.

Jill signaled the end of the observation period by turning off the lights. The excited flutter of children and butterflies waned as the girls and boys returned to their tables.

> The children sit in small groups at tables, rather than at individual desks, to facilitate cooperative grouping, which is used extensively throughout this thematic unit. This seating is consistent with both constructivist and two-way bilingual immersion practice because it emphasizes the social context of the learning process.

*(Continued)*

(Continued)

The sounds of gentle chatter in English drifted throughout the room.

"Mesa seis es la más callada." As with Ernest, understanding Spanish was a prerequisite to understanding Jill's joke. She had declared that table six was the most quiet.

The class giggled. Amber was not yet seated, and Lisette and Azucena had not yet arrived at school, hence nobody was there to sit at table six.

> Jill seizes an authentic opportunity to attempt to change the linguistic environment. In doing so, she exhibits an understanding of the infectious nature of second-grade humor. Second language teachers must be ever vigilant and creative in their role to facilitate communication in a new language.

The children were able to unwind in the brief but focused conversation that followed. Jill initiated a discussion, in Spanish, about the red spots of waste they had seen on the floor of the net cage. She cautioned them that the butterflies were easily frightened and that they needed to talk softly when they were nearby.

> Jill initiates a class discussion on insect observations. Unlike the free-flowing bug observation session, her direct facilitation ensures that conversation persists in Spanish. The separation of languages for instructional purposes mandated by a two-way bilingual immersion theoretical stance not only promotes competence in two languages but also signals to students the appropriate language for classroom talk. Thus, class content (insect observations) signals discourse in Spanish, while the teacher's facilitation sustains it.
>
> Note, also, that a hands-on experience with insects shelters instruction by supporting teacher talk. The context-embedded nature of the learning experiences has been a constant throughout this thematic unit and is consistent with both two-way bilingual immersion and constructivist practice. Furthermore, the inherently constructivist approach of two-way bilingual immersion curriculum is in evidence. Students are encouraged to come to conclusions about insects based on scientific observations as opposed to reading about them in a text; hence we see the integration of content and process.
>
> When viewed collectively we can see the integration of language, content, and process in this second-grade discussion on insects.

Insect observation ended with a most welcome announcement; the class would spend the rest of the morning practicing for the Pan American Assembly.

> Participation in arts-based activities promotes cultural appreciation and is part of the cross-cultural agenda of two-way bilingual immersion programs. In addition, arts-based activities are recommended practice for language arts instruction in a second language.

Several girls pulled full skirts over their school attire. A cassette tape beat African drums, and they were transformed, full skirts whirling like butterfly wings, by the contagious rhythm of the Puerto Rican "Bomba."

❖  ❖  ❖

Change can be unwanted; it can bring pain. On Monday afternoon, a butterfly died and the children grieved. Prior to this they had been nonchalant about the passing of several beetles; but the butterfly—that was a different matter.

The children theorized as to what had happened to cause their butterfly to die. Although no one could be certain, the most accepted explanation was that, in its struggle to free itself from the chrysalis, it had taken a fall and, in so doing, had suffered a mortal injury.

> Jill uses this authentic opportunity to facilitate the development of critical thinking. Constructivist teachers are facilitators of learning environments in which students are encouraged to examine data and come to their own conclusions. This method integrates content and process as well as, in a two-way bilingual classroom, the additional element of language.

The four other butterflies, however, were still in the realm of the living, and Jill reminded the group that those remaining needed care. The children were still in the process of scientific study and thus continued their observations.

> Jill engages the children in scientific study of a subject in which they have inherent interest. She taps their prior knowledge of insects and helps them expand upon it through a scientific process that can later be applied to other areas of study. Here we see the importance of process in knowledge construction.

Jill continued her facilitation, in Spanish, of the scientific study of insects.

> Unlike the previous free-flowing bug observation activity, the majority of the students respond in Spanish for this teacher-mediated discussion. Jill knows when it is appropriate to facilitate conversation in the target language and when it would be counterproductive, and she responds accordingly. She respects the native language of the students, but she also pushes them toward proficiency in their second language. She validates their language and culture while respecting their capacity to develop linguistically in two languages.

They learned how butterflies "chupan su comida" (suck their food) through a "proboscide" (proboscis), or "nariz especial" (special nose).

*(Continued)*

(Continued)

> Vocabulary development in a second language is of the utmost importance in developing academic competence, and here Jill takes advantage of an opportunity to extend this essential ingredient of school success by tapping the students' prior and continuing hands-on experience with insect study.

The students predicted what future changes might occur.

> Process-oriented science study involves generating hypotheses and is consistent with both two-way bilingual immersion and constructivist practice.

Glenna speculated, "Van a ponerse más grande" (They will get bigger). Leticia commented, "Volar más" (Fly more). Jill counseled, "Vamos a mirar más huevos" (We are going to see more eggs). The children liked this idea and embellished upon the theme.
"¡Van a tener bebés!" (They are going to have babies!)
"They're gonna get married!"

> It is normal to revert to one's native language in moments rich with emotion.

The children did not know that their beloved "Damas Pintadas" (Painted Ladies) had only two more weeks to live.

❖ ❖ ❖

"Maestra, ¡ya sé como hacerlo!"
Before Jill could finish her demonstration to the class, Glenna exclaimed that she knew what to do as she pulled back a sheet of tissue paper and, out of her fan, began to form the petals of a flower.
"Maestra, ¿puedo hacer ésto?"

> English dominant Glenna demonstrates her understanding of the appropriate language in which to address her teacher. Although it would be easier for Glenna to speak in English, she is fully capable of communicating in Spanish and is acutely aware that Jill would not respond to a request presented in English. It is essential for teachers to make certain their students understand the linguistic parameters of the classroom curricular environment, and it is equally important to provide them with motivation to do so.

Glenna pulled the tissue petal back further while asking if she could continue. Jill smiled.

"Así," Glenna sighed with satisfaction as she pulled another petal into position. When every tissue was in its place, she called her teacher over to look. "¡Mira maestra!"

Glenna surveyed her flower again, then fluffed out the red, white, and peach petals and pulled them further back until a hollow space was formed in the center of the flower. Balling up the black tissue that she had previously refrained from using, she placed it in the center of her flower as if creating a multicolored black-eyed Susan.

The project of the afternoon was to create an artistic representation of each phase of development in the life cycle of a butterfly; "huevo," "oruga (o larva)," "capullo," and "mariposa." Each of these creations would then be attached to the flower—the egg nestled in the petals, the chrysalis hanging from them.

> Jill frequently engages students in both content and language learning by tapping into the motivational power of arts-based activities. Arts activities can effectively engage students in learning experiences in both two-way bilingual immersion and in constructivist classrooms.
>
> In this instance, the teacher also uses an arts-based activity to reinforce science vocabulary in Spanish and, thus, to enhance possibilities for high academic achievement.

The eggs, caterpillars, chrysalises, and butterflies were all successfully created out of a combination of clay, tissue and construction paper, paint, pipe cleaners, and egg cartons. Of particular fascination to the children was the tempera paint used to color the egg carton caterpillars. When Jill asked the class what they thought the green and yellow paint was for, Glenna correctly responded that it was to make stripes, "Para hacer rayas." As the paintbrushes were distributed, she held one up and asked if the class could start: "Maestra, ¿podemos empezar?"

Jill nodded her consent. Glenna used her paintbrush to cover her egg carton with a green base. Across the room, however, Amber had a different idea; she announced in English that she preferred to use her fingers. Her idea did not receive a positive reception from Jill, but Glenna responded favorably, abandoning her paint brush to rub green paint into cardboard crevices with first her fingers and then her entire palm. The underside of her hand soon turned the deep green color of the paint.

As if a contagious disease, the green hand syndrome spread. At a nearby table, both sides of Azucena's hands were coated in dark green, from her wrist to the tips of her fingers. Ernest, Damion, and Diana had also copied Amber, and their hands were in various stages of color transformation.

Not everything, however, was a shade of green.

"¡Maestra, mira qué pasó!"

Glenna pointed to the yellow paint that had spilled on her desk, asking her teacher to look and see what had happened, then went to the storage area to get supplies to clean it up. She scrubbed her desk top as the cassette player in the back of the room churned out the words to a song about ants—"Las hormiguitas."

Jill was not pleased with the outbreak of green. Azucena, Ernest, Damion, and Diana were soon sent to the storage room to clean up.

"Teacher, can I wash my hands?"

*(Continued)*

(Continued)

Amber, who had started it all, apparently had had enough.

"¿Cómo?" If English dominant Amber was to be permitted to wash her hands, she would have to make her request known in her second language.

---

Jill provides Amber with strong motivation to speak in her second language.

---

"¿Puedo lavar mis manos?"

Amber ended up in the bathroom trying to figure out how she had managed to get green spots on the back of her shirt.

"Las hormiguitas" finished playing on the cassette player and was replaced by a children's version of the "Jarabe Tapatío."

---

Quality children's music in the target language, both contemporary and folkloric, maximizes the connection between music, language development, and memory in second language learning and acquisition. As noted previously, it also utilizes the inherent motivational quality of arts activities, thus encouraging student engagement in the classroom curriculum.

---

"Maestra, that's the music from our dance class!" Marisol announced as she and Glenna began to tap out the familiar steps they had learned in the folkloric dance class held on site at the end of the school day. Spanish dominant Marisol was exhibiting a preference for English in the school environment. Her response, however, unlike that of Amber's, had been made informally in the mix of classroom chatter and required no teacher response.

---

Jill understands the importance of context in deciding when to allow children language choice. This situation highlights an ongoing dilemma for second language educators: the problem of facilitating development of a second language while continuing to validate the native language of the student. In this case, however, the situation is complicated by the fact that Marisol is choosing English over her native language with increasing frequency. Marisol is an academically advanced student, which may be related as much to her family background as to her access to quality instruction in her native language. What may be at stake here is not Marisol's academic and cognitive growth but her attempts at identity construction, as well as her relationship with her Spanish dominant family and extended family.

---

It was important to clean up quickly; today was Josh's birthday, and a small celebration was planned. Her projects complete and her table clean, Glenna rocked her cardboard Spanish dominant caterpillar back and forth, squeaking out a high pitched "qui qui, qui qui, qui qui."

Inventing the sound of a caterpillar by using Spanish phonology suggests that Glenna is internalizing her second language. Internalization is encouraged by student engagement in authentic learning experiences.

Then Glenna picked up her tissue paper flower and began singing *her* version of the traditional Mexican birthday song.

Estas son las mañanitas

Que cantaban el Rey David

Que las muchachas bonitas

Se las cantamos así

Despierta mi bien despierta

Mira lo que maneció

Ya los pajaritos cantan

La luna ya se metió.

Once again, it is significant that Glenna is freely engaging in communication in her second language through the medium of both the visual and performing arts. This supports the notion that the arts hold potential for authentic opportunities for student engagement leading to internalization of the second language.

❖ ❖ ❖

The butterflies had escaped again; the beetles had continued their quest for freedom. Even some of the now bright orange and black "insectos de algodoncillo," the milkweed bugs, had managed to sneak out. Jill caught an "insecto de algodoncillo," and the class watched as it unfolded its "proboscide" while resting on her hand.

The great bug escape happened repeatedly almost every morning. The first time about twenty beetles were discovered under a book. As Jill lifted it up, they squirmed away until Alicia and Damion helped her put them back in their specially constructed habitat. Then a butterfly escaped, and Alicia got a fish net, caught it, and put it back in the cage.

The next day in the middle of math class, Amber exclaimed, "There's an insecto de algodoncillo crawling up the string!"

Jill responded that it was just a cockroach, but Amber insisted that it was an "insecto de algodoncillo."

Just then two more escaped butterflies were spotted; one was caught in a vent. Jill helped it crawl onto her finger. The children watched with silent intensity as she placed it back in the butterfly cage. The other butterfly was caught by a student wielding the fishing net and was put back as well.

*(Continued)*

**(Continued)**

The children were still not satisfied. Despite Jill's claim that it was a cockroach, they insisted that there was an "insecto de algodoncillo" climbing on a string hanging from a poster on the wall. Finally Jill relented, climbed on top of a desk, and discovered that the class was correct. Soon another "insecto de algodoncillo" was spotted crawling on the floor! "Insectos de algodoncillo" were escaping all over the place!

Jill gently removed the insect from the string and placed it on her finger. As she stepped down from the desk, the children clustered around her and gazed at the bug on her finger. Spontaneous insect observations ensued. Of special interest to the children was the "proboside" (proboscis) that sucks food, nutrients, and liquids. They noted that it was like the butterfly's as opposed to the beetle's. The children continued to make observations as the insect crawled around on their teacher's finger and hand, and then it was once again imprisoned in its cage.

Jill creates an environment conducive to extemporaneous and authentic learning situations. As the learning facilitator, she takes full advantage of these moments when they present themselves. In this instance, she uses the medium of "the great bug escape" to promote scientific observation, tapping into a childhood sense of wonder to use it as a springboard for scientific observations and the use of Spanish in the classroom.

She does so by embedding science in authentic experiences, supporting teacher talk by the nonverbal means of simply holding up a concrete object (live insect). All these events are illustrative of both constructivist and two-way bilingual immersion instructional principles.

❖  ❖  ❖

Glenna and Marisol stared down at the mass of black beetles tunneling in and out of the thick oatmeal carpet that lined the plastic container. Rotting pieces of apple were scattered throughout the rectangular bin, and the hungry insects swarmed over them like seven-year locusts on a feeding binge. The two girls, faces frozen in disgust, remained motionless and silent, contemplating their mission. Feed the beetles. Feed the beetles that long for escape.

Once again, Jill facilitates an experience in which the study of science is embedded in an authentic learning situation involving concrete objects (beetles). Although the students find the insects distasteful, they must nonetheless figure out a way to accomplish their task; creative thinking is thus involved and may enhance cognitive development. Constructivist practice makes this opportunity possible.

The fat, crawling bugs needed a fresh supply of fruit. First, however, the remainders of the past week's allotment had to be removed. Neither child volunteered to begin.

Marisol picked up a napkin lying on the table and handed it to Glenna.
"Use this."

Glenna wrinkled her nose.

"It might crawl on the napkin."

Marisol was silent.

Covering her hand with the white paper, Glenna dipped it down to grab a chunk of rotted apple. The soft, brown fruit slid out of her napkin-covered hand.

"It's too slippery."

Marisol remained silent.

Glenna tried again, this time with success, scooping the apple piece up quickly and then dropping it on the table as if it were poison. She repeated the procedure with several other pieces.

"Now you get one. I've done all of them."

She handed the napkin to Marisol, who distastefully obliged.

Only one piece of apple remained, and it seemed that all of the displaced beetles had flocked to it. The children stood frozen above the beetle habitat.

"It's got escarabajos on it," Marisol muttered.

---

Here we can see evidence of vocabulary development in Spanish.

---

The two continued to stare.

"Maybe if we like put a new apple in, they will like go to the new one and we can like get the old one."

Glenna agreed to the plan and began to cut a chunk off of the unused portion of the apple that had been left on the table during the week. The warm, brown pulp resisted the knife; it was useless.

---

This interaction exemplifies the strong friendship between Spanish dominant Marisol and English dominant Glenna that pushes positive cross-cultural interpersonal relations.

It is also important here to note that, although both are bilingual, the two friends choose to communicate almost exclusively in English. This illustrates one reason why linguistic minority children can be so successful in bilingual immersion programs. Marisol has the advantage of literacy instruction in her native language to assist her cognitive and academic growth, facilitate her L1 as a bridge to L2 literacy, and encourage positive self-esteem and identity construction. At the same time, the overriding influence of the majority language and the internal drive to achieve majority language fluency serves to ensure that communicative competence in English will occur and will serve as a bridge to English academic competence. A solid foundation in L1 literacy, coupled with high academic achievement and appropriate cognitive development, then make it possible for these attributes to transfer over to the L2.

---

*(Continued)*

**(Continued)**

The girls went off to speak to Jill, Glenna as their spokesperson.

"Maestra, it's all . . ." she paused. Realizing she was speaking to her teacher about bugs, she switched languages in midstream. "Toda la manzana es vieja y soft. ¿Tienes otro?"

> The influence of the teacher in regard to language choice is once again clearly visible. Not only does Jill's pedagogical stance promote Glenna's second language development, it demonstrates to Marisol, a linguistic minority student, the prestige of her native language. Thus, both students benefit from this brief but significant teacher-student communication.
>
> Note, also, that code switching, as it occurs in this instance, is probably a reflection of limited vocabulary in Spanish and will probably fade with the passage of time and a corresponding increase in second language proficiency.

Jill sent them off to the cafeteria, and they returned with a fresh apple. Glenna sliced off a crisp chunk.

"You can't cut it that big," Marisol protested.

> Note that in Jill's absence the girls immediately resume conversation in English.

"Yes I can. Look at these!" She pointed to the rotted chunks lying on the table. "They ate all of them."

They rotated slicing and dropping the newly cut food into the beetle habitat. As the insects swarmed to attack the fresh fruit, Marisol quickly plucked out the final piece of rotted apple. The two had accomplished their teacher-requested mission. The beetles could now be safely left for the weekend.

The salonito, an oversized closet appropriated by the class for additional workspace, was in use. Glenna looked over her hands, positioned tentatively over the computer keyboard. She first pressed the shift key, then the letter "t," and then glanced up at the screen. A capital "T" appeared in the upper lefthand corner. Looking downward she repositioned her hands. Gingerly, she pushed down the "o," then the "d," slowly followed by the "a" and the "y." With meticulous precision, she finished the sentence.

"Today in class 307 they got new butterflies some have not come out of there cocoons and they are white."

As the news story crept slowly onward, the carefully positioned pressing gave way to random finger poking.

Sammy leaned in the doorway to the storage room, fidgeting with impatience. He was next in line to use the computer, and he knew that time was running out. Jill knew that the week was running out. Everybody knew that school was running out. Soon Jill was seated in front of the computer as Glenna dictated her news story for the class newspaper, *The Daily Bug Garden*, which comprised a component of the English language arts curriculum.

> Both two-way bilingual immersion and constructivist pedagogy encourage an emergent literacy perspective in which literacy development is embedded in meaningful and functional activities, such as the one illustrated in the production of this class newspaper.
>
> Although this narrative focuses on the development of Spanish in English dominant students, we can still see an illustration of the principle of the transfer of literacy skills from L1 to L2. Here, given the thematic similarity of the English and Spanish curriculum, Glenna's literacy development in English (her L1) can be used as a bridge to her literacy development in Spanish (her L2).

When Glenna's news report had been entered in its entirety into the computer, Jill, speaking in English, pointed out that the paragraph was rather long and suggested that Glenna do some editing.

> Jill is not asking Glenna to complete a grammar exercise; she is asking her to produce a written piece about an exciting classroom event for peer consumption. Because she is writing for an authentic purpose, Glenna has strong motivation to follow her teacher's suggestion and, in fact, does so with enthusiasm. It is possible that she is more likely to internalize the aforementioned principle of good writing because it has personal meaning to her.

Before the morning reached its conclusion, Glenna's story was ready to go to press.

> The concept of separation of languages by subject matter is adhered to, and in this case the curriculum in English is thematically related to the curriculum in Spanish. Not only does this arrangement allow engagement in the curriculum conducted in Spanish to extend into the curriculum conducted in English, but it also encourages bilingual vocabulary development without resorting to the problematic concept of translation. This result is of the utmost significance to teachers who, no matter what their philosophical stance in relation to standardized academic proficiency testing, are still accountable for student achievement in that area, to which vocabulary development is so important.

*(Continued)*

(Continued)

Today in class 307 they got new butterflies some have not come out of there cocoons and they are white.

Everybody is excited. Leticia a second grader felt that at first the butterflies were caterpillars then they were cocoons then they were butterflies but one died.

Antwan and Damion said, "They first came out of the cocoon and one died. They put out garbage. It looked like blood."

Leticia also said that the butterflies' color was red, orange, black, and white. Lisette said that the color of the butterflies' are orange white and black. Josh said that he only knew that the butterflies came in May. Diana said that they came to the class on Friday, May 27.

❖   ❖   ❖

Andy, Sammy, and José Luis ran frantically to Jill.

"Maestra, we think a mariposa is dying! It's on the floor on its side, and it's flapping its wings and its proboside is hanging down!"

> Once again, Spanish is lost in the drama of the moment; however, some Spanish vocabulary is retained.

Their teacher calmly advised, in Spanish, that the butterfly be left in peace while they finished their work. They would check on it later.

"Ahora tenemos que dejarle en paz. Seguimos con el trabajo y lo chequeamos más tarde."

> By refraining from taking immediate action in response to the children's concern, Jill builds anticipation and investment in the curriculum, thus strengthening student engagement in the learning process. In addition, critical thinking is promoted, as the students silently speculate as to what will happen next. Finally, by responding in Spanish to a request made in English, the teacher gently pushes Spanish language development.

Only three days remained in the school year, and there was much work to be done. Throughout the room, children were involved in various end-of-the-year activities—putting together portfolios, cleaning out over-stuffed desks and backpacks, and writing letters to their yet unknown third-grade teachers. The three children rejoined the classroom flurry.

Forty minutes later, Andy, accompanied by José Luis, was back talking to Jill.

"Look, it's shaking." Andy pointed toward the cage at the side of the room. "Is he sick? What's wrong?"

Jill, followed by Andy and José Luis, walked over to the cage and visually examined the butterfly.

"Mira en la flor. ¿Qué ven ustedes?" She asked what they saw on the flower.

> Jill persists in her use of Spanish despite student attempts to revert to English. She demonstrates unlimited and unrelenting patience in this regard; indeed, in the face of the societal push toward English dominance, she must do so or she will inadvertently subvert the Spanish curriculum.

"I donno."

"Las cositas negras." Jill pointed out the small black specks on the flower.

"Oh yeah!"

"¿Qué son?" Jill probed, asking what they were.

> Jill continues to press for both the content and the linguistic goals she has set for her students. In addition, she presses them to think critically, consistent with the process-oriented science curriculum. Once again the intersection of language, content, and process can be seen. In this instance, the resulting impact on student cognitive development is evident. The teacher is attempting to build the students' independence in the knowledge construction process. Prior knowledge has been tapped, forming a bridge to new knowledge.

José Luis looked up at Jill wide-eyed. Andy looked as if he couldn't comprehend why his teacher would ask a question with such an obvious answer.

"¡Huevos!" (Eggs!), they both declared, each with his own distinct intonation, using the Spanish vocabulary word that Jill had reinforced in prior lessons.

> Jill's perseverance in speaking in Spanish begins to pay off as evidenced by this simultaneous outburst by both a Spanish dominant and an English dominant student. They have demonstrated content learning, critical thought, and Spanish vocabulary development; yet what is more impressive is that in a moment of epiphany they have responded in the target language. This may suggest an element of internalization of the minority language for Andy, the linguistic majority student.

With exuberance they called over Leticia, Antwan, and Joe. Jill calmly beckoned the others. In an instant children were clustered around the butterfly cage, some standing on the floor in front of it, others standing on the radiators to the side of the cage and gazing down, still others standing on chairs behind the children in the front row. All eyes were focused on one thing—a butterfly with its abdomen angled downward on the red paper flower in the process of laying an egg.

*(Continued)*

(Continued)

Cautioned to be quiet by their teacher, the children reacted in excited whispers.
"¡Están poniendo huevos!"
"Come here, come here!"
"¿Maestra, qué hacen?"
"Where are the huevos?"
"Look, look, look!"
"Uuuuhhhhh!"
"Aaaaaahhhhh!"
"Where are the eggs?"
"Ssssssshhhhhhh!"
"Oh look, I see one!"
"Come here, come here!"
"¡No toques!"
"I don't see them."
"On the flower!"
"Under the net!"

> Although the dominant linguistic mode of expression is still in English, more Spanish has made its way into informal conversation than in such prior occurrences. This result may indicate the effectiveness of the two-way bilingual immersion teaching strategies that have been implemented by Jill.

"Maestra, maestra, the eggs are under the net! They fell down!"
The butterfly that had been reported earlier as dying had laid its eggs on the net covering resting just above the plastic cage floor. Its eggs had fallen through the small openings and lay trapped between the soft net and the hard plastic. A child-sized hand reached inside to rescue them.
"No podemos tocarlos." Jill cautioned that touching was not a good idea.
José Luis was wide-eyed once again.
"So you're telling me that we're gonna have orugas crawling around under the net?"
Jill gave no answer but sent Leticia and Alicia to the salonito to summon Glenna, Marisol, and Sammy, who were at the computer working on *The Daily Bug Garden*.

> Jill promotes critical thinking by setting up learning situations that require student inference. Not only is it important for the teacher to understand the proper context for linguistic choice in response to student commentary, it is equally important to understand the power of silent response.

"The butterflies are laying eggs! The butterflies are laying eggs!"
The three latecomers charged out of the side room and maneuvered their way into the cluster of children standing in front of the butterfly cage, entranced by the

round black specks, smaller than the size of a pinhead, and breathlessly hoping for more. But the children were too late; no new eggs emerged.

Children slowly trickled back to their seats. Jill noted that it was time to visit the sixth-grade inventors' fair.

"Okay niños, ya es la hora para pasar a la presentación."

In a few minutes, the children were walking down the hallway and room 307 was empty. Almost. In a darkened corner, beetles scurried over spoiling chunks of apple. Milkweed bugs sucked nourishment out of wet paper towels as they hung from the wall in plastic bags punched with airholes. Butterflies fluttered their wings, and minute black eggs rested between netting and plastic or on paper petals, hiding within them unborn caterpillars.

Huevo, oruga, capullo, mariposa, huevo. Egg, caterpillar, chrysalis, butterfly, egg. Change is continual. Life goes on.

❖   ❖   ❖

The day after the butterflies laid their eggs, the children entered the classroom to a wonderful surprise. Their teacher relayed that, while she had gone downstairs to use the Xerox machine, Alicia, who had arrived in class early, had made a discovery.

"Yo, esta mañana, miré a las mariposas y yo no vi nada. Entonces yo me fui abajo para hacer copias y cuando subí Alicita estaba en el salón. ¿Qué dijiste, Alicita?"

Jill asked Alicia to reveal her early morning discovery to her classmates. The normally expressive child became suddenly shy, but pride in her achievement compelled her to speak about the caterpillar she had seen earlier that morning on a flower.

---

By discussing this new development with Alicia, Jill takes advantage of an opportunity to model sustained conversation in Spanish to the class.

---

"Vi una oruga." Alicia responded that she saw a caterpillar.

"¿Una qué?" Jill asked her to repeat her answer.

"Oruguita." Alicia revised her answer slightly by naming it as a little caterpillar.

"¿Dónde?" (Where?)

"En la flor." (On the flower.)

"¿Pero tuvimos oruguitas ayer?" (But did we have little caterpillars before?)

"No."

---

In addition to modeling dialogue in Spanish in an authentic situation, Jill is able to reinforce positive self-esteem in Alicia, as well as to promote respect for the linguistic minority children in the classroom.

---

"No. ¿De dónde vino? ¿Glenna?" Jill asked where the caterpillars had come from.

*(Continued)*

(Continued)

"Porque ayer una mariposa puso huevos y ahora tenemos una oruguita."

After Glenna answered that the caterpillar had come from the butterfly's eggs, Jill conversed with the class, using animated gestures and facial expressions. "La oruguita es, ¿qué cosa? ¿Es cómo qué? ¿Es un adulto? ¿Qué es? . . . Una larva. Es una larva. ¿O? . . . O un bebé. Voy a llamarles en parejas. Alicita va a buscar la oruga. Voy a llamarles en parejas para ver si Alicita puede buscar la oruga. Niños, hablen español, por favor."

(The little caterpillar is . . . what thing? . . . it's like what? . . . Is it an adult? . . . What is it? . . . A larva . . . Or? . . . Or a baby. I am going to call you in pairs. Alicita is going to look for the caterpillar. I am going to call you in pairs to see if Alicita is able to find the caterpillar. Children, speak in Spanish, please.")

---

This is an example of both sheltering and scaffolding instruction. Jill shelters instruction by modifying teacher talk through rate of speech, phrasing and rephrasing, pausing, sentence expansion, facial expression, and animated gesture. She scaffolds instruction through questioning and feedback.

Not only does Jill scaffold instruction herself, but she also facilitates a situation in which Alicita can assist in scaffolding sustained conversation in Spanish for her peers. In so doing, Jill addresses both cross-cultural attitude and identity construction through tapping the richness inherent in a bilingual peer group and the social context of learning. Linguistic majority children may benefit from viewing a linguistic minority child as a role model, and linguistic minority children may benefit in self-esteem and corresponding identity construction.

In addition to addressing linguistic goals by sheltering and scaffolding instruction and addressing cross-cultural goals by using a Spanish dominant child as a role model, Jill addresses academic goals by reviewing content area vocabulary in science.

In this one small example, we can see the teacher address the foundational goals of immersion education through the integration of content, process, and language within a social context of learning in which students fulfill the roles of both teacher and learner. Constructivist and immersion pedagogy and curriculum work in unison to maximize learning experiences for the students in this bilingual/bicultural peer group.

---

After reviewing with her students that the caterpillar was a larva, all the while sustaining Spanish, Jill instructed that they would be called, in partners, to the butterfly cage to see if Alicia could find the caterpillar. She reminded them to speak in Spanish.

Spanish dominant Alicita stood expectantly by the butterfly cage. Glenna and Marisol were the first pair sent to view the tiny caterpillar that resembled a short, black, fuzzy thread.

"Aaaaaaaahhhhhhhh!"

Glenna's mouth hung open as she gazed downward in silence at the black spot on the red paper petal. Finally words came to her.

"Now it looks like a huevo."

"En español," Alicita whispered.

"Un huevo chiquito." Marisol pinched her thumb and her third finger together to illustrate how small the egg was.

"No, así." Bringing her fingers still closer, Glenna made the imaginary egg even smaller.

"Es como . . . así." Marisol made her egg tinier still.

Glenna would not be outdone. She declared that the egg was like a dot and indicated so with her index finger. "No, es como esta puntito."

Alicita nodded her agreement. "Está bien chiquitito."

---

A bilingual peer group provides rich resources for second language learning. Jill wisely uses this student resource to promote second language learning for her English dominant students. Constructivist theory posits that learners create their own knowledge. Two-way bilingual immersion programs use a linguistically mixed peer group within a context-embedded curricular environment to maximize the linguistic benefits students can give to each other. This Vygotskyan notion of the social context of learning is a foundational principle of such programs. In addition, the fact that Spanish dominant children can serve as linguistic role models to their English dominant peers promotes higher levels of self-esteem in linguistic minority children. All of these principles are illuminated as Alicia guides the classroom activity.

---

Two at a time, the children were sent to be hosted by Alicia as they observed the "oruguita." Ernest fantasized about what could happen next.

"What if that egg breaks open and a huge caterpillar comes out? What if a butterfly comes out of the egg? So where is he? Where is he? How many eggs are there?"

Alicita patiently responded to each of her classmates.

"¿La ves? La cosa negra. Salió de ese huevo. Do you see that black thing by the leaf? See it move. Y salió de ese huevo. Okay, Ms. Sontag, ya terminé la mesa seis." Alicita called out to Jill that table six was finished.

She continued with the next group, pointing out the egg from which a caterpillar had emerged. "Salió de ese huevo aquí. Mira."

"How do you know it's an oruguita?"

"Because salió de ese huevo y se mueve mucho." Alicia noted that it had come out of an egg and that it moved a lot.

Like her teacher, there seemed to be no end to Alicia's patience. Gently she pressed each small group to communicate in Spanish.

---

The majority of student conversation here is in Spanish. The teacher's facilitation of a Spanish dominant child to scaffold sustained conversation in Spanish is thus successful. It is possible that Alicia, too, benefits in terms of self-esteem and identity construction. Rather than viewing her Spanish language dominance and Latin heritage as a deficit, as would unfortunately be the case in many other educational contexts, Alicia is empowered to see these attributes as strengths.

*(Continued)*

(Continued)

> After all of the children had finished viewing the caterpillar, Glenna returned for a second look. To her dismay, the caterpillar was no longer visible.
>
> "Maybe it fell down in the water," she sadly speculated. In the absence of Alicia, she slipped into English just as easily as the caterpillar had slipped out of sight.

> Here we can see the essential nature of the teacher in facilitating second language development. Even a vibrant, engaging classroom environment and a bilingual peer group cannot ensure the practice in second language conversation that is so essential to immersion pedagogy. The teachers must be always vigilant, perceptive, creative, and skilled in providing the motivational atmosphere in which second language development can occur.

## GUIDELINES FOR PRACTICE

TWI programs promote bilingualism, engage students in learning as a means to promoting academic achievement, and foster positive cross-cultural relations among students. All of these goals have been highlighted in the prior narrative, along with analytical commentary. Salient points that have been illustrated in this fashion are listed below, in categories corresponding with program goals, to facilitate incorporation by the reader.

### Promote Bilingualism

The societal pervasiveness of English is a significant obstacle to educators working within TWI programs. Christian (1996) found that English was the predominant language used by children in two-way immersion programs when they spoke among themselves. To meet the goal of bilingualism for all students, Jill employed strategies to counteract the tendency of students to communicate in English and to promote the use of Spanish in the classroom. Recommended strategies used by the teacher in this chapter include the following:

- Respond to the students in Spanish when Spanish is the language of instruction, regardless of the language used by students to initiate communication. (Likewise, respond to students in English when English is the language of instruction, regardless of the language used by students to initiate communication.)

- Maximize the use of students (both Spanish dominant and English dominant) as language models for their peers.
- Contextualize instruction to promote second language learning.
- Use music to reinforce language memory.
- Structure the learning environment to maximize the social context of classroom language acquisition and learning.
- Teach language (L1 and L2) through content.
- Set the linguistic tone for the language to be used for instruction and stick to it.
- Use teacher modeling incessantly.
- Use humor to motivate language learning.
- Separate languages by content area.
- Be creative in ways to motivate children to use L2.
- Use the visual and performing (creative) arts often.
- Scaffold conversation in L2.
- Support teacher talk in L2 through hands-on experience and context-embedded instruction.
- Shelter and modify teacher talk in L2 through
  1. Rate of speech
  2. Phrasing and rephrasing
  3. Vocabulary
  4. Pauses
  5. Sentence expansion
  6. Gesture
  7. Facial expression

## Engage Students in Learning: Immersion Pedagogy Meets Constructivist Practice

The key to high levels of academic achievement may well be student engagement in the learning process. Students who are motivated to learn *will* learn. Play is the learning vehicle of childhood. Tapping into the childhood drive for exploration and discovery can be a powerful means of promoting student engagement. Structuring the learning environment to allow students to use prior knowledge and to work cooperatively can enhance such engagement. Recommended strategies used by the teacher in this chapter include the following:

- Use cooperative groups frequently.
- Choose curricular topics of inherent interest to students.

- Link different content areas thematically.
- Promote authentic learning activities.
- Promote critical thinking.
- Do not give answers—encourage children to find their own. (Likewise, encourage children to ask their own questions. In addition to promoting critical thinking, children are more likely to engage in seeking answers to authentic questions in which they are personally invested.)
- Do not be afraid of silence; use it as a tool to promote critical thinking.
- Engage children in scientific study through scientific methods, even at a young age.
- Use a process-oriented inquiry approach.
- Teach and reinforce L2 vocabulary within context-embedded learning experiences.
- Use the arts frequently to motivate and engage students in the learning process.
- Seize the moment. Authentic learning promotes engagement that in turn may promote academic achievement. Do not be a slave to the lesson plan.
- Unify the bilingual curriculum through thematic units. Thematic units can be bilingual by maintaining language separation by subject.
- Structure instruction to maximize the social context of learning.
- Facilitate a context-embedded curriculum.

## Foster Positive Cross-Cultural Attitude

When academic achievement, cognitive skill, and linguistic and metalinguistic ability connect within the context of an overall classroom environment supportive of bilingualism and biculturalism, positive cross-cultural attitudes can result. Cross-cultural respect, as well as a motivating and stimulating learning climate, can lead to positive student interpretations of a bilingual/bicultural environment and thus healthier cross-cultural attitudes. Herein lies a possible connection between academic and cognitive gains and cross-cultural attitude. When students experience both social and academic success within a bilingual/bicultural environment, positive attitudes toward bilingualism have a firm foundation in which to grow. Recommended strategies used by the teacher in this chapter include the following:

- Facilitate friendships between students of different cultural and linguistic backgrounds.
- Use arts-based activities to promote cross-cultural appreciation.
- Promote respect for linguistic minority children by using them as linguistic role models.
- Model excellence in all language arts areas (listening, speaking, reading, writing) in two languages.
- Treat children of all linguistic and cultural backgrounds with respect.

# 7 Constructivist Classroom Connections

## *Intermediate Newcomers Meet the Universal Chicken*

*Barbara Nykiel-Herbert*

The program for ELLs presented in this chapter was implemented in an elementary school in Upstate New York. During the years following the Gulf War, the district experienced a sudden influx of refugees from Iraq—both Arabs and Kurds. There had been no Kurdish community in the area previously and only a scattering of Moslem Arabs, so the community resources to draw on for language, culture, and instructional support were extremely limited.

Like all the previous ELL newcomers at the school, the Iraqi children were assigned to mainstream classrooms with forty-five to sixty minutes of daily pull-out ESL instruction. The Iraqi students, however, appeared markedly different from the previous groups of immigrants, who were mostly from Southeast Asia and postcommunist Europe. The children from Iraq seemed to experience many adjustment problems, progressing at a much slower pace than their predecessors. After twelve to eighteen months of instruction, many of the students, including those in the middle and upper grades, performed poorly on both oral and written language assessments; many could not recognize even the basic, high-frequency words in print. The students' performance in the content areas was correspondingly low. Further cause for concern was the Iraqi children's social behavior; they failed to integrate into their classroom communities, acting either passive and withdrawn or defiant and disruptive.

Worried about the Iraqi students' lack of academic progress, the mainstream teachers began to refer the nonperforming Iraqi children to be tested for potential learning disabilities so that they could be placed in special education classes, and over 30 percent of them were diagnosed with "exceptionalities." It was hard to explain such a high percentage of learning disabilities within one immigrant group, leading some district educators to speculate that chemical weapons used by the Iraqi regime against the Kurds might have affected the children's cognitive development. This hypothesis, however, was never corroborated.

It was far more likely that the Iraqi students were not learning because they could not participate meaningfully in the Western thought-based curriculum that was not only linguistically but also culturally alien to them. U.S. public school curriculum is derived from the beliefs, norms and expectations, and general knowledge base shared by the middle class not only in the United States but also throughout most of the Western world. The Western thought paradigm, which merges Judeo-Christian values with an evidence-based approach to scientific knowledge, is difficult for non-Westerners to access, especially if they lack formal education and have not been exposed to Western culture. All of the failing Iraqi students had experienced interruptions in their schooling due to their families' flight from war zones into refugee camps and their subsequent resettlement. Because of such disruptions, some of the children had never had a chance to attend school at all. Moreover, many had come from farming communities in which the level of education was minimal. Because the students lacked the necessary background knowledge, the instructional content in their mainstream classrooms, where they spent most of their school day, was beyond their comprehension, not only linguistically but also conceptually. In Vygotsky's terms, the mainstream classroom instruction was pitched above these children's ZPDs. The only comprehensible input they received was their daily hour of ESL instruction; for the remaining five hours of their school day, the Iraqi children were wasting their precious time, suspended in an abyss of incomprehension. The performance gap between them and their American classmates was not closing, but widening.

Although they lacked the foundations of formal education, the Iraqi children nevertheless had extensive experiential knowledge, broader in some respects than their American peers. What they needed was not special education services but a coherent, comprehensive educational program addressing their specific learning needs and abilities, built on the foundations of their previous knowledge and incorporating key elements of their culture. The solution the school eventually adopted on an experimental basis was a self-contained immersion class for the lowest-performing Iraqi students in Grades 3 to 5, since those students were at the greatest risk of educational failure. Fourteen such students, who scored in the non-literate category at the end-of-year Language Assessment Scales Reading/ Writing test administered in May, were invited, with their parents' consent, to join the class in September.

The leading goal of the program was to accelerate the students' acquisition of literacy so that they could become independent learners. The children faced the complex task of acquiring communicative English, learning the K–2 curriculum (acquiring basic reading skills such as word recognition and developing reading fluency), and at the same time learning the patterns and functions of written discourse necessary for meaningful participation in their grade-level curriculum. They needed to acquire analytical skills to evaluate texts in terms of their informational value as well as their structural, organizational, and linguistic features. They also needed to develop writing skills adequate for accomplishing grade-level academic tasks as well as for their own purposes of creative and personal expression.

Subject content was integrated into literacy instruction. Rather than targeting the content curriculum of a particular grade level, the program emphasized the development of conceptual frameworks of formal knowledge by directing students to think about, connect, and organize the facts they already knew. In this way, the framework for future learning was constructed on the foundations of the students' experiential and cultural knowledge. The initial instruction was based on concrete, observable, and demonstrable phenomena with which the children were already familiar in a practical, nonacademic way; these served as steppingstones toward cognitively and linguistically more abstract planes.

However, to become authentically engaged in reading and writing, the children needed to find personal meaning and purpose in literacy. Engaging, easy-to-read stories that would appeal to Middle Eastern ELLs were scarce, so the children were taught to read and write with materials based directly on their own oral narratives. In the safety of their own group, no longer uninvolved and apathetic, the children talked openly and eagerly about events in their personal lives and the lives of their communities. The children's narratives and conversations were collected on audiotape and then transcribed and edited into short stories for reading and as prompts for writing tasks.

In *Closing the Achievement Gap* (Freeman & Freeman, 2002), an excellent piece on struggling ELLs in the United States (new arrivals with interrupted formal education and older learners who have "fallen through the cracks" of the system), this veteran team of authors and educators formulate four key principles of instruction for academic success:

1. Engage students in challenging, theme-based curriculum to develop academic concepts.

2. Draw on students' background—their experiences, cultures, and languages.

3. Organize collaborative activities and scaffold instruction to build students' academic English proficiency.

4. Create confident students who value school and value themselves as learners. (Freeman & Freeman, 2002, p. 16)

The application of these four principles, consonant with constructivist practice, is evident in the following narrative that takes place in the highlighted self-contained ELL classroom. It is based on transcripts from several sessions recorded on site in the middle of the school year; it also contains samples of students' narratives and their written work.

"Teacher, I go with Mr. Matthew today?"

"Yes you may, Beyar."

"No, it's not fair! It's our turn today! Me and Nigar!"

"But I have a good story. I told Mr. Matthew already I have a story!"

"It's not fair. It's Mercam and Nigar turn!"

"But I already wrote my story at home for Mr. Matthew. See? I told him I have a good story and I said was gonna write it at home and he said, okay, you show me next time!"

A forest of hands shot up; bodies stretched like guitar strings, on ballerina tiptoes, leaned over the edges of desks, while excited, high-pitched sounds collided overhead at high speed. The idea that you raise your hand to signal your desire to speak and then wait to be called on never appealed to this group, and their teacher, Maria, was no longer even trying to enforce the rule. Not all battles were worth fighting.

"Hold on, Beyar. Sorry. I think you'll have to wait. Mercam and Nigar will go now, and I'll ask Mr. Matthew if he has some time afterwards to listen to your story. As a special bonus. How's that?"

"What's bo-nus?"

"Something extra, like a reward or a prize. For writing your story you'll get extra time with Mr. Matthew."

"Teacher, can I have a bo-nus with Mr. Matthew, too? I wrote a story, too!"

Aaargh. Maria grunted with "you kids will drive me insane" mock exasperation, but a secret smile bubbled up inside of her. When she had proposed the idea of an all-day, self-contained class for non-literate ELLs to the district administrators at the end of the previous school year, she did not anticipate that she would end up *rationing* literacy.

Mr. Matthew stood at the door with his audio recorder. The children loved to go off with him to tell and record their stories about their lives in Iraq, their families and neighbors, and schoolwork and games. Even stories about chickens.

> The children's personal stories are embedded in their shared culture, so they are easily accessible to the whole group. Personal storytelling also has a huge affective benefit because it puts the focus of positive attention on students as individuals.

"Why you like chicken stories, Teacher?"

"Well, you know what? People all over the world keep chickens. We all eat chickens, and chicken eggs. That's one way in which we are all the same. And so we all have stories about chickens, and we can all relate to them. We have also been talking about birds and eggs in our science lessons, right? By the way, what kind of animal is a chicken?"

> The teacher identifies an area of "human common ground"—experiences that we can all relate to, regardless of culture. Unlike cows, pigs, or dogs, chickens are safe to talk about because, outside of strictly vegetarian cultures, they are commonly treated strictly as food rather than as deities, pets, or "unclean" animals that must be avoided. Chicken stories are most likely to be told in the context of family and community activities and, as such, provide the teacher with insights into the culture of a child's daily life. Also, many stories about chickens involve situational humor—often of the slapstick kind—which has a universal appeal. While chicken stories are being explored as part of the language and literacy component of the program, the students study flying animals (birds, insects, and bats) in their science lessons. The vocabulary learned through a science activity can be immediately used in a literacy task, and the other way around. Both the chicken stories and the projects comparing birds and insects serve to integrate language, literacy, and content.

"Chicken is a bird because . . . because it has two legs . . ." Shkriya volunteered.

"And feathers . . ." Nigar couldn't help prompting.

"And it has eggs."

"And it has wings, and it fly . . . no?" attempted the usually quiet Zainab.

"Yes, it has wings, and it can fly, but not too high and not too far. But some birds cannot fly, but they are still birds. So flying is not a *defining characteristic* of birds," Maria said slowly and distinctly, putting extra emphasis on "defining characteristics." She did not use small talk with this group.

> Maria uses big words on purpose. The students may not understand what some of the words and phrases mean now, but they will grasp their sense eventually, after the word or phrase has been used in similar natural contexts several times.

*(Continued)*

(Continued)

> "Chicken is not an insect. Because insect has six legs," Shkriya showed off. They had just finished their projects—mini-posters to display on the classroom walls—in which they had to compare a chosen bird with a chosen insect to show their class characteristics and differences.
>
> "By the way, what do you call a chicken in Kurdish?" enquired Maria.
>
> "Mrishik. Mri-shik."
>
> "Mri-shik?"
>
> "Yeah, you say good! Teacher, *you* have mrishik stories?"
>
> "Of course I have mrishik stories. I have a story from my childhood about flying chickens. I'll tell you mine when you tell me yours, okay?"

> Although unable to use the children's native language for instructional purposes, Maria shows an interest in her students' first language, occasionally incorporating a Kurdish word into her speech. By doing so, the teacher communicates to her students that she values their language and culture.

> That was a few weeks ago, and since then the class has enjoyed many mrishik stories—about chickens roaming the roads and laying eggs under parked cars, about mother's chickens getting mixed up with the neighbor's and ending up in the wrong pot, about toddler siblings finding stray eggs and making a mess of them. Maria told her childhood chicken story, too; how she forgot to open the chicken coop for her grandma's chickens, and how they flew up into a tree, one by one, and went to sleep there. Grandma had to wake them up and herd them back to the coop. The story may not have made an impression on urban American children, but Maria's Kurdish students found it hilarious. Of course chickens mustn't sleep in a tree—unless we want to have eggs raining from the tree in the morning!

> Maria's trading of her childhood stories with the students' stories enhances the classroom climate of this learning community.

> With help from their authors, Maria wrote some of the chicken stories on large sheets of lined paper for the students to read, initially together, and then individually. These collaboratively created stories also served as models for the children to try their hand at their own story writing. Gradually, storytelling and story writing became a way of life in Maria's class.
>
> Mercam and Nigar, flashing triumphant smiles at Beyar, followed Mr. Matthew to an old broom closet down the hall, which Maria had transformed into a makeshift "recording studio." In the evening, Maria transcribed the conversation between Mr. Matthew and the two sisters. As she reread the typed transcript, looking for material that could be adapted for classroom use, Maria pondered Mercam's account of playing outside in the light of rocket fire. How real did war and death appear to seven- and eight-year-olds? How traumatized were their families, having had to flee their homesteads, often on foot, carrying babies and toddlers and family belongings on their backs? The tape triggered Maria's own childhood memories. Never having been

directly touched by war, she had experienced it vicariously through the continuously relived trauma of her parents' generation, whose childhoods were painfully scarred by World War II. She realized, once again, how much her own childhood in rural Eastern Europe resonated with the experiences of her immigrant students. But for now, saving the topics of war, guns, mosques, and prayers for perhaps another time, she chose the innocent theme of the two sisters' school-going routine. She underlined the passages that she intended to rewrite as a story about Mercam and Nigar.

---

| Mercam: | Our school in Iraq was about from Saratoga Heights to here. It would take us about 40 minutes. We were tired when we got there. |
| Nigar: | We walked to school. Our mom would give us money and we would buy lemons and candy. |
| Mercam: | She loves lemons. Kurdish people love lemons. We eat it with salt. |
| Nigar: | Lemons are my favorite fruit. We like watermelon, too. |
| Mercam: | Sometimes we would eat flavored ice. Sometimes my mom made them. Sometimes it was cold, sometimes it was hot. We had snow there sometimes. Always our garden had frost on it. We had oranges in the garden. |
| Mercam: | We lived in the mountains. We had three houses, but we gave one to my uncle and one to my cousin. |
| Mr. Matthew: | Can you draw a picture of your house for me? |
| Nigar: | She draws nice pictures. Mercam made a yellow book with pictures about my family and me. Where we were born. |
| Mercam: | I wasn't so good in school. I couldn't write in Arabic. I could only write my name. So I got in trouble. My mother knows how to speak in Arabic and Kurdish. I know how to speak Sorani—it's kind of my language—they lived in my country, but they don't speak the same language we do. I speak Sorani, Kurdish, and English, and my mom is trying to teach me Arabic. My best language is Kurdish. Even better than English. At school, we would stay home Friday. We had to go to the mosque. We stayed at the mosque for as long as you want. It started at 11 o'clock, but it ends at around 6 o'clock, but if you wanted, you could stay until 12 o'clock. |
| Mr. Matthew: | Do your parents get mad that you have to go to school on a Friday in America? |
| Mercam: | No. We never go to mosque in America. |
| Nigar: | I forgot how to pray. Mercam knew some, but I forgot. I was too little. |
| Mr. Matthew: | Do your parents wish that they could go to mosque here? |
| Mercam: | We have a mosque here. It's in Stuyvesant Street. My dad goes to mosque here, but my mom prays at home. During the war, my mom would tell us to pray. Sometimes the soldiers would come and we would bury the guns in the dirt. At nighttime, the sky looked like fireworks. I liked how bright it was and we would go outside to play, but it was scary because if it hit you, you would *die*. |

---

*(Continued)*

(Continued)

> Maria rewrote the story of Mercam and Nigar as a third person narrative:
>
> ---
>
> In Iraq, Mercam and Nigar walked to school every day. It took them about forty minutes to walk to school. They were tired when they got there. Their mom gave them money, and they bought lemons and candy and sometimes flavored ice.
>
> Mercam wasn't so good at school. She could not write in Arabic. She could only write her name. So she got in trouble.
>
> On Friday, Mercam and Nigar did not go to school. They went to the mosque.
>
> ---
>
> In the morning, while the students were arriving in the classroom, Maria copied the story on a poster-sized tablet displayed on a stand. One by one, the children sat down and attentively read what the teacher was writing.
>
> > The students become engaged in reading the text while it is being created on the board. By now they can easily identify the word "Iraq" and the familiar names of their classmates in the first line of the story, which become the "hook" engaging their interest. By the time they read the story as a group, most of the students have previewed the text, and they will be able to focus their attention on the unfamiliar words.
>
> When everyone had settled down, Maria got the group to read the story and made sure that all the vocabulary was understood. Afterward she played the tape with Mercam's and Nigar's conversation, asking the students to observe how the two stories differed. They immediately pointed out the most obvious content differences.
>
> "Mercam was telling about the mosque, and how her dad goes to mosque here, but she and Nigar don't."
>
> "And Nigar says that lemon is her favorite fruit, and she eats it with salt."
>
> "And they have oranges in their garden in Iraq."
>
> "And sometimes it snow. And they have three houses."
>
> "So the story on tape is about many different things, right? And what about this story here on the board?"
>
> Aha! The students realized that only the parts of the narrative relating to Mercam and Nigar's school-going had been included in the written story. But Maria wanted them to notice other important differences.
>
> "Who is telling the story on the tape?"
>
> "Mercam and Nigar."
>
> "And Mr. Matthew. Three people."
>
> "Mercam and Nigar are telling their stories to Mr. Matthew. The three of them are having a conversation, right? Now, how about the written story—who is telling this story?"
>
> The children were somewhat confused by this question. They quickly reread the story.

"Two people are talking, Mercam and Nigar."

"How can you tell?"

"It says there, in the first line, 'In Iraq, Mercam and Nigar walked to school every day.'"

Expecting this answer, Maria played the tape again, guiding the students to observe that Mercam and Nigar referred to themselves as "we," but in the written story they were referred to as "they." The knotted eyebrows and half-open mouths told Maria that she was pulling the students out of their depth. She threw in another rescue line.

---

Working within the constructivist paradigm, Maria deliberately sets up a task that is a little too hard for the students to accomplish independently but one they can do with assistance. This strategy is consistent with Vygotsky's concept of the ZPD. Maria then supplies the necessary scaffolding, in this case, in the form of several easier questions that guide them to the answer. The teacher's guiding questions also provide the students with a blueprint of a problem solving path. If the process is repeated several times, the students will eventually be able to follow the same thinking path on their own.

---

"Mercam and Nigar told their story to Mr. Matthew, but did they also write this story here?"

"No, no. The teacher wrote it. You."

"There you go. On the tape, Mercam and Nigar tell a story about themselves. After I listened to the tape, I wrote the story about Mercam and Nigar. As you've noticed before, I took some details out and changed the order of sentences. It is still their story, but I wrote it, so I could not use 'we' and 'I,' right?"

"Because the story is not about you," Nazdar pointed out.

"Because you didn't go to school in Iraq!" piped in Selwer.

"That's right, I've only retold the story about Mercam and Nigar. I am the *narrator* in the written story. Na-rra-tor. Can you say it?"

"Na- rra -tor. Narrator."

"A narrator is the teller of a story. On the tape, Mercam and Nigar tell their own story, so they are the . . ."

"Narrator!"

"You got it! Mercam and Nigar are the *narrators* of their story on the tape. They *narrate* their story."

---

Maria introduces the terms "narrator" and "narrate" that belong to the academic discourse (CALP) of the English language, as opposed to "tell" and "teller" that are more likely to appear in oral communication (BICS). The new term is introduced only when the students demonstrate that they have understood the concept that it denotes. For an academic term to "take root" in a learner's mind, the concept must be introduced meaningfully—linked to other concepts within a specific framework. In this case, the new concept and term are introduced into the already familiar framework of story structure.

*(Continued)*

(Continued)

Maria warned the students that a difficult question was coming next. The children's eyes lit up. Maria could almost hear a chorus of "Oh, goodie! We love hard questions!"

"Now tell me this: can a story character also be the narrator in the same story?"

"Nooo . . ."

"Yeees. Yes!"

"No!"

"Yes or no? Think hard. Who are the characters in the taped story?"

"Me and Nigar are the characters," said Mercam proudly. Becoming a story character doesn't happen to every Dick, Tom, and Harry!

"Right, Mercam and Nigar are the characters, and they also tell their own story, so they are also . . ."

"Narrators!"

"Right! So a character in a story can also be the . . ."

"Narrator!"

"Bingo! A character can be the narrator."

This was still somewhat confusing to the younger students, but the concept seemed to be sinking in for the older ones. The students were already familiar with the basic elements of story grammar: character, setting, event, problem, and resolution. It was time to deal with more complex elements of writing: narrator, audience, and style. As they learned about the structure and organization of writing by analyzing written stories and nonfiction passages, they also learned to follow the steps of the writing process. Maria wanted her students to understand that a written text is not cast in stone, that it can be taken apart and reshaped if necessary. She wanted them to see language both as a tool of expression and as pliable material that can be molded and shaped to our needs and visions, like a mound of clay in the hands of a sculptor.

---

Constructivist teaching is organized around "Big Ideas," in this case, the forms and functions of written discourse. In the course of the program, the students will learn to differentiate between fiction and nonfiction writing as well as recognize a few genres within each category. This is achieved by integrating reading, writing, content, and classroom talk. Organizing teaching around Big Ideas allows teachers and students to kill three birds with one stone: students acquire content knowledge (factual information), expand their conceptual frameworks (semantic networks), and develop practical skills of oral communication, reading, and writing.

---

The following week, Maria selected Beyar's story, which lent itself easily to the same treatment as Mercam and Nigar's story of the week before. She had brought up Mercam and Nigar's story on several different occasions throughout the week to make sure that the students were comfortable with the concepts they had learned. She believed the students were now ready for the next step.

Maria plans her instruction within her students' ZPD. In Vygotsky's (1978) theory, the ZPD is the distance between a child's level of independent performance (what can be done without help) and a child's current performance potential (what can be done with assistance). Maria carefully structures her instruction by starting with what her students already know and can do without her help, and builds new concepts and skills on that foundation. She will pull her students to the top of their ZPDs through careful scaffolding (in this case, channeling their thinking in the right direction with skillful prompting) so that they can perform at the peak of their current potential. Further engagement with the concepts and practice in their application are going to transform the students' current potential level into independent performance.

Maria's teaching strategy also illustrates Krashen's (1982) comprehensible input hypothesis: when the learners are at Stage I, they are ready for the acquisition of input that is one step higher (I+1). What the learners know and can do helps them process and absorb the new material.

Beyar's story merged at least two themes, so the material irrelevant to the main theme would have to be edited. Maria felt fairly confident that, with some gentle guidance, "her kids" would be able to accomplish the task.

Maria follows the instructional process standard proposed by Vygotsky, which involves modeling a given task first and, subsequently, assisting learners, repeatedly if necessary, until they reach the level of independent performance. In this case, the teacher plans to assist the learners in reshaping an oral narrative into a written story—the process she had previously modeled for them.

Maria made copies of Beyar's story for everyone. She modeled reading the story first, while the children followed in their copies; then they paired up, the less confident readers with their stronger classmates.

Collaboration is one of the cornerstones of constructivist practice. Learners raise their performance levels when assisted by a teacher or a more advanced peer. This multigrade classroom provides many opportunities for older, more advanced students to help their less proficient classmates. The more proficient students may also benefit from this strategy. In addition to enhancing their self-esteem, they are afforded the opportunity to reinforce academic knowledge.

Maria read with Atef, who, as the most recent ELL arrival at the school, was only just being introduced to English literacy. She used a shared reading strategy, first reading the text aloud to him while pointing to the words, then letting him read the words that he recognized and taking over the parts that he could not yet read.

*(Continued)*

(Continued)

---

**Beyar's story (transcript)**

My best sport in Iraq is soccer. I can't play anymore. My mom and dad won't let me. My second year here I was on a team. The fifth game we played championship and a boy on the other team kicked the ball and it broke my nose. It looked like grandma's nose. Now I play basketball.

In Iraq, I played when I was 7. We made a soccer field in the garden with two big rocks for the goal. Part of the garden was for growing and part was for playing.

We grew tomatoes, onions, potatoes, fruit, and lettuce. Both of our houses had a garden, but the country house had a bigger garden. In the summer, people open doors and windows to sleep. Sometimes we slept on the roof because it was so hot.

---

The reading accomplished, it was time to take the story apart, the task some of Maria's budding scholars most enjoyed. Maria would first have them look for the standard elements of story grammar—characters, setting, events, problem, and resolution—to determine whether Beyar's narrative conformed to the story format. She displayed the story grammar diagram that the students were already well familiar with and distributed hand-out copies of it so that they could take notes as they identified the relevant elements.

> The students are involved in a hands-on (and minds-on) task of story analysis. The diagram provides the scaffolding to facilitate the task.

"Okay, now," Maria got the students' attention. "What's this story about?"

"The main idea is about sports," offered Zerin.

"The main idea is that . . . about sports, about playing games," echoed Shkriya.

"The main idea is about soccer," Aram climbed on the shoulders of his predecessors.

"The story is about . . . the boy liked to play soccer. And when he was playing the other boy kicked the ball and hit it . . . hit him in his nose and his nose break. And then his parents didn't let him play soccer anymore," Mercam expertly summarized the plot of the story.

> The students listen to each other attentively and elaborate on each other's contribution; each previous comment serves as a scaffold for the next, and the initial idea expands and takes a more definite shape. The children demonstrate that they are perfectly capable of holding a productive dialogue without the teacher's intervention. This is a more natural pattern of communicative interaction than the Teacher-Student-Teacher model predominant in more traditionally oriented classrooms. In a constructivist classroom, the teacher allows the students to take charge of learning situations that they can handle independently; the teacher's role is to guide the learning process by setting challenging but achievable goals, and providing assistance for reaching them.

The students successfully identified the characters and the problem (they argued that there were actually two problems) with no difficulty, but they hit a wall when trying to identify the setting and the resolution. Beyar's story, being essentially a transcript of an oral narrative, was not structured like the written stories they had analyzed before. Beyar's narrative was organized around his interest in soccer, and it tied his past life in Iraq with his current life in the United States. It also digressed into a second theme, a somewhat nostalgic description of his home in Iraq. Maria's objective was to get the students to discover differences between the structure of oral narratives and that of written stories. Awareness of these differences would make them better critical listeners, readers, and writers. So she pressed on.

"What happens at the end of the story? After Beyar's nose got broken?"

The children took a quick look at the bottom of the page, to the last lines of the passage.

"In the end they had to . . . the people had to open the door and windows," ventured Shkriya.

"Because Beyar's nose was broken?"

"Nooo . . ."

Shkriya realized that the strategy of looking for the end of the story in its last line had failed for some reason. She looked around for assistance from her peers, but none was offered. Instead, more questions followed.

---

The teacher deliberately introduces another challenge, paving the learners' way toward understanding with searching questions.

---

"What is the setting of the story? Where was Beyar when his nose got broken?"

"The setting is in Iraq. Did he get his nose broken in the garden?" wondered Nazdar.

"No! Yeah . . . yes. No."

"We don't know," Aram resolutely summed up the confusion. By then the students knew that, unlike in their schools in Iraq, which operated along traditional, rote-learning principles, it was okay to admit to not knowing. Not knowing was a starting point for finding out. "If you knew everything you wouldn't need to come to school. Just imagine how boring your lives would be then," Maria often affectionately teased. Everyone knew how much they all enjoyed school. Aram missed the school bus once, and instead of going back home to watch TV, he walked for a good hour in rainy and windy weather to be with his classmates.

"Then read the beginning of the story again. It says, 'My first year here, I was on a team.' What do you think the word 'here' means?"

"The United States."

"New York?"

"At our school?"

"Aha! So the soccer game in which Beyar's nose got broken took place after he came to the United States, right? But in his story he also talks about . . ."

"His home in Iraq."

"His garden."

"Fruit!"

"You're right. I want you to take a pencil and underline all the sentences that do not have anything to do with the story of the broken nose."

*(Continued)*

(Continued)

Heads bent over the typed pages; pencils got to work on a search and destroy mission. A minute or two later, several hands went up: Awdar, Zerin, Mercam—the fifth graders. They all concluded that the last five sentences of the story should be scrapped.

"Because he say a story about soccer, and this part is about garden. It doesn't go in the soccer story," explained Awdar.

Maria asked Zainab, who had been sitting quietly throughout the discussion, if she understood Awdar's point.

"The main idea of the story is about Beyar playing soccer, and this part here is about garden," Zainab recited without hesitation. Although silent, she seemed to be on top of it.

> Maria is satisfied that Zainab, one of the youngest students in the group, follows the discussion even though she does not actively contribute to it. Zainab is learning from more knowledgeable peers. Zainab does not repeat Awdar's statement verbatim but phrases it in a different way, which shows that she understands the point he has made.

Shkriya was trying to get the teacher's attention, circling the first paragraph with her finger.

"This part, this one is enough for the story, but this right here . . ." Shkriya's finger moved down the page, "Beyar did more . . . this was about like, garden and things . . ."

"This whole part . . . what do we call this unit of writing?" Maria didn't miss a chance to revise an academic word.

"Paragraph!" offered Beyar.

"Paragraph," repeated Shkriya. "This whole paragraph . . . it's not good for the story. We don't need it."

"So what are we going to do with it?"

"Take it out," said Mercam, with all of her fifth-grade self-confidence.

"Take it out. *Delete* it. Very good." Maria emphasized the word "delete."

> The teacher introduces a new word, delete, more specific and appropriate in the academic context, to replace the word that is already familiar. Once again the new information is supported by the old. From now on, Maria will use the new word interchangeably with the old one until the students incorporate it into their own speech.

"Sometimes we can make a better story not by putting more into it, but by taking something out. Let me tell you this. Good writers throw out a lot of their stuff."

"What do you mean?" demanded Aram, puzzled.

Maria realized that her comment was a little too cryptic. She sometimes forgot that these students were ELLs and that, for all of their growing sophistication, their real life literacy experiences were still fairly limited at this point. But she also realized, not without satisfaction, that Aram would not have asked this kind of question when he sat in his mainstream classroom the previous year, completely "out of the zone." Aram's request for clarification gave Maria a sense of success.

> The students are beginning to take comprehension for granted and have the courage and confidence to ask for an explanation, a sign that the communication between the teacher and the students is genuine, purposeful, and meaningful.

"I mean, you become a better writer if you learn to get rid of a lot of stuff that you don't need. Sometimes you have many ideas in your head when you work on a story and you write them all up, but when you read what you have written you see that some of the stuff you don't need, because it takes you away from your main idea. And it can confuse the reader. And so it's better to delete it, to take it out. It's called *editing*. It's a new word for you. To *edit* means to fix what is wrong with a story. To delete what we don't need, and to correct mistakes. Can you say *edit*?"

"E-dit. Edit."

Maria wrote the word on the board, and the students grabbed their pencils to copy it into their notebooks.

"Edit. And it means . . ."

"Fix the story."

"Make your story better."

"Right. And now I want you to cross out all the sentences that we don't need in Beyar's soccer story. What do we call this task?"

"Edit."

"We edit the story. We call the process e–di– . . ."

". . . ting! Editing?" Zerin takes a risk.

"Editing! Bingo!"

> The two words "delete" and "edit" are introduced in the same conversation; however, the word "edit" receives more emphasis because it has higher conceptual value and will be more useful to the students. "Editing" refers to an activity, but also to a specific step in the writing process. The teacher consequently uses several techniques to facilitate definition of the word: she makes the students repeat it, she writes it on the board, she again checks for understanding, and she uses the word in two different grammatical contexts (edit, editing) to elicit its different morphological forms.

"But . . ." Beyar, usually at the heart of a class discussion, had been listening silently until now. "But when we look at the ending, should we use a little bit of this . . . this sentence at the end . . . not like a resolution, but like . . . to give some information . . . ?"

"Some background information, you mean? In the introduction, perhaps?" Maria suggested.

*(Continued)*

(Continued)

"Yeah, introduction. Maybe put some of this sentence at the beginning."

"That's an excellent idea, Beyar. Let's look again at the second paragraph. Is there any information in it about soccer that we could use in the story?"

"*We played when I was seven.* And the other one, *We made a soccer field in the garden with two big rocks for the goal.*" Selwer was the first one to hit the target.

"Good. We can use some of this information at the beginning of the story, as Beyar suggests."

"The second part that is good for soccer, we can put that in the first place, and then the first paragraph will go second," Awdar mentally reorganized the story material, to confirm for himself that he was on the right track.

Maria asked one more question—on identifying the narrator of Beyar's story, which by now appeared to be an easy task. Of course Beyar was the narrator; he was telling a story about himself. He was both the narrator and the character. They backed up their point by referring to the story grammar chart. The children were sucking up literacy like a colony of sponges.

> The concept of narrator introduced the previous week is revisited here. To help the students internalize the concept, their writing task is set up in such a way that they have to make a conscious choice about the narrator of their story.

"But when you rewrite Beyar's story, you can be the narrator. You can write about Beyar, like I did about Mercam and Nigar, remember? Or you can make up another name, and add your own details. You can rewrite the story with your own sentences." Maria encouraged creativity.

"I'm gonna write my own sentences," declared Aram.

"Me too," seconded Shkriya.

"I'm gonna use *one day* at the beginning," announced Aram.

"What about the title?" inquired Awdar.

"That's easy. I already know my title," boasted Mercam.

"Me too," Nigar basked in the confidence of her older sister.

"I'm gonna make a real good story now," promised Beyar.

> Excitement, motivation, and desire to succeed are direct benefits of treating all students as competent partners in the teaching-learning process and holding them all to the same high standards.

Within a few minutes, everyone was busy writing. Mercam and Nigar were working together. As usual, Mercam wrote her story first, and then helped her sister. She would probably dictate to Nigar what to say. But that would be okay if Nigar could write it down and then read it back, as long as she was learning. She was beginning to shed her insecurity; her increasingly assertive behavior on the playground showed that the self-confident Nigar was slowly emerging.

Shkriya was working alone; she had moved her desk away from the others. Proud, ambitious, and fiercely competitive, she rarely asked for help. She didn't like to work with anyone, and both the teacher and her peers respected her need for personal space. Shkriya was the only girl among her siblings, sandwiched between two older and two younger brothers, a hardly enviable position for a female in her culture. This classroom was virtually the only place where she could show her independence and have her own way over things she could control, such as her writing.

---

Constructivist practice is particularly sensitive to individual differences among learners in personality, ability, previous experience, attitude, and so on, which may affect their work preferences and achievement patterns. Even though this group is fairly homogenous from a cultural and linguistic perspective, there is enormous individual variation. Nigar and Shkriya, who are the same age and in the same grade level and who both have older siblings in the class, exhibit radically different approaches to their learning tasks. The teacher recognizes the differences and allows the students to work within their own comfort zones while ensuring that they make the expected progress.

---

Maria asked the students to finish their stories at home and bring them to class the next morning. Homework was never an issue in Maria's class; the students knew that they didn't have to do it if they didn't know how. All they needed to do was ask for help in the morning. But that almost never happened. One student confessed that she would be too embarrassed to do so. Instead, they did the best they could, which was often better than what Maria had expected, even though she had learned to expect a lot from this group.

In the morning, the class quickly went over the previous day's work. Maria wanted to make sure that the younger, less advanced students understood what they did and why. With some prodding and prompting, accompanied by inevitable eye-rolling from the older students (as in, "How many times do we need to do this?"), Maria got them to reconstruct and justify the steps of the process.

---

A quick review session activates the previously acquired language, concepts, or content knowledge for a new application or further expansion. A review is especially useful for less advanced students who may not have gained an adequate understanding of the material and thus may not be ready for the next installment. A review also gives less confident learners a chance to demonstrate their knowledge; verbalization aids both comprehension and memory.

---

"Beyar say the story and then Mr. Matthew write it and then he type it on the computer and then we read it." Nigar hijacked the turn without raising her hand, before anyone had a chance to gather their thoughts. She stopped suddenly, as if completely surprised by her own courage.

*(Continued)*

(Continued)

"It was about..."

"Soccer!" Atef shouted out victoriously. He had come to the United States just this past summer and, at ten years of age, had never been to school prior to his arrival in Upstate New York. Completely disoriented at first and frustrated to the point of causing deliberate disruptions, Atef was beginning to "get it" and finally seemed to be enjoying learning.

"About nose broking..."

"About getting hurt."

"And then we wrote the story again."

"Because the other part, was, actually, the writing was not about soccer. The writing was about garden."

"About growing things in the garden."

"And sleeping on the roof."

"So we, like, we cross some words out and we write...like, like...," Nigar's voice trailed off; she looked pleadingly at her older sister.

"Why did we cross out some words? Come on, you know it," Maria helped Nigar to get back on track without Mercam's help. Nigar's budding confidence needed reassurance.

"Because the story would be good...would be better without them." Nigar caught the teacher's nod and grinned happily.

"Because there were some...mistakes," offered Zainab.

Mistakes??? "Noooo!" the group protested in unison.

Zainab shrank back in her seat at her classmates' unequivocal reaction. If those were not mistakes, then what should we call them? Zainab's self-esteem had taken a punch and needed immediate restoration.

"Zainab is trying to say that there was some irrelevant information in the story that needed to be edited." Aiming for two birds with one stone once again, Maria put extra emphasis on the word *edited*. "She used the word 'mistakes' because there is no word in English that means *unnecessary details*. That's not Zainab's fault. We *edited* the story by *deleting* the unnecessary details."

"They are not mistakes.... They are good...for, like, a story about garden, but not about soccer," explained Awdar.

"Precisely. Beyar can use these ideas in another story," Maria confirmed.

> Constructivist teaching requires learners to take risks, and so the teacher must be particularly sensitive to potential ego damage. This diligence is especially important in teaching ELLs, who are aware of their own lack of linguistic and other skills and may be easily discouraged by unsuccessful attempts.

A smile of relief spread over Zainab's face. The only student in the class wearing a tell-tale black headscarf, as was more typical of Arab than Kurdish girls, Zainab seemed to have a fragile ego. Maria often wondered if the headscarf difference contributed to her insecurity. But the real roots of her insecurity went deeper than that; as deep as her life, which almost didn't happen at all when one of Saddam Hussein's soldiers viciously hit her pregnant mother in the stomach. Shocked into a premature birth as a result of her mother's trauma, Zainab fought for her life, and won. Now as a newly literate eight-year-old, Zainab attempted to re-create the story of the astounding circumstances of her arrival in this world. But words seemed to be failing her, and she kept crossing them out, then slashing with her pencil through whole paragraphs before, invariably, tearing the pages out of her notebook and starting over again. Witnessing this silent, tense, private struggle, Maria hoped that one day Zainab would muster enough courage and confidence in her writing to share her story with the world.

> Literacy acquires a personal value for students like Zainab; it becomes the tool for self-expression, which is likely to have a therapeutic effect on trau-matized children.

"And now I'd like to hear how you edited, or rewrote, Beyar's story. Who wants to go first?"

As usual, almost everyone wanted to read, but the group voted to let Zerin go first because she had to go to her gym class in about twenty minutes.

---

**Zerin's edited version of Beyar's story**

My best sport in Iraq was soccer. I played soccer in Iraq when I was seven. We made a soccer field in the garden. We put two big rocks for the goal. Part of the garden was for growing, and part was for playing.

My first year in here, I was on a team. In the fifth game we played Washington and the boy on the other team kicked the ball and it broke my nose. It looked like grandma's nose. And I went home, and my parents took me to the doctor.

Now my mom and dad won't let me play soccer anymore. When my parents told me I can't play soccer anymore, I felt bad. So I played basketball with my friends.

---

Zerin beamed with pride as she finished reading. Maria refrained from comments until Zerin's peers had expressed theirs, but her body language was sending a clear message to Zerin that she had done an excellent job. Maria asked the students to look again at the original version of Beyar's story to appreciate Zerin's improvements. They observed that Zerin had indeed incorporated all the comments that were made during the previous day's discussion. Nazdar also noted that Zerin had changed the tense from present to past because "the story took place a long time ago so we must use *was*, not *is*." In Nazdar's comment, Maria recognized her own words, repeated so often in this class. Nazdar, Zerin's younger sister and only a third grader, was a self-appointed grammar watchdog; grammar-wise, she never missed a beat.

*(Continued)*

(Continued)

> When a new language is learned holistically, through exposure and meaningful use rather than through formal instruction, grammatical rules are internalized in roughly the same way as the rules of the native language. However, Nazdar's functional explanation of the use of past instead of present tense is the result of writing instruction. Although Maria's teaching is not grammar based, she consistently offers minimal, strictly-to-the-point explanations when a grammatical change or correction is required. In this way, the students acquire not only the practical command of the language but also gain academic knowledge that allows them to make conscious grammatical choices in their writing. This doesn't mean, of course, that when learners understand a certain grammar rule and its application domain they will automatically stop making grammatical errors. Accuracy develops with sufficient practice over time.

Selwer questioned Zerin's use of the first person narrative. Selwer was Beyar's sister, and Maria suspected family loyalty fueled her discomfort; Selwer didn't like anyone appropriating her brother's story as his or her own. "It was Beyar's story, but Zerin said, 'My best sport in Iraq was soccer.' She was supposed to say, 'Beyar's best sport in Iraq was soccer.'"

Aha, there we go again, thought Maria, as she seized an opportunity to revisit the concept of character, narrator, and author and the newly acquired idea of editing.

"Okay, is Zerin's story about Zerin?"

"Nooo . . . it's about Beyar."

"Right, it's about Beyar's experiences. So Beyar is the character in this story, right?" The children nodded their agreement.

"Who is the narrator in Zerin's story? Is it Zerin?"

Yes. No. Nooo? Confusion.

"Who in the story says, *my nose, my mom and dad?*"

"Beyar."

"Aha! So who is the narrator?"

"Beyar . . . ?"

"Yes, Beyar is the character and also the narrator."

"Oh, yeah." There was a spark of recognition. "A character can be the narrator."

"Right. The story is told from the point of view of the main character. Zerin is not the character, and she is not the narrator, either. In fact, this is not really Zerin's story. She only *edited* Beyar's story, to make it better, less confusing to readers. She did an excellent *editing* job, didn't she?"

Maria was sure the children would be tripping over these concepts again and again, but they would sort them out eventually.

> Conceptual knowledge cannot be memorized, and it may take learners some time to gain deep understanding of concepts so that they become useful as analytical tools. Constant reviewing and recycling in a variety of new contexts is necessary to help learners incorporate new ideas into their cognitive repertoires.

The chorus of appreciative noises from her classmates made Zerin blush. Zerin and her twin brother, Awdar, would be going to sixth grade in the fall. In this district, the sixth grade was housed at the middle school, so they would be moving into a completely new environment. The twins were anxious about the change and were determined to do their best to start sixth grade well prepared.

"Can I read my new story now?" asked Beyar. "I changed a lot of things, and I have more details."

Beyar read his new story with pride and afterward handed Maria the hard copy.

---

### Beyar's story (written)

In Iraq, I played soccer when I was 7 years old. We made a soccer field in the garden with two big rocks for the goal and I priktis shoting goals. And every day I priktis goaling and stelling. But the game was coming. And my mom washed my clothes for the game. But the game was in 30 seconds. And we went to the game, then I went to my kaptin. And we start the game. But it was the championship game. But one boy pass to me. And I kick the ball very hard. And the goaler kiked the ball bake. Than the ball hat my noise. And the referee say time out and they toke me to the hospitel. And I stay in hospitel for 2 week. And they hope me to get better. But they sayd that of your bad come bake to the hospitel. And my mom and dad toke me home. And that was 4 months, then I was OK.

---

Beyar had incorporated much of the classroom discussion into his written story. Unlike his oral narrative, his written story was well focused on his soccer experience, with the reference to the garden skillfully incorporated into the introduction. The events were well sequenced, ending with a natural resolution.

Once again the concept of the ZPD becomes a constructivist's teacher tool, this time as the basis for assessment. A traditional, skills-oriented teacher is likely to assess Beyar's writing statically, in terms of what it currently contains and what it still lacks. A constructivist teacher will use a more dynamic model of assessment, looking at the progress Beyar has made and at the direction in which Beyar's writing is progressing. A traditionalist would look at Beyar's imperfections as errors; a constructivist will look at them as a learner's intellectual decisions made in the absence of sufficient data. A traditionalist would probably dismiss Beyar's writing as decidedly "below standard" for a fourth grader, but a constructivist teacher would assess Beyar's potential performance and see extremely encouraging signs of a young learner on his way to becoming academically successful. In five months, Beyar has progressed from the non-literate to limited-literacy category for his grade level. He seems to be passing through roughly the same stages in his writing development as English-speaking beginning writers, but at a faster pace. Beyar's use of invented spelling shows that he has a high

*(Continued)*

(Continued)

> level of phonological awareness; his invented morphological forms, such as "goal-ing" and "goaler," testify to his native-like morphological productivity. It is not the independent level but, rather, the level of assisted performance that tells the teacher where a student is in his/her cognitive development. The appreciation of a learner's progress and potential rather than his actual performance is especially important in second language classrooms, which is why ELLs who fail in tradi-tional mainstream settings are more likely to thrive in constructivist environments.

But things could always be improved. Beyar got some serious editing advice from his classmates.

"You must change some sentences. You say *but, but, but* all the time," advised Mercam.

"And when you say *they* we don't know who you are talking about," added Awdar. He sounded exactly like Maria whenever she cautioned her students, in pre-cisely those words, about the consequences of overusing pronouns.

"Ah, you monkeys," she mused affectionately to herself, wondering which of her other lines and behaviors the children imitated, perhaps behind her back; she vividly remembered doing so to her own teachers.

> A teacher serves as a model to students whether or not she is conscious of it. This incident illustrates how the students have adopted Maria's way of talking and explaining grammatical points. The fact that they also know when and how to use these points demonstrates their firm grasp of the underlying gram-matical concepts. Due to young learners' innate propensity for imitation, mod-eling is a powerful scaffolding strategy.

Recovering quickly from her personal moment, Maria saw an opportunity for another instantaneous mini-grammar review.

"What do we call words like 'they?'"

"Puh . . . pur . . . Ah, that's hard word!"

"Close. Try again. Pro . . ."

". . . nouns! Pronouns!"

Even though Maria had been fairly sure that they knew the answer, she was impressed.

> Maria uses questioning and prompting as a scaffolding strategy to get her students to recall the information. The students again demonstrate that they have "absorbed" grammar through both natural use and the teacher's model-ing of specific usage patterns. The teacher has introduced the basic grammat-ical terminology, such as the names of lexical categories. This example, however, is not about teaching formal grammar but, rather, of teaching aca-demic language. Students are likely to encounter references to word classes such as nouns, verbs, pronouns, and so on in their language arts textbooks.

"So what do you think Beyar should use instead?" she asked, but Beyar was already a step ahead.

"Oh I know, I know. I can change this."

> The concept of the ZPD manifests itself here again. Beyar understands his misuse of a pronoun, and he knows how to correct his error. He demonstrates that his potential level of performance—in this case, achieved with the assistance of a peer comment—is higher than his independent performance.

Beyar crossed out the confusing pronouns and confidently scribbled replacements over them in his highly idiosyncratic script. Entering the American school in third grade, with no English literacy experience, he had missed penmanship practice and had invented his own way of forming the letters, often moving from right to left as in Arabic. Maria's attempts to help him correct his handwriting had failed; attending to letter formation slowed him down, and Beyar was an impatient, even overactive child with lots to say and to write. He was a fourth grader and didn't want to spend time on what first graders were learning. And, frankly, he couldn't afford to. Maria believed that terrible handwriting had never stopped anyone from achieving success.

"Anything else?"

"And you have too many *ands*," Nazdar threw in.

"But I need them!" Beyar got defensive. "Because I like long sentences. Because some people, they only write short sentences, they maybe have three words. That's not good in a story."

Beyar was aware of the stylistic effects he wanted to achieve, but his linguistic tools were still inadequate for the job.

> Beyar's taste for literary language has undoubtedly been shaped by the children's literature, nonfiction, and poetry that is read and discussed in class on a daily basis. Quality children's literature provides valuable models of language use to which developing ELLs are as sensitive as native language speakers.

Maria made a mental note to address the issue of combining sentences in the near future. More and more complex sentences emerged in her students' writing—temporal clauses, relative clauses, conditionals—evidence of their growing language competence and of the need to express more complex relationships among objects, events, and ideas.

"I have looong sentences!" boasted Aram. "Can I read my story next, please?"

Aram, Shkriya's older brother, was more reflective than the quick, impulsive Beyar. Aram took his time to compose his stories; the numerous cross-outs and corrections testified to the intellectual struggle that drove the process. He read slowly and accurately, pausing at all the right places. Maria suspected that he actually practiced reading his story aloud to himself at home so as to impress his audience with his impeccable performance.

*(Continued)*

(Continued)

### Aram's story

One day a boy named Awdar played soccer with a team. On Saturday, Awdar and his team played soccer against another team. When they played soccer with the other team a boy on the other team kicked the ball very hard. When he kicked the ball it hit Awdar' face and broked his nose. Then Awdar went home to tell his mom and dad that he got a broken nose at the soccer game. Then his dad said, we have to take you to doctor. When they took him to doctor, he never played soccer again. Because he knew that if he played soccer he will get his nose broken again. Then he started to play basketball.

Aram's efforts paid off—his audience was indeed impressed. Although they could not explain it in words, they recognized that Aram's style was more mature than Beyar's. Maria praised Aram's sentence combining and his organization of the story. Aram's sentences showed a higher level of grammatical complexity than Beyar's. Aram's use of grammatical structures accentuated the connectedness between adjacent events, giving his story a better flow; Beyar's story sounded choppy by comparison. But of course Maria didn't say that out loud. While she explained, in as simple terms as she could, why Aram's story held together so well, she gave herself an invisible congratulatory pat on the shoulder for the kind of talk she consistently encouraged in her class: "Don't just recount the facts—elaborate and explain. For example, when exactly did X happen? What else was going on? Why do you think it happened? Why didn't Z happen? What if? What if not? Now, imagine this . . . and that." And so on. Now her constant "nagging" was beginning to bear fruit.

In the meantime, eager critics were dissecting Aram's story, searching for weak spots that could benefit from their insights.

"When you said, his nose broke and he went to home, how . . . how he went home when his nose broken?" Nigar enquired cautiously.

"It wasn't his leg," retorted Aram, more than a little patronizingly. Maria immediately gave him one of her special looks reserved for less than courteous behavior, and he checked himself. "Well, I mean, he walked. He walked home and he did this with his nose . . . ," Aram demonstrated by cupping his nose with his hand. "He put clean . . . on his nose . . . tissue . . . tissue."

The answer satisfied Nigar; for her, asking a question was an act of challenging herself. By raising a question she demonstrated that she was finally "with it," on the same page as her older sister and her more advanced classmates.

"How could he know his nose will get broken again?" demanded Beyar.

"You said he went to the doctor, it should be hospital," threw in Aram's sister, Shkriya.

Aram realized that the criticisms were fairly insubstantial; his critics were clearly grasping at straws just to make a comment. He had faith in the quality of his story. He straightened up in his chair and looked his classmates in the eye: "Whatever I want, I'm gonna say it," he declared.

Attaboy! Maria was proud of Aram's assertive stance. Aram had made tremendous progress, both academically and socially, within the past five months; it was exciting to see him thrive. Like his sister, Shkriya, he was one of the neediest students at the beginning of the program. Their parents, Kurdish subsistence farmers from the mountains of Iraq, were essentially illiterate. Aram had started school in Iraq—a long daily walk along a mountain road—but had never had a chance to learn to read and write in either Kurdish or Arabic. Now a fourth grader, he was becoming a sophisticated consumer of English-based literacy.

Shkriya nevertheless continued to pick apart Aram's story. She used every chance to remind him that, even though at home she was his younger sister, in this classroom she was his equal. Maria suspected that Shkriya did so only because she knew that Aram could stand his ground; had he been under attack, she would have shown her sisterly loyalty. Now she challenged Aram's authorship of the story. Looking pointedly at her brother, she observed that his story was "a little bit the same as Beyar's story. Awdar nose broke and Beyar's nose broke too, so it's little bit the same. And they both played basketball at the end. So Aram took that from Beyar's story."

---

Even in a culturally homogeneous and essentially harmonious classroom, problems do arise, and conflicts among students do occur. The more the teacher knows about the lives of her individual students, and the better they know each other, the easier it is to take steps to prevent potential disruptions, or at least moderate their intensity. Once again, teaching strategies based on constructivist principles, and especially those that bridge the students' home and school experiences, afford the teacher deeper insights into her students' life situations and allow a wider range of academic and nonacademic interventions.

---

This was clearly a case of sibling rivalry, and Maria thought that she might have to intervene, but it was Beyar who inadvertently saved the day: "But my story is different. The difference between my story and Aram's story, for example, he didn't say, when I was seven years old I began to play soccer, he didn't say where I began to play soccer. My story has more details."

Quite so. Maria had been thinking that she would have liked to have had Aram help Beyar edit his story, eliminate some of his repetitive coordinate conjunctions and recombine the simple sentences into complex ones. But that seemed tricky; Beyar was too proud to accept help from Aram. And then a window suddenly opened.

"Of course the two stories are somewhat similar because they are both based on the same facts, remember?" she began. "But the stories are also a little different, and each one has different strengths. Beyar's story has more details, because he tells about his own experience. Aram included fewer details, but he paid a lot of attention to his grammar and style. So now, Aram and Beyar, do you think you two guys can work together and produce one super story? You can include all of Beyar's details and use Aram's sentence ideas."

*(Continued)*

(Continued)

> The teacher skillfully maneuvers the two competing students into collaboration—the hallmark of constructivist practice. Maria doesn't merely tell the students to "work together" on this; she recognizes their individual strengths and how they can contribute to the quality of the final product. Maria's emphasis on the goal of the activity, and on each learner's assets rather than deficiencies, boosts the students' confidence and motivation to complete the project. The teacher will, of course, provide her assistance and guidance throughout the process.

The two boys looked at each other, and then at their teacher. Each one was a little possessive of his literary output. Finally Beyar gave in.

"Yeah. I was going to change some things again anyway," he said.

"You both have a good thing going here, and two heads are better than one." Maria offered more encouragement, and then she threw in a bribe: "And when you are done, I'll make copies of your story for everyone to read. How's that?"

> Without forcing the students to complete a task, the teacher negotiates by providing incentives that motivate them to make their best effort. Because of the unique classroom dynamics created by the interplay of cultural factors and constructivist philosophy, writing for "peer review" has become a motivating and highly satisfying endeavor.

"That will be excellent," Aram assured his teacher, suddenly taking charge. To show that he was up to the task, he used Maria's favorite word, the word that each child hoped for, strived for, competed and cooperated for, every single day. The word they wore with pride, like a badge. Excellent.

Maria could relax. She was in good hands.

## GUIDELINES FOR PRACTICE

Self-contained classes for ELLs are not common in U.S. public schools, and so students like those in the above narrative are more likely to be found in mainstream classrooms. The following suggestions, taken from Maria's classroom practice, offer guidelines for teaching ELLs effectively and productively in constructivist mainstream classrooms:

- Establish ELLs' positive presence in your class. A silent period should not be an invisible period. Call on them often, even if only to ask a simple yes or no question. Be patient and help them comprehend your question and give an answer. Prompt the answer when necessary, and offer plenty of positive reinforcement afterward.

- When you plan a thematic unit, incorporate some relevant information that pertains to the students' background: country, language, history, art, famous people, and so on. (All such information is usually within reach on the Internet; draw on the students' knowledge as well.) ELLs will feel included. Remember, your attitude toward ELLs is a model for your mainstream students.

- Make sure that ELLs participate in the content curriculum even though their level of participation may be lower than that of the native English speakers. Establish what the students know and are able to do before you give them tasks. An integrated, theme-based approach lends itself to differentiating the levels of difficulty while addressing the same content goals. Always support content instruction with visuals and practical activities and provide extensive scaffolding. Incorporate the students' experiential knowledge as much as possible into your academic content instruction. If necessary, devise alternative (nonlinguistic) ways for them to demonstrate what they know.

- Try to adapt instructional language to the needs of ELLs. Make sure that they can see your face when you speak. Try to speak slowly and distinctly, pronouncing all the words, especially if your ELLs are real beginners. Always announce verbally what you are going to do next. Talk through your demonstrations, using the simplest language possible for beginning English learners. Use linguistic terms denoting specific concepts only after the concepts have already been introduced (and, hopefully, understood).

- Ask questions frequently, starting with those requiring yes/no answers. If necessary, model the answers and have the students repeat them. Use many repetitions in your talk; restate ideas using simpler grammatical structures and vocabulary.

- Use outlines and graphic organizers (even if the students cannot speak or read English), and refer to the relevant elements in them frequently. Exposure to both spoken and written language, as well as visual maps of ideas, will help ELLs acquire both language and concepts.

- Capitalize on peer assistance and promote teamwork, but make sure that ELLs don't just "sit there" while the other group members are working. Put two ELLs, preferably those who speak the same language, into one group so that they can support each other. Give ELLs a task that they can do either by themselves or with assistance from another group member. Make sure their contributions are acknowledged.
- Literacy is key. Literacy learning is hard in a second language, especially if a student has never acquired native language literacy. Making literacy activities personally rewarding to students increases their motivation. Try some of the strategies used in Maria's classroom; for example, involve the whole class in storytelling and choose some stories as the basis for further work (rewriting, editing, etc.). Use stories provided by ELLs for whole class activities; this is beneficial for them, as well as for the rest of the class, academically as well as socially.
- Allow ELLs to use their native language if anyone in the class (including the teacher or other ELLs) can understand and translate their responses into English. The goal is to communicate, in whatever language.
- Encourage verbal participation in lessons, but don't correct language usage mistakes; ignore them if the message is clear. Re-state a student's message in more correct English only if comprehension is compromised.
- Learn some words from the native languages of your ELLs (greetings, expressions of praise, or words for school environment and classroom objects) and incorporate them into your classroom talk, alternating them with English words. Let the native speakers teach you and correct your pronunciation. Encourage mainstream students to learn some of the words. You will be sending positive signals about language to all of your students.

# 8 Critical Classroom Connections

## *Eighth Graders Face a Fence on the Border*

The classroom in which we did our field research for this chapter was one in which there was a significant representation of Guatemalan, Mexican, Columbian, Puerto Rican, and Honduran cultures (M. Gonzales, personal communication, July 18, 2006). The majority of students in this eighth-grade classroom were from homes in which the parents' native language was Spanish. Although the majority of the students were fluent in oral, communicative English, they did not necessarily have grade-level proficiency in academic English. The teacher was thus charged with integrating the teaching of content (social studies) with the teaching of language (academic English).

The particular unit of study was quite timely because the topic of immigration was gaining national attention. Across the country, rallies were being held, and the students in Monica Gonzalez's classroom critically examined President Bush's speech regarding our borders. Regardless of the timeliness of this unit, however, the quality of the interactions that occurred can take place around any topic that relates to students' lives. It was the way in which Monica taught, not necessarily the content, that afforded students the opportunity to critically reflect. We hope you enjoy your foray into this classroom!

"There is something going on right now in our society that is very important to all of us. A lot of you participated in one of the events that just happened. Could someone mention what that is?"

Monica stood in front of five tables of eighth-grade students who were remarkably focused despite the approaching graduation date. "Immigration rights!" The response was swift.

"Immigration rights, or the rights of immigrants. How many of you participated in that day? One . . . two . . . three . . ." Monica counted nine students who had been involved in the immigration rights demonstration and rally of the prior weekend.

> Monica connects her lesson to current events in society. This strategy allows the students to examine their social identity and to read both the word and the world.
>
> Monica's encouragement to students to position themselves in society gives them a place to pose problems; they will ask some difficult questions that get to the heart of their perception of immigration law.

"I didn't buy anything that day!"

"Oh that's right, you can participate in different ways. How many of you went to the march? How many of you participated in a different way? Okay, what was the way you participated. . . . He participated in the other part, which was the economic boycott in which you decide not to buy any products . . . you didn't eat tacos that day."

"No, I was going to go eat some, and then they were closed."

A lively conversation ensued about Puerto Rican restaurants that had closed the day of the immigration march. Yolanda suggested that this phenomenon was due to Mexican cooks in Puerto Rican restaurants. Monica made no attempt to resolve the issue but took advantage of student enthusiasm to more formally introduce the unit.

> As Yolanda talks about the "Mexican cooks," she builds on her own background. Monica allows this reflection, important because Yolanda is thinking about how the march affected her and how the immigrants may have exercised their power because the restaurants were closed that day.

"We are going to examine how immigration policy has shaped the U.S. by including or excluding immigrants based on their race, class, gender, sexual orientation, national origin, and disability. What do I mean by policy?"

> Monica gives purpose to the unit by asking the students to look at how U.S. policy has either excluded or included immigrants.
>
> Once again, she is looking at society through a critical lens as she raises questions about public policy. This is a wonderful starting place for her unit.
>
> By questioning policy, Monica is *problem posing*. Problem posing, which is more than problem solving, looks beyond the curriculum and encourages students to ask questions (Wink, 2000) about things relevant to their lives—in this case, immigration.

"Like a rule," Alex responded.

"Like a law," continued Marta.

"Like a right," chimed in Yolanda.

"Like a bill, like the bill they are trying to pass," contributed Mario.

"Something that you try to follow," added Yolanda.

"The way things are supposed to be done," finished Alex.

"So, the United States, throughout history, has enacted different policies that affected different immigrant groups, based on all these things that I mentioned . . . race . . . gender . . . national origin . . . sexual orientation . . . . The second goal is to look at current examples of immigrant rights violations that have a historical connection between what has happened in the past and what is happening now."

Monica finished her opening remarks and introduced the day's activity by example. She distributed manila paper to the students. Next she wrote her first name vertically, in large capital letters, on an overhead projector transparency. For each letter in her name, she wrote a word that had something to do with her own immigrant history, all the while modeling for the class her thoughts on word choice.

coMmunity

Oppression

Negligence

Immigrant

aCtivist

trAnsition

As Monica introduces the unit, she shares her own story. She suggests that as a Peruvian immigrant she has experienced oppression. In this way, Monica makes the environment safe for her students (many of whom have family members who are—or are themselves—immigrants) to share their stories and tap into their lived experiences.

Before she could finish her demonstration, Rosa, Cesar, and Jessica had already begun consulting with each other on what words they would choose for their papers. By the time Monica had reached the word "transition," about half of the class had already begun to write.

As Monica circulated among the students, Alex grabbed her attention.

"Can we put how it is?" he inquired. His teacher answered in the affirmative, and in a flash the word "harsh" was added to his page.

Monica allows her students to write what they are feeling. She encourages critical dialogue in an emotionally safe learning environment. As we learned from Freire, love and trust must be present for meaningful dialogue to occur. Monica

(Continued)

(Continued)

> creates the kind of classroom where students feel they can be who they really are, even if it means saying, "I'm an immigrant," or "I'm bilingual," in a society where these things are not necessarily valued.

Lynelle had a problem; her name contained three of the same letter.

"Gimme one for D," Dalia leaned across to Jonah's table.

"Shut up. I can't."

"Can I just write in Spanish?" inquired Luisa. No one responded, so she wrote "Apoyo." Across the room, a few other students had figured out that thinking bilingually would double their word choices.

"I don't think of myself . . . I think of others," Rosa remarked to her tablemates.

With such high motivation levels, it did not take long for the students to finish their name projects. Monica taped a long sheet of chart paper to the chalkboard at the front of the room, and the students contributed words of their choice.

Dalia contributed "border" because of a news report she had seen. Other students had a similar approach, putting distance between themselves and the concept of immigration. Alex noted that immigrants are unappreciated, Rosa said they want an affordable life, Cesar declared that they need to be hired, Zenaida remarked that they are determined, and Salvador acknowledged that they suffer. Jonah was of the opinion that immigrants are being terrorized by their fear of deportation. Dalia put a piece of tape on her name poster and stuck it onto her nose. She moved her head from side to side. No one seemed to notice. Sam said he was confused about immigration because his parents were always talking about it. Even if students did not feel a personal connection to the concept, they clearly understood its contemporary significance. Gilbert contributed the word "reality" because "it's really happening."

> Once again, students are situating their studies within society and their lived experience.

Only Yolanda noted a connection between the concept of immigration and her personal history. She highlighted the word "recomendaciónes" and discussed how people come to the United States based upon the recommendations of others. If her dad had not gotten a recommendation in Mexico he would not have come to the United States.

The school day had come to an end, but the students did not want to stop. The name activity ended in spontaneous word calling.

"Deception!"

"Dreams!"

"Harsh!"

"Impatient!"

"Inspiration!"

"Immunity!"

"Our names are powerful," concluded Monica. She reminded the students that the purpose of the activity was to help them start thinking about the issue of immigration and asked how many class members were immigrants themselves. Luis, Luisa, and Jessica raised their hands. Monica, a native of Peru, brought the classroom total up to four.

> By reminding students of the power of their names, Monica provides a catalyst for seeing their own ability to transform.

"Why are there only four immigrants in this class?" inquired the teacher.
"Because we are Americans," a lone voice announced.
It was time for dismissal. "Tomorrow we will talk about who is an immigrant. Tomorrow we will see who is an immigrant . . . ," Monica paused to listen to Rosa. "Rosa wants to talk about who is an American."
The children filed out of the room. Rosa lingered for a moment. "Ms. Gonzalez, but I *do* want to go back to who is an American . . ."

❖　❖　❖

"America must be kept American."
"What comes to mind when you read this?" Monica was referring to the words projected from the overhead, in large print, on the front wall. They served to reactivate student interest in the immigration unit, which had started to wane during a brief rainy season and corresponding lack of recess.
Rosa was first to respond. "No immigration, no nothing else."
Her teacher requested that she be more specific, but Rosa had difficulty, so Mario took the opportunity to speak.
"What comes to mind for you, Mario?"
"Racism!"
Yolanda was more specific. "I think what they are saying is the United States is for people born in the United States."

> Monica's use of dialogue here reflects Freire's idea that dialogue itself must teach. It is not prescriptive, it emerges from the students, and Monica uses it to teach content. For ELLs this is an effective way to develop cognitively and to explore notions of identity.

"Okay, you think they are trying to say that only people within the United States should be kept within the United States. What did we say last week about who is an American?" Monica was cognizant of the wish Rosa had expressed several days ago, which had most likely been influenced by prior class discussion on this topic.
"Anyone in North, South, or Central America is considered an American. But they are trying to say only those in the United States are worthy of being an American," Jonah volunteered.

*(Continued)*

(Continued)

The conversation continued until Monica refocused the students' attention on the words still projected on the front wall. "Who wants to take a guess at who said this? Was it a public official, or someone like you or me?"

The students guessed that it was a public official.

"How high in politics?" the teacher probed.

"Really high."

"A president."

"Do you know which president?" Monica asked.

"Bush!"

"Bush!" The theme gained instant popularity and was echoed several times.

"Bush? This is something you think President Bush would say?" Monica was not content with a one-word response.

"No!" chorused a multitude of voices.

"No?" asked their teacher.

This time it was a mixed chorus of "no" and "yes."

Gilbert was adamant. He was convinced that it was President Bush.

"Gilbert, yes, why? Why do you think this is something President Bush would say?"

"Because that's how he is."

Luisa supported her classmate. "He does not want any immigrants here."

Luisa's support encouraged Gilbert to continue. "Because when they asked him if the national anthem should be sung in Spanish, too, he said, no, it should be kept American."

---

Monica provides a framework for students to examine past immigration policy. Yet, she does not in any way limit their reactions or discussion. What comes as a result is a group of students who are engaged in answering authentic questions—questions that relate to their own reality. Nothing is contrived in their responses. Monica lets it flow.

---

Monica pointed to the quote. "Okay, President Coolidge, in 1924."

Salvador noticed that 1924 was covered on the immigration time line handout that they had examined some days ago. Monica reminded the students that thousands of Mexican workers, including many U.S. citizens, had been deported during that period of time. With attention focused on the time line, the teacher directed the students' attention to a chart at the side of the room. It contained the headings, "Policies that give economic benefits," "Policies that discriminate," and "Both." Each table was assigned a part of the time line and was responsible for writing each policy listed during the corresponding time frame on a Post-it note, to be stuck on the appropriate section of the chart.

Gilbert asked his teacher if he could get a drink of water. Monica rolled her eyes. Gilbert sprawled across his desk and groaned. His teacher moved on to a discussion of Proposition 187, passed in 1995 and later repealed, which denied immigrants access to education, health care, and other basic services. She asked the students what they thought of Proposition 187.

Yolanda declared that it was unfair, because California used to be a part of Mexico. No other students volunteered ideas.

"Have you ever heard of human rights? I'm denying Gilbert his basic human right to water!" She giggled as she explained her objections to Proposition 187 and sent her example on his way to the water fountain.

Next on the agenda was a brief description of Proposition 4487. When Monica noted that, if passed, Proposition 4487 would criminalize illegal immigrants, Mario gasped, "How are they going to arrest all those people?" No one had an answer. The conversation moved on to other current developments, such as the proposed use of the National Guard to stop immigrants from crossing the Mexican/U.S. border. The students were asked to work within their groups to extend the time line handouts beyond its current ending point, the USA Patriot Act of 2001. Later, they shared some of their work with each other.

Rosa volunteered that in 2001 racism in the United States began to increase as a result of 9/11.

Jonah announced that in 2006 a group known as the Minute Men threatened to put up a barbed wire fence along the border to stop immigration from Mexico.

Amanda stated that on March 11, 2006, the first big immigration march took place, and then on May 1 another one was held.

Only a few minutes remained. Monica announced that President Bush would be addressing the nation that evening to discuss his proposal to use the National Guard to stop immigrants at the Mexican border. The homework assignment was, amazingly, to watch TV.

❖　❖　❖

"We are going to take ten minutes, and I want you to write a reaction to one point Bush made in his speech."

The students wrote furiously during the time allotted by Monica. Then, one at a time, they read their reactions to the class. Improvisation, elaboration, and summarizing were not allowed; only the printed word was to be shared. While each student read, the others listened, and some jotted down notes that later would become part of the group discussion.

---

Monica uses a strategy called "write and share," which involves students writing their responses to a prompt, or in this case President Bush's speech, and then sharing them with the class. When the students share, everyone listens—including the teacher. This technique allows the students to share their thoughts, which reflects the emergent nature of critical pedagogy. Notice that Monica does not come to class with a list of components of the speech *she* believes is important for the students to know. Rather, she elicits that response *from the students* and shapes the dialogue around their impressions.

*(Continued)*

(Continued)

> Jonah was first. At the top of his paper he had written "english = Power?" He read:
>
> ah, Bush. Trust like him to try and please Both sides. First, we must "crack Down on immigrants then its "Give them a chance." Rinse and reapeat, RIght? "Mexico is our friend and neighbor" yet "we must stop Drug Dealers and immigrants." Pathetic really. He says he wants to be Fair to families oF immigrants, then trys to save himself with "Its not amnesty, no way." next, his "TemPorary worker Program" he says it nicely, with a thick layer of cream on top, but with words like "to keep our economy UP" to them say "they must then exit the country, his Program Basically says:
>     1. You, give me cheaP labor to keep the U.S. rich
>     2. work like crazy to please U.S.
>     3. your beginning to lose your value, so get out.
>     4. what a nice man, that Bush?

While not all the students reflected Jonah's level of sophistication, the prompt elicited a strong response from almost all of them. Spanish dominant Luis read in his native tongue.

> Monica places no restriction on students using their native language. In fact, she encourages them to do so when the use of English will impede communication. Interestingly, students use their native languages several times during this unit. The assumption can be made that they are doing so because their language and culture are so closely tied with their identity that, when they are encouraged to position themselves within the broader context of society, for some students, their second language is not the language with which they choose to do so.

Jessica, who was not often verbally expressive, was able to write the following:

> He said that he was going to do more technology. I don't think anyone would believe him because he says so many things but doesn't take his word for it so I don't think that he will really go anywere with the immigration he could say it but in real life its hard it not that easy.

Jessica had her teacher read her passage aloud for her. Lynelle, however, could not be convinced to either read her response or to let someone else do so. Monica chose not to force the issue.

"Do we want to start conversing?" Monica asked when the students had finished sharing their responses.

Group consensus was affirmative.

"We are conversing and talking, we are not arguing, because these are our personal feelings, our opinions, our emotions, our reactions. Reactions and feelings are not ever wrong."

Cesar said that Bush is fixating on the southern border while ignoring the northern one. Alex liked Cesar's point. Yolanda agreed; she couldn't understand why "he never talks about immigrants coming from Canada." Salvador explained that immigration from Canada is not a problem. Jonah reinforced Salvador's point of view, reminding everyone that the largest numbers of immigrants were coming from the southern border.

The room became silent. Despite the teacher's prodding, no one seemed to have anything else to say.

"So, you all agree with each others' opinions?" she asked.

A universal "yes" filled the room and propelled the students to support each other further.

Alex felt that "George Bush is trying to make himself look good."

Salvador said, "He is saying bad things in a nice way."

"Like saying 'Be quiet' is the same thing as saying 'Shut-up,'" added Alex.

"Oh, I see. You are saying that Mr. Bush is saying bad things but he is putting it in a nice way. It's like saying be quiet instead of saying shut up when you really want to say shut up."

"Yeah," confirmed Alex.

Jonah explained how Alex's point supported his own written reflection—by projecting an image of generosity for letting immigrants work when they had been working all along, the only real change was that the government had more control over their lives.

---

Here, the students are critically reflecting on their society, and they are doing so while identifying what they perceive to be inequities. Remember, critical pedagogy essentially examines oppression in society in order to work toward transformation. Monica allows her students the luxury of critical reflection—something that may become a lost art in classrooms driven by high-stakes standardized testing.

---

"Do you think that our personal experiences as immigrants or as the children of immigrants or knowing lots and lots of people who are immigrants, do you think that that experience or that connection makes us react more negatively to what President Bush proposes in his immigration bill? Do you find anything in the bill that perhaps could be helpful to immigrants?"

The class was silent.

"Nothing at all?" she pressed.

More silence.

"Okay, maybe not to immigrants. Do you find anything in the bill that he proposes that is helpful to the nation?"

Finally Yolanda spoke. "I just don't agree with him . . . ."

" . . . I didn't like his tie!" Salvador interjected. The class giggled.

"Right, the president has only two terms?" Apparently Alex had more important concerns than the president's tie.

*(Continued)*

(Continued)

"Yeah," his teacher responded, amidst side chatter of "What?" and "He's outta here!"

Monica, however, was in the middle of instructional time and was not that easily distracted. "Okay, Yolanda said that she just doesn't agree with him. But, is there anything, Yolanda, that he may be proposing in this bill that may be helpful to the nation, to the United States? Okay, Alex."

"I don't think that us being Latinos or immigrants doesn't make us not like this bill because most of us aren't illegal now, and even though nothing is going to happen to us, I don't know how to say this . . ."

"Okay, I know what you want to say, but I want you to come back to it. Thank you. To rephrase my question, I know some of the feelings toward President Bush have to do with, maybe his politics, maybe that we are immigrants ourselves, but is there anything in his policy that may be considered good for the country. That is the question I asked."

Salvador and Elena mentioned boosting the economy, but without much vigor. Luisa, along with a number of the students, noted her personal connection to the issue. Monica conceded that personal histories and families do indeed influence how you think.

"I agree with Luisa; if they were in our shoes they wouldn't say anything about it," remarked Dalia.

"Okay, who is 'they'?" probed Monica.

A number of children responded simultaneously, "Them."

"The legislative body? The president?"

"Yeah," again it was a general response.

"If they were in our shoes—what do you mean? If they were recent immigrants like we are?"

---

Notice that, while only three students acknowledged that they were immigrants on the first day of the unit, there is a strong connection and identification with immigrants.

---

Again, in unison, the students responded, "Yeah."

Then Salvador asserted, "In my opinion, I feel that immigrants should be let across the border but at a certain limit; if they do bad things they should be sent back to their country."

"So you are saying that if immigrants come here just to do bad things they should be sent back to their country. That's what you're saying. Okay, we have about five minutes, and I have to give you the homework. I want to say a couple of things before we go."

"Why don't we unite with Mexico and become the United States of Mexico?" Alex broke the intensity of the moment.

"Why don't we unite with Mexico, Alex suggests, and become the United States of Mexico?"

"Of Amexico," he said, grinning.

"Of Amexico. Before I give you the homework, I just want to say one thing. Our personal feelings sometimes get in the way of really clearly evaluating something."

"I was just joking."

"I know that's a joke," she responded matter-of-factly, then asked Rosa to help with collection and distribution of papers and continued without missing a beat. "What you have with you is a copy of the actual speech; this is the text of the speech. . . . We are reading the speech that I just gave you, then, for homework you are going to do a T-journal. Take a quote, write the quote on the left side of the page, and on the right side of the page I want you to respond to the quote. . . . After you respond to the quote, leave a little space so you can have another person, another adult member of your household, respond to the same quote, not to your response, please, make that clear to your parents. . . . Three or four quotes would be sufficient. . . . Thank you . . . I will see you guys tomorrow."

> Monica uses a T-journal, which is also called a double entry journal. On the left side of the journal, students are to write something that impresses them (from the speech). On the other side, they are to write their reaction. This strategy allows students' views to emerge just as the write and share did earlier.

❖  ❖  ❖

"Yesterday we were discussing that we may have a certain way we feel about immigration because it is affecting us directly based on our experiences and the people we know. . . . But the homework was to look at the written text, for you to take a quote and to respond to it." Monica displayed a blank copy of the T-journal, along with the text of the president's speech on immigration, and continued. "Now, when you respond to written information, by reading it, you have a little bit more time to think. You can reread it, you can rethink it, you can analyze it. When you are responding immediately (verbally) to somebody else's thoughts, ideas, or speech, you don't have time to do that really because you have to immediately respond. . . . But when you have something in writing, you have something to go back to. Think about it. So what we are going to do at this moment is to share one of the entries. . . . You read your quote, you respond, and share the response of the adult."

Amanda was the first to volunteer to read from her T-journal:

"It is important for Americans to know that we have enough Guard forces to win the war on terror, respond to natural disasters, and help secure our border." My thoughts: I don't think we do. We've got to send troops to help the victims of Hurricane Katrina. Now the border and so many people have died in Iraq trying to win the war on terror. We can't afford to send more troops. My mom said "I disagree with this statement. The responses in the Gulf Coast Region after Hurricane Katrina from the Guard was not particularly effective because many of the area Guard had been deployed elsewhere in the world, Afghanistan and Iraq."

*(Continued)*

(Continued)

> Notice the critical reflection in which the students are engaging. This level of sophisticated thinking is helping to develop CALP; it reflects quite a different philosophical perspective and methodology than a teacher who supports the ideas of, for example, E. D. Hirsh. A teacher holding to that perspective would teach this unit very differently, likely following a banking system of education as explained by Freiere (1970).
>
> Notice, also, how this student's identity is closely aligned with that of her mother. By encouraging students to include their families in this assignment, Monica gives them another way to explore what they think.

Alex was next:

"We will fix the problems created by illegal immigration." My thoughts: This guy is saying that we created problems. Look how many problems he has created, the gas prices are going up, and we're at war supposedly looking for weapons of "mass destruction."

Elena used her "homework certificate," which entitled "the bearer to a free day off any homework." Although Luis wrote in English, he used his native Spanish to express himself to the class. Lynelle had a full page but would not share.

When the students had finished, Monica continued. "As I walked around I noticed some of you had the same feelings or sentiments that you had before. This validates what you were saying yesterday. Yesterday you were angry at some of the policies that are being discussed. After reading this, some of you may still be angry, at the same level, or some of you will be more angry because this is in black and white—it's in writing, I can see it. So it makes a bigger impact. I wish I had more of your parent responses, but it seems to me, from what you guys shared, that many of your parents share the same sentiments. Okay, now I am going to collect that. Tomorrow I have invited, and you won't know until tomorrow . . ."

"Who is it?"

"Tell us!"

"Com'on, who is it?"

". . . you know the people so I'm not going to tell you . . . ."

There was a groan of collective disappointment.

"Tomorrow I have invited two people to come and share their immigrant experience. But . . . in order for us to get the best dialogue, the best conversation with them, we are going to prepare for their visit . . . we are going to generate questions to ask them. I am going to give you index cards, and individually I want you to come up with two or three questions that you are going to ask this immigrant. After you have two to three individual questions, as a group come up with one or two, then put one on the front and one on the back so tomorrow we are prepared. It's only for one hour; tomorrow is Friday. So we have two people, and sometimes they have lots to share, and sometimes you want to know a whole lot about them. So we are ready, we need to agree on the questions we want to ask; for example, a question such as when did you come to the United States may not take a whole lot of dialogue. So, we can look at our questions and move from there. When I come to give you the index cards, I will collect the T-journals. . . . Alex wants to know if I know if our two guests for tomorrow saw the president's address. . . . You can ask them."

"Are you one of the speakers?" Dalia asked.

"No."

"Are they very important people?"

"Yolanda wants to know if they are very important people. No, they are people just like you and me."

"It's you and Ms. Orellano!" If it wasn't their own teacher, perhaps it was another. "Are they illegal?"

"You can ask them yourself."

Dalia was still trying to figure it out. She pointed at Salvador. "Your mom!"

> Note, once again, the personal connection to immigration; the students are relating to their own lived experiences. No matter what the content is, students will relate to their own lives.

The children began to work. Although an individual activity, a sharing of ideas occurred naturally within students grouped at the same table.

"Remember you are doing two or three questions individually. Once you have your individual questions ready, you may discuss them together."

Alex wrote his questions in English with Spanish punctuation. ("¿Where you able to read between the lines on the Presidents address about immigration?" "¿Do people feel different about you when they find out that you are a immigrant?") Salvador and Lynelle did likewise. Magda and Luisa wrote exclusively in Spanish.

> Notice the high level of oral English fluency of this class. Yet, Spanish (L1) literacy is still an influence and consequently an academic consideration. The teacher will need to address the issue of English punctuation when the students engage in more formal written discourse. There is often a false perception of more advanced Cognitive Academic Language Proficiency (CALP) in English because Basic Interpersonal Communicative Skills (BICS) are in place in that same language. However, to read and write in an academic manner in the L2 (in this case English) requires much more time and process.

The children continued to work. Monica circulated and offered support. Finally, she determined that intervention was in order.

"Okay, I have to clarify something. A lot of you are asking questions to these people about when they first became immigrants. Like, when did you come, did you cross the border or not, are you still illegal? Suppose they had been here a long time, what are the questions you would ask them if they had been here a long time? . . . Okay, when you are done with the individual questions, I am going to give you

(Continued)

another card. The next step is to share your questions with each other. You are going to come up with one or two questions that together, as a group, you want to ask these two guests tomorrow. If you have only one question, we run the risk that two tables may have the same question. So, if you put one on the front of the card and one on the back of the card, if a question is repeated, you have a back-up."

As the children finished their individual index cards, they began to converse in groups to try to come to consensus. Monica spent time with each group, helping them clearly formulate questions.

Monica began at the table occupied by Cesar, Jessica, and Rosa. Jessica and Rosa read their questions aloud, but even with urging, Cesar hesitated. Monica leaned over and read his index card to herself and noted to the others that his question was similar to theirs. She worked with the group until they were ready to begin composing their back-up question, and then moved on. In each session she first let the children read their questions to each other and then offered support in refining them. When she had finished facilitation of every group's discussion, she offered feedback to the entire class.

"Some of you obviously are right on task, but some of you finished like this," Monica demonstrated with a snap of her fingers, "and you are done. But you're not done. Because this is what is going to happen. Choose the questions you have selected, and . . . maybe Sam will ask the question to Alex, or the other way around, exactly the way you have it written. If it is clear, you should be able to start answering. If it is not clear, then you need to rewrite it. But don't change your question. They are very good questions. Just change the way it is written so it's clear, okay?"

Mario, Jonah, Lynelle, Luisa, and Magda summoned Monica to their table to assist them in the process of clarifying questions. Next, Jessica, Rosa, and Cesar summoned their teacher. They wanted to know if she thought the mystery guest would understand their questions. Jessica read from the index card. "'Where were you born and explain your childhood, did you live a rough life and when you came here were you an illegal immigrant?'"

"It's clear, it's very specific, and it's a multiple step question. So when you give that question to someone you're interviewing, you need to repeat it because that person may want to answer it in parts. . . . You have to give the person warning that your next question requires several different answers. So, where were you born, and explain your childhood, and then there is another one . . ."

"Did you live a rough life and were you an illegal immigrant," Jessica supplied.

"By the time I tell you I was born in Peru, explain my childhood, I was there until I was fourteen years old, I may have to ask you what was the last part of your question."

Rosa concurred. "You have to like tell them that this is a multiple set question."

"Or you may want to break it down into two different parts. So the first one, where were you born and explain your childhood, sort of go hand in hand, but the last one requires you to ask the question again, so maybe you want to hold off on that question. . . . "

"And then our back-up question is, 'When you first came to America were you treated differently?'" Rosa added.

"Okay, that one is fine, but work with the other one—whether you want to eliminate the last part or you want to have it as two completely separate questions—because otherwise they may ask you to do that."

Luisa, Gilbert, Yolanda, and Luis were next. Yolanda read their question and elaborated. "'Do you think that a person who knows English and Spanish has the same opportunities in the United States as a person who just knows English?' And then it goes like this, it says, 'Do you think they'll be treated differently if for example we're talking about a Caucasian with a Hispanic?' That's our first question. Okay, the second one is, 'Do you think that racism still occurs today in the United States society?'"

"Woooow!" Monica paused and savored the group's work. "Interesting."

Yolanda was anxious to hear her teacher's reaction. "Do you like it?"

"I think it is very good! That's why I am saying 'wow.' Now the first one is a very complex question. What does it require for you to answer a complex question?"

"Organize your thoughts."

"Organize your thoughts and . . . you may have to do what?"

"Think," Gilbert stated.

"Think a whole lot," affirmed Monica.

"Yeah."

"So in a complex question like that, that you are using to interview, it's not for me to answer that in writing, because in writing I have it there, I can do what? I can go back to the question."

"Reread it," said Yolanda.

"Reread it! Answer it in parts. So if you are using the question to interview someone in person, what do you think that person is going to require you to do?"

"Say it again," said Luisa.

"Say it again."

"Yeah," affirmed Yolanda and Gilbert.

"Break it down a little bit for them," Yolanda continued.

"Break it down a little bit for them, okay."

---

Notice Monica's strategy of repeating back to the students. Not only is she facilitating content, but she is also facilitating language development.

---

Yolanda concurred and indicated the group had already been discussing this.

Monica continued, "You are asking something very powerful that has to do with the language that's part of the culture that immigrants bring. With me comes my culture and part of my culture is my language. So you are asking whether it is important to maintain the language, whether it's Polish or Spanish, and then you are saying, but would it be different if it were Spanish versus another language. Do you think your own experiences with language have helped you to write this question?"

---

Monica guides the students toward critical consciousness. They are questioning what some might consider a basic human right—that of access to one's native language. Through powerful dialogue, she facilitates their thinking *and* their language development. As they read and write the questions together,

---

*(Continued)*

(Continued)

> they are examining academic language and the thinking process, which allows for the development of academic writing. Additionally, they are naming the *white elephant* (refer to Chapter 5) and problem posing as they learn.

"Yes." It was a communal response.

"Yes. Okay."

"And I also wrote this question because of my mom," Yolanda added.

"How about you Luis? Is this a question that is powerful and important to you?"

"Yes."

"To you, too, right Luisa?"

"Yeah."

"So you see, a lot of our experiences shape how we see things. That's a very good question. All I would recommend that you do is develop it into smaller portions."

The discussion wound down. Monica told the group to use another index card to develop their question and break it down in steps. When all of the groups had finished their work, she collected the index cards and read each one aloud, engaging the students in a critique of each question. Alex listened intently to each one but reserved his commentary for the right moment.

"'Do people feel differently about you when they find out that you are an immigrant?'" read Monica.

"Aw . . . that's an awesome question!" Alex's grin spread from ear to ear.

"Let's see who wrote it!" Monica knew it came from Alex's group.

"Ahhhh, that's like the best question . . . the best!" Alex continued the self-adoration.

Monica nonchalantly continued to flip through the cards. "'How did you immigrate to the United States? Was it hard? How long did it take?' Oh, I wonder who wrote it!"

"Great question! Wow, who wrote that? That is beautiful!" Salvador exclaimed. Unlike Alex, he was not praising himself, but authors Sam, Amanda, Alex, and Elena.

"This one. This one, listen carefully," the teacher moved on. "'Do you think that a person who knows both English and Spanish has the same opportunities in the United States as a person who just knows English?' Wow. 'Do you think they would be treated differently, let us say, a Caucasian versus a Hispanic?'"

Response was mixed. Some of the students thought the question was a good one. Jonah, however, stated, "The way the question was formed was biased," and with the help of his teacher clarified that a comparison between a bilingual and a monolingual was different than a comparison between two monolinguals, each with a different native tongue. The conversation continued at length. Monica noted that the group was going deeper into issues of immigration and discrimination. "Let's be very honest, some of us with accents are not treated equally, so I know where they are going with that question, so let them ask that question and have the two people here answer it."

As the class discusses the way in which immigrants are treated, the idea arises that immigrants are discriminated against. Monica confronts this assertion directly, stating that it may indeed be true. We see an emergence of critical discussion, which focuses on oppression. Can transformation be far away? Will the students want to act on what they are beginning to see as injustices? If the answer is yes, then we see exactly what critical pedagogy is—a way of teaching in which inequities are examined and through which society is transformed to eliminate those inequities.

Also of significance is the way in which both the teacher and students examine their identities. As stated in the previous chapter, these classrooms are fluid, with the identities of both the students and the teacher being examined—and perhaps changed.

Excitement was mounting as to the identity of these mystery guests.

"Are they coming tomorrow?"

"Yeah. If they feel that the question is biased or they don't agree with it, they will say so."

"And we'll discuss it, too."

"Exactly."

"Are they older?"

"One person is in her sixties . . ."

"Hijole, wow!"

"Wow!"

"That person immigrated a long, long time ago. You may have questions about that."

"And we'll respect her, too."

When students feel safe, their cultural values may be more easily expressed, as illustrated by this comment about respect.

"Is it your mom?"

"No."

"Is it somebody else's mom?"

"Obviously! . . . And the second question, do you think they will be treated differently? Who is 'they'? . . . We need to work on that part of the question. . . . Are they asking about someone who speaks English and Spanish and who is Latino, or are they saying anyone who speaks English and Spanish will have more opportunity? Do you mean if the Caucasian speaks English and Spanish or the Hispanic speaks English and Spanish? Let's rephrase this question. I think it is a very powerful question. You are going beyond the issue of immigration; you are going to some of the issues of race and discrimination, but you will need to rewrite this one. You need to break it down. Who will ask our guests the questions tomorrow?"

*(Continued)*

(Continued)

Dalia's hand shot up in the air like lightning as she shouted, "Me, me, me, me, me!"

"Ahhhh, this is what we'll do. Each one of you who want to will read a question here, as if you were doing an interview. The rest of us will listen and see how you perform as an interviewer. Okay? So I think it would be fair if everyone asks the same question.... Okay, so all of you who want to will read the same question, it will be question number one on this card. Stand up and ask the question as if you were asking it to the two individuals coming here."

The first person to ask the question was Jonah. The normally reticent Lynelle followed him. "Next person," called out Monica. "Dalia."

The same child who was jumping out of her seat a few moments ago stumbled miserably, tripping on almost every word.

"You need your glasses!" Monica laughed. Dalia was busted; she avoided wearing her glasses because she thought they were too thick. "You cannot do this without your glasses!" Monica paused to enjoy the moment, and then continued, "Who's next?"

Marta was much more successful than Dalia. She read smoothly in a clear voice. Next was Amanda, who not only read clearly but also projected well. Elena and then Alex followed. The class voted on whom they wanted as their representative. When her own name was called, Dalia's hand shot up like lightning. When Alex's name was called, he put up both of his hands.

Monica laughed. "You are trying to be two people!"

Alex's classmates began to question whether Alex should be allowed to vote for himself.

"Technically, you can vote for yourself. In any election you can vote for yourself." She counted the votes for Alex. "One for Alex."

Despite Alex's attempt at vote mongering, Amanda was the clear winner.

> As the students are working on their questions, an authentic opportunity to learn about elections occurs.

"Tomorrow you may be surprised by one of our guests."

"It's a teacher; I betcha one of them is a teacher!" Despite his electoral loss, Alex was invested in the upcoming activity.

"It's someone you have known for a long, long, long time!"

Alex shouted triumphantly, "Yes, one of them's a teacher!"

Excitement mounted, and random guesses were shouted out. Alex was the loudest. He declared it was going to be Ms. Cifuentes, the assistant principal. Energy was at an all-time high as Monica collected the index cards. Yet, as the day ended and the children left the classroom, the mystery names still had not been revealed.

❖   ❖   ❖

The day that the mystery guests were to appear had finally arrived, and the pre-approved questions were ready on index cards. Anticipation was mounting, and so was the corresponding level of noise as the students entered the room.

"I'm going to give you each an index card in case you need to jot down something that is important," announced their teacher. "It's more important for you to listen and pay attention to our guests, but if you feel there is a phrase, a key word, or something that really touches you, write it down."

> This strategy accomplishes many different things. First, it allows curriculum to be shaped by the students; we see the emergent nature, once again, of critical classrooms. Curriculum is not predetermined but, rather, comes about as a result of students using their own cultural background to interact with content. Monica interjects several open-ended ways for students to respond. In this way she repeatedly allows them a forum to express and examine their own views.

Amanda helped her teacher arrange chairs for the guests at the front of the room. The class radiated with excitement. Monica asked if anyone would like to introduce the class to the visitors and briefly let them know about the topic they had been working with. Jonah volunteered.

The moment had arrived. Two guests appeared in the doorway to room 208.

"Oh my God!" gasped Dalia.

"I knew it was Mrs. Cifuentes!" Alex proclaimed triumphantly.

"I'm sorry to disappoint you," responded the school's assistant principal.

"Noooo..."

Alex interpreted the collective no. "We're not disappointed."

"They are not disappointed," confirmed Monica. "Okay, let's introduce the two people who have graciously agreed to talk to us. Eduardo Miranda, he is a parent here, ... and Ms. Milagros Cifuentes, who I have known since I started working here eight years ago and many of you have known since first grade. And your mom knows her. She is very familiar to all of us, but maybe we can find out a little bit more about her."

The applause was genuine and spontaneous.

Jonah gave the introduction. "This is room 208. This is an eighth-grade class. We have been covering the topic of immigration and other things related to this topic."

Amanda followed up with the first question. "'Where were you born and tell us a little more about your childhood?'"

Milagros began. She was born in Chicago but raised in Mexico. Her father had been considered a "wetback." Eduardo left his native country for political reasons. He wanted to provide a safe haven in which to raise his children. Although a university educated professional in South America, he had to start from the bottom of the job market when he immigrated to the United States.

The children listened intently to the real life stories from members of their own school community. Not a murmur was heard; they sat erect in their chairs, faces intent on the guest speakers in front of them.

Amanda continued with the preapproved questions, and the guests answered enthusiastically.

Eduardo was more comfortable speaking in Spanish, and he rotated between his two languages once he warmed up to the class. All the children faced the front, eyes glued on the speakers, intent on listening to their stories. Milagros and Eduardo

*(Continued)*

(Continued)

began to interweave their comments, sliding easily back and forth to reinforce shared beliefs. When Eduardo spoke in Spanish, Milagros followed his lead and switched to her native tongue for a sentence or two. By the time Amanda presented the third question, the lines between everyone in the room had been blurred well enough for the guests to start asking the students questions. Milagros and Eduardo were having such a good time that Amanda could not get them to stop. She had lost control and had to be rescued by Monica, who graciously thanked the guests and sent them, glowing, on their way.

❖    ❖    ❖

"[Let's] think about what happened on Friday," announced Monica as she led the students in a summarizing discussion of not only the Friday session with Milagros and Eduardo but of the entire immigration unit. Then she moved on. "We are going to think and brainstorm ideas. If you were in the position to help shape policy for immigrants, what kind of policy, what kind of laws would you say are important? Let's suppose you are a lobbyist. Do you remember what a lobbyist does?"

"Influence lawmakers."

"Yes, and you want to influence lawmakers for immigration policy. What would you want?"

"Fairness," Alex announced.

"But what would fairness be in terms of immigration policy?"

Alex was silent.

"Do you want to think about it more?"

---

Several times throughout the unit, Monica allows students to quietly reflect. This is helpful in that it gives them time to process both language and content that is developing in the classroom. Reflection is also an essential component of critical pedagogy, and we see it here as in other places as the classroom unit progresses.

---

Alex nodded his head in affirmation.

Yolanda raised her hand and offered "equal rights," which she clarified to mean the same rights as citizens. Monica began to list student ideas on the chart paper at the front of the room.

Amanda stated that if immigrants were going to be sent away they needed some money. Monica suggested Amanda meant that, if deported, immigrants would need start-up funds. Yolanda stated that immigrants should be able to get work permits. Monica asked who would qualify and how long the permits would be for. Grinning, Alex announced, "Working permits forever!" Marta was a bit more serious and suggested that more permits need to be issued than are currently allowed. The class struggled with this issue. Jonah suggested that priority be given to those who had been here the longest. The teacher explained the difficulties in determining how long a person has been in the United States. She asked the class how they could make a fair determination. Luis suggested giving permits based upon the date of application for citizenship. Monica explained the quota system for immigration. She said that it sounded like Luis was suggesting that the citizen eligibility lists be utilized, and she explained how priorities are set for those who can enter the United States. By way of example, she explained that if your mother wants to bring her sister it is not the same priority as if she wants to bring her children or her husband. Jonah suggested that English proficiency levels could be used to determine how long an immigrant has been here.

"How many of you would agree or disagree that English proficiency, knowing English, should be one of the requirements for immigrants to be granted residency?" inquired Monica. About half of the class raised their hands. "How many disagree?" The other hands went up. "Gilbert, why do you disagree?"

Gilbert explained that you couldn't force people to learn a language. Mario noted that many immigrants are here only to work and earn money to send home to their families, not to learn English.

Amanda asked, "What if it's too hard for them, like with Mr. Miranda?" She remembered Eduardo's difficulty expressing himself fully to the class in English. She expressed concern that, like Eduardo, some immigrants may be trying to protect their families politically through relocation and that it would not be fair to expect them to speak English first before they could do so. Yolanda countered by asking how immigrants could get around if they did not know English.

> Students are codifying, or naming, the problems. Here, they say that families need access to their native language. They represent their thoughts through language. Freire did the same with the peasants with whom he worked.

"If immigrants come here, because they are trying to find a job and everything, and they're learning English and they're trying their best, then I think Americans should also learn Spanish or another language." Rosa spoke forcefully.

"Why is that?" inquired her teacher.

"Because they are coming to America and it really wouldn't be fair if everyone has to speak English only. It's not fair."

Jonah reconsidered his prior opinion. He volunteered a new idea: If everyone were required to speak only English, Latinos would lose their value because there would no longer be a need for translators!

Marta stated that her dad "took a test for English" when he applied for residency, so the English requirement was already in place.

> As students engage each other in debate, they are learning that difference of opinion is healthy. They are examining issues from different perspectives and, consequently, changing their opinions. Rich dialogue allows this to happen.

*(Continued)*

(Continued)

Monica used the opportunity to mention the current discussions in the legislature to make English the official language.

> Monica is positioning her instruction right in the midst of the debate over whether English should be a national language. In a clear way, she is facilitating discussion in which the students are learning about the legislative processes at work and how their involvement in such processes is a way by which they can have a voice and power in society.

According to research statistics, she noted, only a tiny percentage of illegal immigrants don't speak any English. Based on this statistic, she questioned the necessity of mandating an official language. "You don't have to tell people who come to the United States to speak English. If you go to Mexico, what's the official language?"

"Spanish."

"It's the official language, right. No one has to tell you that."

The students were not pleased about the news of possible official English language legislation. They talked among themselves, and Jonah stated, "Speaking only English takes away from our culture." Monica expressed the opinion that having English as an official language would not stop people from speaking Spanish. Some potential problems might arise as a result, however, such as the loss of translator availability in hospitals and a lack of access to public service information in two languages.

Refocusing attention on the chart paper, Monica reviewed all the information offered by the children thus far and announced that tomorrow there would be a speaker from an immigrant advocacy organization.

Alex interrupted, "Is it someone who works at the school?"

"No."

"Thank God!" with great drama, Alex gave a tremendous sigh of relief.

The featured guest, continued Monica, could deliver letters to someone who had input on the formation of immigration policy and implementation. The students would have twenty-five minutes to write the draft of such a letter, and then she would choose partners to edit their writing.

During the "free write," the most dominant theme had to do with the pending legislation to make English the official language of the United States. Tablemates Rosa, Cesar, and Jessica all agreed that English should not be a requirement for residency or citizenship. Cesar remarked that there is not enough time to learn English if someone is working every day. Zenaida suggested that English speakers should learn another language.

After circulating among the groups, Monica addressed the class collectively, noting that they were having some difficulty with both content and the correct technical format for letter writing. She first discussed the need to identify which policy ideas they liked and which ones they didn't like. She next addressed the difference between a letter of complaint and a letter that might actually be considered in shaping policy, a letter with suggestions for policy development and implementation.

To be more effective, she urged them to move beyond language like "I feel" or "I disagree," and she provided encouragement for making their own unique suggestions. The letter's form and content were different things; what to include in the content was their decision, but the letter format followed specific rules. They had already worked on the correct format for writing a letter; now was the time to use that information. Noting that some of the students were ready to edit, she assigned editing partners. "When we edit, what are we looking for?" she asked, and the students responded, "grammar and content."

"No repetition."

"Order, sequence."

"Don't mix ideas, and separate them by paragraphs."

> Monica takes this opportunity to teach a mini-lesson on standard grammar. She discusses the audience as well as the format of the letters the students are writing. Once again, she masterfully integrates content and language within an authentic context.
>
> Also of interest is the attempt to affect change by writing to someone of official importance about English as a national language. It may seem like a small step, but the fact remains that the students are taking action toward social change. They are putting praxis (or action) to their ideas—ideas that have come about as a result of this rich, critical, and divergent social studies unit.

As in past editing work, they could make suggestions to the author at the bottom of the paper, Monica reminded them. Seating assignments were shifted so that the editing pairs could be closer together, and the students were reminded that, when the letters were written, they would be sent out.

"Is someone actually going to read this?" Salvador inquired.

"Yes."

Alex was skeptical. "What is that going to do?"

"Wouldn't you like to know that someone is going to read your strong opinion and your strong suggestion? What is it going to do? Suppose all of you decided to write letters to me about my homework policy, and I decided to do nothing with it. What would be your reaction?"

> Monica takes this opportunity to give a context-embedded example to help the students understand what effect their letters might have.

"We would stop doing homework."

"Someone just suggested that the reaction would be to stop doing homework. So I would have to take into account all your letters and make some changes. I would have to say, okay, the entire eighth-grade class feels that I overwhelm them with homework."

*(Continued)*

(Continued)

"Yep!"

"So I need to change that, and I have, this quarter. Yes or no?"

"Yes, thank you." Cesar was genuinely grateful.

"I have this quarter, a lot. So, yes, someone is going to read this, . . . and they're going to see that you have strong feelings about this English language policy."

Salvador was surprised that they would be doing only one draft. Normally, three were required. Monica explained that the speaker was available only the next day.

The students continued to write. Lynelle, in particular, was a voracious writer in terms of both volume and intensity. She would not put down her pen until her classmates were ready to file out the classroom door.

❖   ❖   ❖

Classroom life is unpredictable. The representative of the immigration advocacy group was unable to visit the class. Furthermore, the students were having difficulty recalling the prior instruction they had received on proper letter-writing format. Monica had a double dilemma, but she also had practice in making lemonade out of lemons. She let the students know of the cancellation and announced that this time would be well spent working on letter format.

"Let's take out the letters that you were working on yesterday. . . . Remember, when we edit, we're not only looking for composition; that's important, but we are also looking for content. . . . You are the reader; you are getting this letter from somebody. This person is asking you to do something. If it is not clear, . . . nine times out of ten, the reader will put the letter into the garbage. You know, you're like, what does this person want? It doesn't make any sense. So you have to be clear, focused in your writing."

She allowed time for the students to continue editing in partners and then refocused the attention of the class.

"We are not deciding the content together because that is yours, that's personal, but together we can decide the format. You have your address," she used the chart paper displayed at the front of the room, conversing as she wrote. "Some of you don't want to put down your address. What we can use together is the school address," she said while continuing to write. "What comes next in a letter?"

"The date."

"The date," repeated their teacher.

"May 23, 2006," said a lone voice.

Monica wrote, "May 23, 2006," on the chart paper and continued, "suppose it's May 23rd . . ."

The rest of the class laughed good-naturedly. They knew that it was actually May 22nd.

"Well, I said suppose because maybe you're not finalizing it today." The laughter subsided, and Monica talked them through the rest of the parts of the letter—address, salutation, introduction, and so on—discussing the various stylistic choices available as she went along. Since the immigrant advocate would not be visiting the class, no one knew where the letter would be going, so the chart remained incomplete.

"Let's think about who we want to send this letter to.... You have this letter about a concern to you, a concern to us. You don't want the letter to just go into Monica's file, okay, because as much as I would like to address your concerns, I don't have the power to do so. So where do you think we may want to send these letters?"

The question was met with silence, but Monica did not pressure them.

---

Monica teaches the students how their letters might have influence. Once again, dialogue becomes the method by which students come to new understandings.

---

Gilbert broke the silence. "To the governor."

"To the governor." Monica repeated his words deliberately, for all to hear.

"Congress." This time it was Luis.

"Congress. Okay, how many members are there in Congress?"

A variety of numbers were called out.

"Wait, wait . . . you're missing it! The Congress has the Senate and the House of Representatives, right? So how many, you don't have to give me the exact number, roughly, how many . . . ?"

"400," volunteered Luis.

"Over 400," expanded his teacher.

"Thousand!" filled in an anonymous jokester.

"No! . . . Are you going to send it . . . excuse me, Luis, didn't you say Congress? So, if we have over 400 members in Congress, who are you going to send it to in Congress?"

"One of them."

"One of them! Let's say we choose one of them. Either a member of the House of Representatives or . . ."

"What if we made a lot of copies and sent it to each?" suggested Cesar.

"You could do that, make 535 copies, to be specific, and you will cover the entire Congress. Do you want to do that? How effective would that be?"

"Very! Very!" was the group response.

---

Monica facilitates the discussion. She does not tell the students they are incorrect. She guides them through questioning.

---

"Maybe, but who do you think will actually read your letter and pay a little bit more attention?"

"Our parents!" Cesar continued.

"No, we're still with the Congress, Luis?"

Cesar tried again, "A teacher!"

"A senator," volunteered Luis.

"A senator. What senator *maybe* will be more likely to read it than others?"

*(Continued)*

(Continued)

Several students simultaneously offered, "Barack Obama!"

Alex disagreed. "No, let's send it to Richard Durbin and tell him that we are the class that he met when we were in Washington DC!"

"Yeaaaaaaah!" the class yelled their consent.

"Okay, let's see, someone said Obama . . ."

"Obama."

"Why?" asked Monica.

"He's an African American."

"He's an African American so maybe he can see what bad things happen to African Americans and be a little more sensitive with us. Okay. . . . And you say Richard Durbin. Why Richard Durbin, Alex?"

"Because we met him in DC, and maybe if we write that we are Southwest School and this and that . . ."

Monica continued to converse with the students. "Okay. Maybe if you want to write Senator Durbin and say we met you during the month of April because we were there during our class trip; we are from Southwest School, a public school. Now, what do Obama and Durbin have in common?"

"They are both senators."

"They are both senators, and . . ."

"They are Democratic."

"They are Democratic, okay, what else?"

"They are closer to home."

"They are closer to home. Where are they from?"

This time the entire class responded, "Illinois."

"Illinois! Okay, so you are saying that Obama, he's an African American, maybe he will be more sensitive to the issue because he is a minority. And Durbin, because we met him in DC, and he may say these are the same students that came, took the time to come to the Capitol, and maybe they are interested in this issue. They also are from Illinois. So out of the 100 senators, maybe these two would be more likely to read your letters and do something about them because they are from Illinois, and you are from Illinois. You also met one of them."

"Briefly only," said Cesar.

"Briefly," agreed Monica.

"I don't think he remembers us," continued Cesar. "Does he have gray hair? He looks younger on TV. He should take off ten pounds!"

Monica discussed congressional representatives as alternate possibilities. The students were not as enthusiastic about this idea. Rosa balanced a book on her head and then passed it on to Cesar, who did the same.

Their teacher seemed not to notice. "Let's assume we all want to send it to Richard Durbin because maybe you think we have a connection. You can say in your letter, we met you once, during the week of April 5th when we were visiting the nation's capital. You can say we took a picture with you . . ."

"Put the picture right there. You will have proof!" suggested Alex with glee.

But nothing could derail Monica. "We are Southwest School, or I am a student at Southwest School."

"We were waiting in the rain and cold for like . . ." the class was on a roll.

"...an hour!" Cesar completed the sentence.

Rosa's attention was recaptured. "Yeah, so he'll feel sorry for us."

Collective chatter of remembered commiseration filled the room, but Monica was not slowing down.

"Let's narrow it down. Let's say we want to send it to Richard Durbin, state senator, because we may feel we have a little connection because we met him, okay." As she spoke, she began to write on the chart paper hanging on the front board. "So the name up here will be what?"

"Richard Durbin," was the collective response.

"What's his title?"

Again the response was collective, "Senator."

"Senator. Now, what is the organization he works for?"

"The Senate."

"The Senate, right, or the United States Congress. The address...do we know the address?...It is easy to find because he is a public figure. If you go on the Internet, you will find his address."

This time the response was individual, as Salvador announced, "I know the White House address. Do you know the White House address?"

"Yes. What is the White House address?"

Salvador was happy to supply the answer, "1600 Pennsylvania Avenue."

"Sixteen hundred Pennsylvania Avenue. How many of you think sending the letters to Senator Durbin would be the route we may want to go? Do you have a comment? What's your comment?"

"He's not going to read our thoughts."

"How many of you feel that what we say will not be that important to a senator?"

About half of the students raised their hands, and there was general spontaneous discussion in support of the idea that Senator Durbin would not read their letters.

---

As the class discusses the likelihood of their letters actually affecting change, students are continuing to position themselves within the context of those who have power in our society. Perhaps their new understandings will continue to grow. Certainly, Monica's classroom has given them a place to critically reflect upon these issues.

The students' apparent realization that their power is limited is part of the *process* of critical pedagogy. Examinations of identity and realizations of disempowerment are not objectives that can be easily measured on a unit test. The issues raised in this classroom community will likely be issues with which these students will engage during their entire lifetimes.

---

"Let me just give a little side note about Richard Durbin. He communicates with his constituents through e-mail. I have e-mailed him, and he has responded."

"Oohs" and "aahs" filled the air.

"But was it really him?" someone inquired.

*(Continued)*

(Continued)

The chatter that followed focused on this supposition. Someone asked if another person could be answering for the senator.

"It could be, but if it's not really him, it's gotta be someone who shares his views, because otherwise I have an e-mail here that is signed, well, it's not signed, but it's got Richard Durbin, senator, and his point of view is, 'I agree with you on immigration issues.' And then later on, he comes out and says," she changed the pitch of her voice in mock imitation, "'Well, I don't agree with that.' What would you say?"

"I would print it out . . ."

"Okay, so, even if he personally won't answer those e-mails, someone on his staff that answers has to have the view and philosophy of Richard Durbin, senator. So, let's say we are going to write to Senator Durbin. What would you want to include in your letter that you do not have right now?"

Once again the teacher allowed silence to fill the room, but after a respectable amount of time had passed, she prompted a response.

"You mentioned it. What do you want to add to your letter that you don't have right now? What?"

"About our visit."

"About our visit," repeated Monica.

"How did you get him to come meet us?"

"How did I get him to come? Through an e-mail, an e-mail to his office. . . . By the way, Richard Durbin and Senator Obama, every Thursday . . . have a breakfast with anyone from Illinois that happens to be in the nation's capital; every Thursday they have an eight o'clock coffee and bagels. You can just show up. As a matter of fact, we couldn't do it because we had booked a visit to George Washington's home."

The moans of disappointment were distinct and genuine.

"But he had invited us to be there with him . . . both of them. . . . What? . . . Yeah, I wanted to be there, too, but we couldn't do it. So we can mention our visit. Rosa, do you think mentioning our visit would be a good idea?"

"Yeah!" she responded eagerly, and her classmates chattered their agreement.

"Okay, it would show that there actually is a connection, that it did matter, what he told us that day. So, in your introduction you say, 'Dear Senator Durbin,' or 'Your Honorable,'" she spoke as she wrote on the chart paper, "depending on how you want to write it, and then an introduction, you have to introduce yourself and introduce the reason why you are writing. 'Dear Senator Durbin,' right, 'My name is Alex Feliciano. I am a student at Southwest School. Perhaps you remember our group. We visited the nation's capital during the month of April,' and I'm gonna put it here so you guys can remember, the week of April . . ." Her voice trailed off as she wrote the date.

With his teacher facing the other direction, Gilbert tried to attach a scrap of paper to the back of Alex's shirt. Alex was so intent on following the conversation that he completely ignored these antics, and Gilbert soon stopped.

"You see, if you write that there, he may say, 'ooooooooooh . . . I know!'" She dramatized the last three words, and the class giggled. Gilbert did not stand a chance next to Monica!

"We had a meeting . . ."

"Yeah, yeah!" Monica conversed with the students. "We could say, we were there visiting. You could say, I am writing you with a concern of mine, then you present your point of view. You could say the Senate is considering making English the official language of the United States. Okay, this is how you introduce it. Now, all you need to do is add your suggestions. Okay, I'm gonna come around and look at your letters."

With the more formal instruction complete, Monica began to circulate among the students. They were editing in pairs and, sometimes, in the groups inadvertently formed by tables. After about forty minutes, she moved the students into a new activity. They choose the most important portion of their letter to read to the class. The children were initially reluctant to do so. No one volunteered to go first. The normal flash of arms shooting upward did not occur.

"Okay, let's begin."

"I don't want to."

"Oh, you know what? You guys have very good things on paper. Maybe what's going on is that there is a different type of writing here. You're writing, you read it to yourself, you understand exactly what you want to say, but there is also the listening part. Do I really convey, do I really send the message I want to send to others? And if other people don't understand my message, then I have to clarify exactly what I want to say." She turned toward Jonah. "Would you like to start here?"

Again silence.

"No?"

"Yeah."

"Okay. Good. Just the point you want the senator or anyone reading your letter to get."

"'My name is Jonah Gonzalez and I am from . . .'"

"No, not the introduction, I'm sorry. We all know who we, okay, we all know we come from Southwest School, we all know that we went to Washington DC and met Senator Durbin . . ."

"I didn't!" cried out Nancy.

"I'm sorry, most of us. So this is what we are doing—we are reading the part where we say what policy we agree or disagree with and why, and our suggestions. That part. Okay. Begin."

Each student, in turn, read the heart of his or her letter. Marta kept with the serious tone. She wrote:

> The reason I am writing is to voice my opinion about the law that is trying to be passed about making English the language of this country. I don't think this is such a good idea because this country is made up of many cultures and languages. *It would be very difficult for a person to make them speak a completely new language. Everyone deserves to still have their native language and stay with their cultural roots.* Instead of this I propose for the government to help out some immigrants to continue their studies financially. This is a great idea. It will benefit the country and educate more people.

Notice how Marta addresses issues of inequity; she gets to the heart of the issue—the oppression, if you will, of denying people access to their native language and cultural roots. She also gives an alternative solution. She is working toward transformation.

*(Continued)*

(Continued)

Amanda had quite a bit to say:

> Suppose you didn't really want to come to the U.S. and you're forced to come because your country is having some problems. All you want to do is protect your family and help them live better lives, and then tell them they have to learn English. It's not fair that they should learn English. It's like telling everyone in the U.S. that they have to learn Spanish. Why make someone do something they don't want to do if all they want is to live a better life and start fresh. But if the United States government is going to make learning a certain amount of English a requirement, then they should at least be helping them learn. I think the government should put some money to the side to help hire teachers that can teach at night so the immigrants can work in the day. Or maybe jobs that are willing to have special teachers teach them at work, they can do that. Overall, I don't like the idea of making learning English a requirement to become a citizen. I think the government should stop wasting money trying to put up a wall to keep immigrants out and instead try to help them.

True to his nature, Cesar looked at things from a more humorous angle:

> First of all immigrants can home school themselves and meet up with a mentor once a week. While they visit this educated and paid mentor they will revise their grammar and quiz them. Later in about a year or two, depending on how they are progressing, they will take a final grammar test. The passing percentile will be 85% and *anything* below that would be failing. If they fail then there could be a makeup test the following month. If they receive a better score than the ones before then they keep studying. If they fail to show they are trying and have no progress then they will be deported.

The written word once again gave voice to the normally silent Lynelle:

> I am writing you this letter considering your policy on immigrants coming to the United States to speak only the English language. I do agree that immigrants should speak the English language if they are going to live in America then they should. I think it should be recommended because English is the United States official language. If they don't know English then it's going to be hard for them to get around and apply for jobs and go to school. But I don't believe that they should speak and write *only* in the English language. I mean they should speak the language that they are most comfortable with then they should. And it's difficult for someone to learn another language. But it wouldn't hurt for Americans to learn Spanish as well.

In critical classrooms, students are encouraged to think, to reflect, and to critique through written language. For Lynelle, who is often reticent to express herself verbally in front of her peers, the written word provides a forum for her to share her views. Lynelle has been processing the classroom curriculum all along, even when she was silent.

Virtual silence reigned, and all eyes focused on the reader... well, all eyes except those of Jessica and Cesar, whose eyes were only on each other. They took turns throwing paper across the table at each other's faces and seemed not to be the least bit upset when the other person scored a hit. This activity, after all, provided a perfect rationale for gazing endlessly into each other's eyes.

Amanda, on the other hand, had no time for such foolishness. As Luisa read, a commotion in the hallway was heard. Amanda got up and discretely shut the door so that her classmate's voice could ring out loud and clear.

## CONCLUDING THOUGHTS

Because critical perspectives are not prescriptive, we do not give a list of strategies to use at the end of this chapter as we did in previous chapters. We reflect, rather, on the impact this approach had on the teachers and researchers. Monica's social studies unit is a good example of extending critical pedagogical principles into the classroom. In a post-unit interview (M. Gonzalez, personal communication, July 16, 2006), Monica talked about how her students were engaged beyond her expectations. Even though it was the end of the year, they were attentive and even sought to go above and beyond what was expected. For example, one student traveled around school with a video recorder and asked teachers, staff, and students their feelings about the issues they were discussing. Further research about student engagement in critical classrooms would be a useful addition to the literature.

What stands out to these researchers is the process of critical reflection in the classroom. As students began to read the word and the world, they looked deeply at themselves and critically at society. What if they are not given those opportunities in the future? What if classrooms are simply places where educators regurgitate information deemed important by legislators? Where will students learn how to think, to reflect, and to transform? Certainly, these issues are important for ELLs, but we suggest that they are also important for all learners.

# 9 Toward Critical Constructivist Practice With Second Language Learners

Spring has arrived slowly, cautiously after a long, cruel Midwest winter. Sun does not flood through the windows of room 307; the shades are not drawn. Outside thin branches test the fragile breeze and buds peer tentatively from slender stalks. Inside, however, there is nothing tentative about room 307, which is full to bursting as 19 pairs of arms and legs continue to investigate life. The four walls are plastered with almost a year's worth of children's discoveries. Their painted people portraits collide with dinosaur skeletons; posters with lists of synonyms in primary grade printing have taken over the rear chalkboard. A poster at the front of the room names children who have performed kind and heroic deeds on the recess playground, or at any other time or place. Hanging from the ceiling are mobiles of geometric shapes, paper birds, and a large paper sun, all crafted by young hands. The number line circling the room has Roman Numerals on hand made cards taped below the corresponding Arabic numbers from one to 120. A sign reads, "If I were in charge of the world." Below, student compositions describe a world free of dentists and vegetables and full of chocolate ice cream and people who are successful in life despite the fact that they forget to take baths.

The words to "Hablemos el mismo idioma" (We speak the same language), as sung by Gloria Estefan, are printed neatly on the top page of a flip chart. In the library Tupperware bins of books in English and Spanish line the shelves, and a sofa cushion and two rug pieces have been tossed on the floor beneath. Four clusters of desks and chairs form tables that are arranged within the room in a shape that is a cross between a square and a circle. Counter tops and tables are full. Nothing resembling a teacher's desk is anywhere to be seen. This is a room that has been taken over by children; this is clearly their domain.

Student made big books travel back and forth between tables. Computer cards manufactured by children at work in the teacher's small storage room are passed secretively under desks. I am dizzy from my observations. Words and colors and sounds overlap and swirl and transport me to a hundred different places.

These are the words a university graduate student used to describe the school in which she completed her fieldwork. They stand in glaring contrast to the words of the university student we highlighted at the beginning of this book. Both students wrote about specific educational contexts for ELLs, but that is where the similarity ends. The mobile unit represents a stark reality for many ELLs, but the vibrant classroom described above represents a bold vision of the future; a future you, like Jill, Maria, and Monica, can help shape in your own classroom and school.

But exactly how will you get to this future classroom? An examination of the contextual factors that Jill, Maria, and Monica considered for creating vibrant and engaging classrooms may shed light on your own journey. We begin by looking at our students, their socioeconomic, cultural, and family backgrounds. Next we examine the local school context, including educational program and resources. Finally we look at the unique gifts of the educators who facilitate student learning. When we bring all these elements together, we can see the contextual background that made possible the three stories highlighted in this book. And when we examine classrooms in this manner, it becomes easier to tell the story of your own classroom.

Jill's students come from diverse socioeconomic and cultural backgrounds. They include children from middle-class professional households as well as working-class and low-income homes. Although predominantly Latino, her class includes a significant number of African American and white students, as well as a few students with parents from two different cultural backgrounds. The Latino students range linguistically from Spanish dominant to English dominant and are at varying stages of bilingualism. However, they are all attending a TWI school, and it is expected that they will continue to develop bilingual language and academic proficiency. Pedagogy and curriculum that drive bilingualism and biculturalism are supported by the school's two-way design; thus the ground is ripe for Jill to weave her artistry. She takes full advantage of this opportunity, even bringing her musical interest into the classroom. It is not unusual to hear the sounds of strumming guitar chords accompanied by children's bilingual singing drifting down the hallway. Jill is an English dominant bilingual who has chosen to not only sing but to teach in her second language: Spanish. In this way, she nurtures her own bilingualism along with that of her students.

Jill maximizes the social context of learning to promote bilingualism. She understands that children learn from each other, and she enables this to happen both linguistically and academically. Furthermore, when linguistic minority students serve as role models for linguistic majority students, she understands that benefits may go beyond language and academics. She facilitates identity construction and positive cross-cultural attitudes in this multicultural environment.

Maria's students are Arab and Kurdish refugees from Iraq who previously experienced failure in mainstream classrooms with daily ESL pull-out instruction. Coming from a war-torn region, many with little or no formal schooling, their lack of academic success could hardly be considered surprising. Educators on the local school level recognized that they were not prepared for this new influx of refugee students. The flexibility to consider an alternative curriculum and empower the ESL teacher to implement it allowed for the academic success of the students most in danger of failure.

Maria brings her personal strengths to this task. Although she is not fluent in any of the native languages of her students, she is a fully fluent bilingual who learned English as a second language. Although at a glance it might seem that her cultural background and family history is completely dissimilar to that of her students, she is able to find points of convergence. Further, she uses the students' lived experiences in their homeland as an entry point into the curriculum. Thus, the classroom she creates is both linguistically sensitive and culturally responsive. When combined with constructivist practice, these factors add up to student engagement and, consequently, higher levels of the second language literacy that lays the groundwork for future content area success.

Monica's students are predominantly from low-income Latino families with a strong immigrant heritage and representation from Puerto Rico, Central and South America, and Mexico. Although a range of bilingualism is present in the class, with the exception of three recently arrived immigrant students, they are all proficient in oral communicative English. Instruction in Monica's departmentalized social studies class is in English; the three new students receive native language instruction in another class. Because she is an immigrant herself, Monica has a special sensitivity to the life circumstances of her students. She is able to use her own life experience to tap the prior knowledge base that her students bring into the classroom.

Monica knows that, although her students possess basic communicative proficiency in English, many are weak in academic English. In her social studies curriculum, English is the mandated language of instruction, and she is thus faced with the challenge of simultaneously facilitating development of academic language and academic content. She does so successfully because she views her students' backgrounds as strengths upon which to build. Their tangible immigrant backgrounds give them special insights, and Monica uses this experience to facilitate dialogue and motivate writing. The end result of her creativity in meeting this challenge is that not only do the students absorb social studies content and improve in academic English, but they experience empowerment as they send their feelings, opinions, and ideas, *their words*, out into the world.

We have situated Jill, Maria, and Monica's classrooms within the contexts that enabled their respective success. Each classroom curriculum was developed within a unique set of circumstances and contextual factors, yet each resulted in student engagement and consequently linguistic and academic success. Like Jill, Maria, and Monica, your educational context is unique. You hold the ultimate responsibility for shaping the curriculum and facilitating the educational environment that may best meet the needs of your students. We cannot provide a magic formula that will engage students in learning; that is up to your artistry. What we can do, however, is to suggest a philosophical stance from which best practice can emerge. Our journey into three classrooms where practice is grounded in a sound theoretical foundation leads us to recommend practice for ELLs that:

- Is constructivist
- Is critical
- Integrates language, content, and process
- Uses modifications to make the curriculum more accessible
- Encourages identity construction and fosters positive self-esteem through validation of native language and culture

We have chosen to name this practice Critical Constructivist Education for ELLs. It is grounded in principles of educational equity, second language acquisition, constructivism, and critical pedagogy. It holds that literacy and critical thought are the *basic skills* needed by *all* students and that reading, writing, and critical thinking are the cornerstones of democracy, that literacy is empowerment, and that all teachers should be critical literacy educators. Critical constructivist practice is maximized when it takes place within program models for ELLs that are additive; however, because pedagogically it is both linguistically sensitive and culturally responsive, critical constructivist practice can take place in multiple contexts.

Changing your instructional practice to a critical constructivist stance can make the curriculum accessible not only to ELLs but to all students. After a professional development session led by Sharon, Bridget A. Cahill, a special education teacher in Evanston/Skokie School District 65 in Illinois, pointed out that Universal Design for Learning (UDL) is a parallel concept, "which in part has grown from the best practice of differentiated instruction. Differentiated instruction is the framework that supports the belief that instructional approaches need to be varied in relation to the unique and diverse learner needs in a classroom." Bridget further noted that,

> by the nature of their design, many special education classrooms need to accommodate multiple learning styles, physical/environmental needs, academic levels, chronological levels, and behavioral issues. In these environments, UDL effectively addresses learner needs by focusing on how the specific objective of the lesson can be accessed by all learners, through modifying materials, content, and teaching strategies to reach all learners.

> One can think of the benefits of universal design theory and its impact in a larger arena by looking at some architectural designs specifically conceived to accommodate one group—people with disabilities—that have subsequently emerged to assist many of us on a daily basis. Curbing cuts in sidewalks at corners, originally intended to help people using wheelchairs, made life much easier for the use of baby strollers and luggage rollers! Escalators and moving sidewalks, also intended to make mobility easier for those with disabilities, provide benefits to seniors, parents with young children, and those traversing malls and airports. The use of larger print media, originated for helping people with visual impairments, provides less eyestrain for seniors (and even advancing baby boomers).

> In public schools, education cannot be "off limits" to any child. Just as curbs and stairs provided physical barriers to those with

disabilities in the past, a singular design for teaching and learning has been a barrier for children to access a quality education. Thanks to the application of a Universal Design for Learning, those barriers no longer need to exist in our schools.

Universal Design can thus be thought of as "inclusive design" or "design for all," just as critical constructivist practice with modifications can be considered inclusive education, or education for all. The benefits do not end there, however. Critical constructivist practice can keep us all wide-awake in this world; it can engage teachers just as it engages students. It can keep us all alive as learners in a multilingual and multicultural world.

We have seen educational equity in action as exemplified by the classroom teachers and the narratives in this text. Like Jill, Maria, and Monica, we all have stories to tell. Issues of equity play themselves out in all of our schools and in many of our lives. We invite you to tell your stories and to unleash your creativity in designing classrooms and programs designed to meet the unique needs of students and families within their educational and community context. And if we are in town, invite us in. We would love to see your learning community in action. Who knows, perhaps it will be featured in our next book!

# Appendix

## Questionnaire for Use in Classroom-Based Oral History Project

*Irma M. Olmedo*

### 1. Grandparents

What do you know about your parents (and grandparents)?

Where and when were they born?

Did they have an opportunity to go to school? What was school like for them?

How did they earn a living? What kind of work did they do?

Did you know them well? Did you spend any time with them?

What kinds of things did you do with your grandparents? What did you enjoy doing together?

If they were born in another country, when did they come to the United States?

Why did they come to this country?

Did they ever tell you about their experiences when they first arrived in the United States?

What kinds of holidays did they celebrate? How?

Did your grandparents tell you any stories when you were young? Do you remember any of them? Can you tell me one?

## 2. Childhood

Where did you live as a child? Can you describe the place (town, city, neighborhood)?

What kind of house (or apartment) did you live in? Can you describe it?

Did you have an opportunity to go to school? What kinds of areas did you study?

Was your family similar or different from other people in the community or neighborhood? In what ways?

What holidays did you celebrate when you were young? How were these celebrated?

Were there any religious traditions that were practiced by your family? How important were these?

What kinds of things did you do for entertainment (for fun)?

Did you have to work when you were young? What kinds of jobs did you have to do?

Were there any historical events that had an impact on your family? For example, did a change of government or a war have any effect on them? How?

Who did you admire when you were young? Why?

How were the following events celebrated or observed when you were young: weddings, birth of a child, birthday, death of someone?

## 3. The Migration Experience

When did your family come to the United States?

What did you know about the United States before you came here?

Why did your family leave their country to come here?

Who made the decision to come?

What kinds of things did your family have to do to get here?

Did many other people from your neighborhood, hometown (city, country) come also?

Where did you live when you first came here?

What was the apartment like? Can you describe it?

What kind of work did your parents do when they came here?

What were your first impressions of this country?

## 4. Life in the New Land

How was life similar in the new country and the old country? What did you continue to do that did not change?

What kinds of activities did you change when you came here?

How did other Americans treat your family when you came here? Were people helpful or not?

Can you describe a typical day in your childhood?

Did you have any problems adjusting to your new home? Which ones?

Are you very similar to other "Americans" or different in some ways? How?

Are you happy that your family made the decision to move here? Why?

Has your family been involved in any organizations in this country? Why?

Has your family ever returned to the country that they came from? How did they feel about this experience?

What kinds of hopes do you have for your grandchildren?

What do you like most about living in the United States? What do you like least?

Adapted from *Oral History Questions* by Irma M. Olmedo.

# Glossary

**Additive bilingualism:** The acquisition of a second language while maintaining and developing the first.

**Affective filter:** An emotional barrier to language learning that must be overcome or set at a lower level so that the learner can progress from the input to the output stage of second language development.

**Authentic assessment:** Ways of assessing student learning that are embedded in classroom instructional practice and that serve to inform educators on an ongoing basis of student learning progress in the day-to-day activities of the classroom.

**BICS:** The Basic Interpersonal Communicative Skills needed for everyday linguistic communication.

**CALP:** The Cognitive/Academic Language Proficiency needed to excel in school.

**Code switching:** The ability of fluent bilingual individuals to alternate between two languages within or between sentences for a specific stylistic or lexical purpose.

**Codification:** The process that occurs simultaneously with dialogue during which students represent their reality.

**Codifying:** The process that occurs during codification wherein students name problems.

**Cognates:** Words that have similar sound and meaning in multiple languages.

**Comprehensible experience:** Embedding content area studies in real life experiences; parallel to comprehensible input in the language arts.

**Comprehensible input:** The continuous modification of speech to facilitate the development of students' L2.

**Comprehensible input hypothesis:** Krashen's (1982) hypothesis that second language learners are ready for the acquisition of language input that is one step higher (I+1) than their current levels.

**Comprehensible output:** The ability to communicate in a second language with native speakers of that language.

**Conscientization:** The development of critical consciousness, which occurs as students codify and problem pose through dialogue.

**Constructivism:** A theory of knowing; it examines the way in which we learn and acquire knowledge.

**Context-embedded instruction:** Instruction that takes place within an environment that offers concrete, real life examples of what is being taught, such as teaching about the life cycle of frogs by raising tadpoles.

**Critical pedagogy:** The art of teaching, or a way of teaching, in which the world is viewed through a critical lens; pedagogy of (and for) oppressed people.

**Culturally and linguistically sensitive pedagogy:** An approach to teaching that considers and validates the linguistic and cultural heritage of the student.

**Culturally responsive pedagogy:** An approach to teaching that draws upon students' identities and backgrounds as central to the formation of meaning in the educational process, thus validating prior knowledge and cultural heritage.

**Disequilibrium:** The state of being we experience when things are not what we expect; it is in this frame that learning occurs.

**ELL:** English Language Learner; the term in current use to denote students in the process of acquiring and/or learning English as a second language.

**Emergent literacy:** A perspective on literacy in which such development is embedded in meaningful and functional activities.

**ESL:** English as a Second Language.

**Enrichment:** Models of bilingual instruction that are by nature additive, usually designed for children from a linguistic majority background; such models assign value to bilingualism in English dominant students.

**Equilibrium:** The cognitive state we experience when things are what we expect them to be and our knowledge is validated.

**Ethnic identity:** The part of personal identity that is embedded in perceptions of ethnic group membership.

**Funds of knowledge:** The knowledge and skills available in students' homes and communities.

**Hegemonies:** Subtle forms of oppression in which those who are oppressed accept their oppression.

**Immersion education:** A model of second language education governed by the basic tenet that second and subsequent languages are best internalized in a manner that simulates first language acquisition. Language is therefore not explicitly taught, but, rather, context-embedded content area instruction is provided in a second language. All immersion education, therefore, highlights the integration of language and content.

**Integrated model:** A program model in which ELLs continue to receive their primary instruction within bilingual classrooms but come together with mainstream classrooms for some content area instruction, usually science, social studies, or math.

**Interdependence hypothesis:** Cummins's (1978) hypothesis that development of the learner's L1 will have a direct impact on future acquisition of the learner's L2 and will further the transfer of knowledge across the learner's two languages.

**L1:** Language one; the native language.

**L2:** Language two; the language being learned or acquired after the initial acquisition of the native language.

**Language maintenance:** A model of bilingual education in which linguistic minority students continue to develop linguistically, academically, and cognitively in their native language even after their English language proficiency is adequate for participation in mainstream classrooms.

**Metalinguistic awareness:** The ability to think flexibly and abstractly about language.

**Motherese:** The language rich in sheltering and comprehensible input that parents and/or primary caregivers use with infants and very young children;

also referred to as "child-directed speech," "foreigner-talk," or "caretaker speech."

**Perturbation:** The disappointment that is one of the conditions necessary for cognitive change to occur; disequilibrium.

**Praxis:** The continuous transformative cycle of reflection leading to action and action leading to further reflection that is the culmination of dialogue and of students and teachers finding ways to *affect change* as a result of their discoveries.

**Problem posing:** The process by which reality is critically examined; it looks beyond the curriculum and encourages students to ask questions about things relevant to their lives.

**Scaffolding:** A way of providing support to students through modeling, feedback, instruction, and questioning. It is based on the premise that, what the learner is able to do with assistance today, the learner can do alone tomorrow.

**Second language acquisition:** The process of developing a second language naturally, in the same manner as the first, without substantive formal instruction.

**Second language learning:** The process of developing a second language through formal language instruction.

**Sequential bilingualism:** Exposure to a second language after the age of three.

**Sheltered instruction:** Instruction given in a second language that maximizes communicative opportunities in the social environment for comprehensible input and context-embedded instruction in order to make the core curriculum accessible to students.

**Simultaneous bilingualism:** Exposure to two or more languages before the age of three.

**Structured English immersion (SEI):** A highly structured model of immersion education that highlights an entire peer group dominant in a minority language (or languages) being instructed entirely in English, with the goal of fluency in English. Considerable controversy follows this model due to its highly structured and subtractive nature, which is unlike other immersion models.

**Submersion:** An educational environment in which learners are instructed in a second language without support or accommodation for their linguistic and academic development.

**Subtractive bilingualism:** The acquisition of a second language at the expense of the first, potentially resulting in monolingualism in the second language.

**Target language:** When used within the context of a two-way bilingual immersion program, this term refers to the minority language being used for communicative and instructional purposes.

**Teacher radar:** The realization that one does not understand the response or interaction of a student or of a group of students. This awareness should trigger the informal research process that teachers use to access information that will illuminate the situation.

**Threshold hypothesis:** Cummins's (1987) threshold hypothesis theorizes that a learner needs to attain a high level of native language proficiency to achieve a high level of proficiency in a second language, and that the attainment of high levels of bilingual language proficiency in turn paves the way for maximum academic and cognitive benefit.

**Transitional program of bilingual instruction (TPI):** The most common model for the bilingual instruction of ELLs. In such programs, students get support in native language literacy and content in decreasing amounts of time as part of a transitional process to an English-only curriculum. This process is usually complete in three years.

**Two-way bilingual immersion programs (TWI):** Sometimes referred to as dual language programs, this is a model of immersion education in which language minority and language majority students become bilingual in classrooms together, as language is learned through content with the majority of curriculum (at least initially) presented in the minority (target) language.

**Zone of proximal development (ZPD):** The distance between what a student knows and what a student can learn with the help of a knowledgeable adult. It is within this zone that students have the optimal or proximal development, and it is also where social interaction becomes the mode by which new learning occurs.

# References

Andersson, T. (1977). *A guide to family reading in two languages: The preschool years.* Los Angeles: National Clearinghouse for Bilingual Education.

Andre, C., & Velasquez, M. (1998). What Johnny should read. *Issues in Ethics, 1*(4). Retrieved April 30, 2007, from http://www.scu.edu/ethics/publications/iie/vln4/homepage.html

Baker, C. (2001). *Foundations of bilingual education and bilingualism.* New York: Multilingual Matters.

Bean, T., & Thomas, K. (2003). Developing students critical literacy: Exploring identity construction in young adult fiction. *Journal of Adolescent & Adult Literacy, 46*(8), 638–649.

Bialystok, E., Craik, F., & Freedman, M. (2007). Bilingualism as a protection against the onset of symptoms of dementia. *Neuropsychologia, 45*(2), 459–464.

Bialystok, E., & Hakuta, K. (1994). *In other words.* New York: Basic Books.

Bransford, J., Zech, L., Schwartz, D., Barron, B., Vye, N., & Cognition and Technology Group at Vanderbilt. (2000). Designs for environments that invite and sustain mathematical thinking. In P. Cobb, E. Yackel, & K. McClain (Eds.), *Symbolizing, communicating and mathematizing: Perspectives on discourse, tools, and instructional design* (pp. 225–273). Mahwah, NJ: Lawrence Erlbaum Associates.

Brisk, M. E. (1998). *Bilingual education: From compensatory to quality schooling.* Mahwah, NJ: Lawrence Erlbaum Associates, Inc.

Carleton College, Science Education Resource Center. (2006). *Starting point. A short glossary of assessment terms.* Retrieved March 23, 2007, from http://serc.carleton.edu/introgeo/assessment/glossary.html

Cavallaro, F. (2005). Language maintenance revisited: An Australian perspective. *Bilingual Research Journal, 29*(3), 561–582.

Cho, G. (2000). The role of heritage language in social interactions and relationships: Reflections from a language minority group. *Bilingual Research Journal, 24*(4), 369–384.

Cho, G., Cho, K., & Tse, L. (1997). Why ethnic minorities want to develop their heritage language: The case of Korean Americans. *Language, Culture, and Curriculum, 10*(2), 106–112.

Christian, D. (1996). Two-way immersion education: Students learning through two languages. *Modern Language Journal, 80*, 66–76.

Christian, D., Genesee, F., Lindholm-Leary, K., & Howard, L. (2004). *Project 1.2 two-way immersion final progress report.* Retrieved August 27, 2007, from http://www.cal.org/twi/CREDEfinal.doc

Christian, D., Montone, C. L., Lindholm, K. J., & Carranza, I. (1997). *Profiles in two-way immersion education.* Miller Parkway, IL: Center for Applied Linguistics and Delta Systems Co.

Collier, V. P. (1989). How long? A synthesis of research on academic achievement in a second language. *TESOL Quarterly, 23*(3), 509–531.

Core Knowledge Foundation. (1999). *Core knowledge sequence content for grades K-8.* Charlottesville, VA: Author.

Crawford, J. (2004). *Educating English language learners.* Los Angeles: Bilingual Educational Services.

Cronin, D. (2000). *Click, clack, moo cows that type.* New York: Simon & Schuster.

Cummins, J. (1978). Bilingualism and the development of metalinguistic awareness. *Journal of Cross-Cultural Psychology, 9,* 131–149.

Cummins, J. (1981). The role of primary language development in promoting educational success for language minority students. In California State Department of Education (Ed.), *Schooling and language minority students: A theoretical framework* (pp. 3–49). Los Angeles: Evaluation, Dissemination, and Assessment Center, California State University.

Cummins, J. (1987). Bilingualism, language proficiency, and metalinguistic development. In D. Aaronson, P. Homel, & M. Palij (Eds.), *Childhood bilingualism: Aspects of linguistic, cognitive and social development* (pp. 197–221). Hillsdale, NJ: Laurence Erlbaum Associates.

Cummins, J. (1994). Primary language instruction and the education of language minority students. In California State Department of Education (Ed.), *Schooling and language minority students: A theoretical framework* (2nd ed., pp. 3–46). Los Angeles: Evaluation, Dissemination and Assessment Center, California State University.

Cummins, J. (2000). *Language, power, and pedagogy: Bilingual children in the crossfire.* Clevedon, UK: Multilingual Matters.

Daniels, H. (2002). *Literature circles voice & choice in the student centered classroom.* York, ME: Stenhouse.

Darder, A., Baltodano, M., & Torres, R. (2003). *The critical pedagogy reader.* New York: Routledge Falmer.

de Jong, E. (2006). Integrated bilingual education: An alternative approach. *Bilingual Research Journal, 30*(1), 23–44.

deKock, A., Sleegers, P., & Voeten, M. (2004). New learning and the classification of learning environments in secondary education. *Review of Educational Research, 74*(2), 141–170.

Dewey, J. (1916). *Democracy and education: An introduction to the philosophy of education.* New York: The MacMillan Company.

Diaz, R. M. (1983). Thought and two languages: The impact of bilingualism on cognitive development. In E. W. Gordon (Ed.), *Review of research in education* (No. 10). Washington, DC: AERA.

Diller, J. V., & Moule, J. (2005). *Cultural competence: A primer for educators.* Belmont, CA: Thomson Wadsworth.

Dinkha, J. I. (2000). *The psychological effect of immigration on Arab-American adolescents: A review and case study.* Unpublished doctoral dissertation, Illinois School of Professional Psychology, Chicago.

Espinoza-Herold, M. (2003). *Issues in Latino education race, school culture and the politics of academic success.* New York: Pearson Education Group.

Feuerstein, R. (1980). *Instrumental enrichment: An intervention program for cognitive modifiability*. Baltimore: University Park Press.

Feuerverger, G. (1991). University students' perceptions of heritage language learning and ethnic identity maintenance. *Canadian Modern Language Review, 47*(4), 660–677.

Finn, P. (1999). *Literacy with an attitude*. New York: State University of New York.

Fosnot, C. T. (Ed.). (1996). *Constructivism: Theory, perspectives, and practice*. New York: Teachers College Press.

Freeman, Y. S., & Freeman, D. E. (2002). *Closing the achievement gap: How to reach limited-formal-schooling and long-term English learners*. Portsmouth, NH: Heinemann.

Freire, P. (1970). *Pedagogy of the oppressed*. New York: The Continuum International Publishing Group, Inc.

Freire, P. (1998). *Pedagogy of freedom: Ethics, democracy, and civic courage*. New York: Rowman & Littlefield Publishers, Inc.

Freire, P., & Macedo, D. (1987). *Literacy: Reading the word and the world*. South Hadley, MA: Bergin & Harvey.

Freire, P., & Macedo, D. (1995). A dialogue: Culture, language, and race. *Harvard Educational Review, 65*(3), 377–402.

Giroux, H. (1988). *Teachers as intellectuals*. Granby, MA: Bergin & Garvey Publishers Inc.

Gottlieb, M. (2006). *Assessing English language learners: Bridges from language proficiency to academic achievement*. Thousand Oaks, CA: Corwin Press.

Hakuta, K. (1986). *Mirror of language*. New York: Basic Books.

Hamers, J. F., & Blanc, M. H. A. (1992). *Bilinguality and bilingualism*. New York: Cambridge University Press.

Hawkins, M. R. (2005). Becoming a student: Identity work and academic literacies in early schooling. *TESOL Quarterly, 39*(1), 59–81.

Herrera, S. G., Murry, K. G., & Morales Cabral, R. (2007). *Assessment accommodations for classroom teachers of culturally and linguistically diverse students*. Boston: Pearson Education Inc.

Howard, E. R., Sugarman, J., & Christian, D. (2003). *Trends in two-way immersion education: A review of the research* (Report No. 63). Baltimore: Center for Research on the Education of Students Placed at Risk. Retrieved August 27, 2007, from http://www.csos.jhu.edu/crepar/techReports/Report63.pdf

Hruska, B. (2000). *Bilingualism, gender, and friendship: Constructing second language learners in an English language dominant classroom*. Paper presented at the annual meeting of the American Association of Applied Linguistics. Retrieved January 5, 2006, from ERIC.

Jesness, J. (2004). *Teaching English language learners K-12: A quick-start guide to the new teacher*. Thousand Oaks, CA: Corwin Press.

Joyce, B., Weil, M., & Calhoun, E. (2004). *Models of teaching* (7th ed.). New York: Allyn & Bacon.

Katz, P. A. (1982). *Development of children's racial awareness and intergroup attitudes* (Report No. PS 012 321). Norwood, NJ: Ablex Publishing Corporation. (ERIC Document Reproduction Services No. ED 207 675)

Knight, J. (2002). Crossing boundaries: What constructivists can teach intensive-explicit instructors and vice versa. *Focus on Exceptional Children, 35*(4), 1–14.

Kohn, A. (2004). *What does it mean to be well educated?* Boston: Beacon Press.

Krashen, S. D. (1982). *Principles and practice in second language acquisition.* New York: Pergamon Press.

Ladon-Billings, G. (2006). From the achievement gap to the education debt: Understanding achievement in U.S. schools. *Educational Researcher, 35*(7), 3–12.

Lessow-Hurley, J. (2005). *The foundations of dual language instruction.* New York: Longman.

Lindholm, K. (1992). Two-way bilingualism/immersion education: Theory, conceptual issues, and pedagogical implications. In A. Benavides & V. Padilla (Eds.), *Critical perspectives on bilingual education.* Tempe, AZ: Bilingual Press.

McKay, S. L., & Wong, S. L. C. (1996). Multiple discourse, multiple identities: Investment and agency in second-language learning among Chinese adolescent immigrant students. *Harvard Educational Review, 66*(3), 577–608.

McLaren, P. (2003). *Life in schools: An introduction to critical pedagogy in the foundations of education.* New York: Allyn & Bacon.

McLaughlin, B., Blanchard, A. G., & Osani, Y. (1995). *Assessing language development in bilingual preschool children.* Rosslyn, VA: Clearinghouse for Bilingual Education.

Moll, L. C., Amanti, C., Neff, D., & Gonzalez, N. (1992). Funds of knowledge for teaching: Using a qualitative approach to connect homes and classrooms. *Theory Into Practice, 31*(2), 132–141.

Morgan, G. (1982). Yes! We should have bilingual immersion programs. *Interchange on Educational Policy, 13*(2), 44–49.

Mueller, J. (2006). *Authentic assessment toolbox.* Retrieved March 23, 2007, from http://jonathan.mueller.faculty.noctrl.edu/toolbox/whatisit.htmn

National Research Council. (2005). *How people learn: Brain, mind, experience, school.* Washington, DC: National Academy Press.

National Teacher Recruitment Clearing House. (2003). Retrieved August 3, 2004, from http://www.recruitingteachers.org

Nieto, S. (2004). *Affirming diversity: The sociopolitical context of multicultural education.* New York: Pearson Education, Inc.

O'Brien, J. (2001). Negotiating critical literacies in the classroom. In B. Comber & A. Simpson (Eds.), *Children reading critically: A local history* (pp. 37–54). New Jersey: Lawrence Erlbaum Associates, Inc.

Ocampo, K. A., Knight, G. P., & Bernal, M. E. (1997). The development of cognitive abilities and social identities in children: The case of ethnic identity. *International Journal of Behavioral Development, 21*(3), 479–500.

Olmedo, I. M. (1993). Junior historians: Doing oral history with ESL and bilingual students. *TESOL Journal, 2*(4), 7–10.

Olmedo, I. M. (2006). Creating contexts for studying history with students learning English. In B. Lanman & L. Wendling (Eds.), *Preparing the next generation of oral historians: An anthology of oral history education.* Lanham, MD: Rowman & Littlefield.

O'Malley, J. M., & Valdez Pierce, L. (1996). *Authentic assessment for English language learners: Practical approaches for teachers.* Reading, MA: Addison-Wesley Publishing Company.

Ovando, C., Collier, B., & Combs, M. C. (2006). *Bilingual & ESL classrooms: Teaching in multicultural contexts.* New York: McGraw-Hill.

Partin, R. (2003). *The social studies teacher's book of lists* (2nd ed.). San Francisco, CA: Jossey-Bass.

Peregoy, S. F., & Boyle, O. F. (2005). *Reading, writing, and learning in ESL.* New York: Longman.

Perez, B., & Torres-Guzman, M. (2002). *Learning in two worlds.* Boston: Allyn & Bacon.

Piaget, J. (1952). *The origins of intelligence in children* (M. Cook, Trans.). New York: International Universities Press.

Reiss, J. (2008). *102 content strategies for English language learners teaching for academic success.* Upper Saddle River, NJ: Pearson/Merrill/Prentice Hall.

Reyes, S. A. (1998*). "!Mami, yo toque una mariposa!": An alternative to linguistic and cultural loss.* Unpublished doctoral dissertation, University of Illinois, Chicago.

Reyes, S. A., & Vallone, T. L. (2007). Toward an expanded understanding of two-way bilingual immersion education: Constructing identity through a critical, additive, bilingual/bicultural pedagogy. *Multicultural Perspectives, 9*(3), 3–11.

Roe, B., Smith, S., & Burns, P. (2005). *Teaching reading in today's elementary schools.* New York: Houghton Mifflin Company.

Rolstad, K., Mahoney, K., & Glass, G. (2005). The big picture: A meta-analysis of program effectiveness research on English language learners. *Educational Policy, 19*(4), 572–594.

Saville-Troike, M. (1981). *Bilingual children: A resource document.* Arlington, VA: The Center for Applied Linguistics.

Slavin, R., & Cheung, A. (2005). A synthesis of research on language of reading instruction for English language learners. *Review of Educational Research, 75*(2), 247–284.

Smerdon, B., Burkam, D., & Lee, V. (1999). Access to constructivist and didactic teaching: Who gets it? Where is it practiced? *Teachers College Record, 101*(1), 5–34.

Tomlinson-Clarke, S. (2001). *Good guy don't wear hats: Children's talk about the media.* New York: Teachers College Press.

Tse, L. (1997). Affecting affect: The impact of ethnic language programs on student attitudes. *Canadian Modern Language Review, 53*(4), 705–728.

U.S. Department of Education, National Center for Education Statistics (NCES). (2007). *The Condition of Education 2007* (NCES 2007-064). Washington, DC: U.S. Government Printing Office. Also available at http://nces.ed.gov/programs/coe/2007/pdf/06_2007.pdf

Van Groenou, M. (1993). Interaction between bilingualism and cognitive growth. *Montessori Life, 5*(1), 33–35.

von Glasersfeld, E. (1989). Cognition, construction of knowledge, and teaching. *Synthese, 80*(1), 121–140.

Vygotsky, L. S. (1978). *Mind in society.* Cambridge, MA: Harvard University Press.

White, E. B. (1952). *Charlotte's web.* New York: HarperCollins.

Whitmore, K. F., & Crowell, C. G. (1994). *Inventing a classroom: Life in a bilingual, whole language learning community.* York, ME: Stenhouse Publishers.

Wiesner, D. (1991). *Tuesday.* New York: Clarion Books.

Windschitl, M. (2002). Framing constructivism in practice as the negotiation of dilemmas: An analysis of the conceptual, pedagogical, cultural and political challenges facing teachers. *Review of Educational Research, 72*(2), 131–175.

Wink, J. (2000). *Critical pedagogy notes from the real world.* New York: Addison-Wesley Longman Inc.

Wink, J., & Putney, L. G. (2002). *A vision of Vygotsky.* Boston: Allyn & Bacon.

Wong, P. C. M., Skoe, E., Russo, N. M., Dees, T., & Kraus, N. (2007). Musical experience shapes human brainstem encoding of linguistic pitch patterns. *Nature Neuroscience, 10,* 420–422.

Wong Fillmore, L. (1991). When learning a second language means losing the first. *Early Childhood Research Quarterly, 6,* 323–346.

Zentella, A. C. (2005). *Building on strength: Language and literacy in Latino families and communities.* New York: Teachers College Press.

# Index

Academic content, language
and, 7–9, 135–165
Acquisition, language, 2–5, 135–165
Additive, definition of, 177
Additive and subtractive models, 16–17
Additive bilingualism, 177
Additive models, 16–17
Affective filter
defined, 177
linguistic self-consciousness, 8
lowering, 8, 9, 47, 55, 56, 76
raising, 58
Amanti, C., 13, 41
Andersson, T., 2
Andre, C., 70, 72, 73
*Assessing English Language Learners*
(Gottlieb), 58
Authentic assessment, 41, 54, 58, 59–60, 177

Baker, C., 11
Basic Interpersonal Communicative Skills
(BICS), 3, 6, 115, 147, 177
Bean, T., 79
Bernal, M. E., 10
Bialystok, E., 7, 9
BICS (Basic Interpersonal Communicative
Skills), 3, 6, 115, 147, 177
Bilingualism
bilingual whole language community
program models, 26
immersion education and,
102–103
sequential, 3, 4, 51, 179
simultaneous, 3–4, 97, 179
Bilingual whole language community,
program models and, 26
Blanc, M. H. A., 10
Blanchard, A. G., 3
Boyle, O. F., 40, 53, 55

Bransford, J., 8, 39
Brisk, M. E., 25
Burkam, D., 28
Burns, P., 44

Calhoun, E., 48
CALP (Cognitive/Academic Language
Proficiency), 3, 6, 115, 147, 177
Carleton College, Science Education
Resource Center, 59
Carranza, I., 22
Cavallaro, F., 11
Cheung, A., 5
Cho, G., 11
Cho, K., 11
Christian, D., 22, 102
*Closing the Achievement Gap*
(Freeman & Freeman), 109–110
Code switching, 94, 177
Codification, 77, 177
Codifying, 155, 177
Cognates, 54, 177
Cognitive/Academic Language Proficiency
(CALP), 3, 6, 115, 147, 177
Cognitive constructivism, 31–33
Cognitive development, language and, 5–7
Collier, B., 10
Collier, V. P., 2, 6
Combs, M. C., 10
Communities
bilingual whole language community
program models, 26
constructivist practices and, 41–42
Comprehensible experience, 55, 56, 177
Comprehensible input
academic content and, 8, 9
content areas instruction
practices and, 53, 54
defined, 40, 177

immersion education and, 22, 23
language arts and, 46
Comprehensible input hypothesis, 177
Comprehensible output, 9, 53, 177
Conscientization, 77, 177
Constructivism
cognitive constructivism, 31–33
defined, 29, 177
overview, 31
social constructivism, 31, 33–35, 36
Constructivist curriculum
activities and, 61–63
assessment and, 58–61
bilingualism and, 102–103
content areas and, 53–57
critical perspectives and, 165
cross-cultural attitudes and, 104–105
described, 29–31
ELLs and, 39–41
engaging students in learning and,
103–104
families/communities and, 41–42
guidelines for practices,
102–105, 132–136
guiding principles for, 35–38
guiding principles for constructivist
curriculum, 35–38
immersion education and, 81–83
Iraqi students and, 107–110, 169
language arts and, 42–52
self-contained immersion classes for
Iraqi students and, 105, 110–132
traditional curriculum vs., 27–29
TWI and, 40
Content areas instructional practices
cooperative learning strategy, 54
embedding content area studies, 55–56
immigration and, 135–165
Iraqi students and, 109
molding and think-aloud
strategy, 53
oral history activities, 56–57, 173–175
problem solving activities, 56
social studies activities, 57, 135–165
Think Pair Share strategy, 53
vocabulary building activities, 54–55
Context-embedded instruction, 8, 9, 103, 177
Cooperative learning strategy, 54
Core Knowledge Foundation, 67
Craik, F., 7
Crawford, J., x
Critical Constructivist Education
for ELLs, 167–171
Critical pedagogy

defined, 178
guiding principles, 73–78
identity formation and, 79
purpose of, 65–66
Critical perspectives, constructivist
curriculum and, 165
Cronin, D., 44
Crowell, C. G., 26
Cultural Literacy: What Every American
Needs to Know (Hirsch), 69
Culturally responsive pedagogy
constructivism and, 12, 169
critical constructivism and, 171
defined, x, 178
equity and, xi
ESL and, 19–20
guidelines, 13
models and, 16
quality education and, xi
SEI and, 24
teachers and, 17, 26
Culturally sensitive pedagogy, 21, 178
Culture, language and, 9–13
Cummins, J., 2, 3, 6, 8, 16, 20, 22, 39, 178

Darder, A., 77, 78
Dees, T., 4
De Jong, E., 25
DeKock, A., 36, 37
Democracy, ELLs and, vii, xii–xiii
Democracy and Education (Dewey), xii
Dewey, J., xii
Dialogue journal, 51
Diaz, R. M., 4
Diller, J. V., 9
Dinkha, J. I., 10
Disequilibrium, 32, 35, 37, 178.
See also Equilibrium

ELLs (English language learners), 178
Embedding content area studies, 55–56
Emergent literacy, 42, 57, 95, 178
English as a Second Language (ESL),
17–20, 178
English language learners (ELLs), 178
Enrichment model, 25, 178
Equilibrium, 31–33, 178. See also
Disequilibrium
Equity, educational, vii–ix, x–xiii,
168–172
ESL (English as a Second
Language), 17–20, 178
Espinoza-Herold, M., 79
Ethnic identity, 9, 10–11, 13

Families/communities, constructivist
    practices and, 41–42
Feuerstein, R., xi
Feuerverger, G., 11
Finn, P., 78
First language (L1), 5, 178
Fosnot, C. T., 31, 33
Freedman, M., 7
Freeman, D. E., 109, 110
Freeman, Y. S., 109, 110
Freire, P., 73, 74, 75, 78
Funds of knowledge, 13, 41, 178

Genesee, F., 22
Giroux, H., 74, 78
Glass, G., 5
Gonzalez, N., 13, 41
Gottlieb, M., 58
The Great Second-Grad Bug Invasion unit,
    83–102, 169

Hakuta, K., 2, 4, 6, 9
Hamers, J. F., 10
Hawkins, M. R., 11
Hegemonies, 77–78, 178
Herrera, S. G., 59
Hirsch, E. D., 69–70, 72, 78
Howard, E. R., 22
Howard, L., 22
*How People Learn* (NRC), 27
Hruska, B., 34

Identity formation, critical
    pedagogy and, 79
Immersion education. *See also*
    Self-contained immersion classes
    bilingualism and, 102–103
    comprehensible input and, 22, 23
    consistency across grade levels and, 83
    constructivist curriculum and, 81–83
    content and, 82
    cross-cultural attitudes and, 104–105
    defined, 178
    described, 21–24
    engaging students in learning and,
        103–104
    The Great Second-Grad Bug Invasion
        unit, 83–102
    motivation and, 82
    program models, 21–24
    SEI, 24
    submersion vs., 21, 81
    teachers'/students' roles and, 82
    TWI and, 82–83

Immigration content curriculum, 135–165
Informal reading inventories, 35
Integrated model, 24, 178
Interdependence hypothesis, 6, 178
Iraqi students
    constructivist curriculum
        and, 107–110, 169
    content areas instructional
        practices and, 109
    self-contained immersion
        classes for, 105, 110–132
    Western thought paradigm and, 108

Jesness, J., 55
Joyce, B., 48

Katz, P. A., 10
Knight, G. P., 10
Knight, J., 27, 31, 32
Kohn, A., 36
Krashen, S. D., 117
Kraus, N., 4

L1 (first language), 5, 178
L2 (second language), 5, 178
Language arts, 42–52
Language maintenance, 20, 24, 178
Language minority/majority students,
    effects of TWI on, 82–83
Learning disabilities, Iraqi
    students and, 108
Lee, V., 28
Lessow-Hurley, J., 8, 9, 22, 25, 26
Lindholm, K., 5, 22
Lindholm, K. J., 22
Lindholm-Leary, K., 22
Linguistically sensitive pedagogy, 21, 178
Linguistic self-consciousness
    (affective filter), 8
Lisa enters first grade story, ix–x

Macedo, D., 74, 75
Mahoney, K., 5
Mainstream with curriculum modifications,
    program models and, 17
McKay, S. L., 11
McLaren, P., 65, 78
McLaughlin, B., 3
*Merriam-Webster's* dictionary, xii
Metalinguistic awareness, 5, 10, 178
Molding and think-aloud strategy, 53
Moll, L. C., 13, 41
Montone, C. L., 22
Morales Cabral, R., 59

Morgan, G., 82
Motherese, 22, 82, 178
Moule, J., 9
Mueller, J., 58, 59
Murry, K. G., 59

National Research Council, 27
National Teacher Recruitment
   Clearing House, vii
Native language, 5, 178
Native language maintenance
   component, 20
NCES (U.S. Department of Education,
   National Center for Education
   Statistics), vii
Neff, D., 13, 41
Newcomer programs, 25–26
Nieto, S., x, 13, 42, 78

O'Brien, J., 79
Ocampo, K. A., 10
Olmedo, I. M, 56
O'Malley, J. M., 59
Oral history activities, 56–57, 173–175
Osani, Y., 3
Ovando, C., 10, 24

Partin, R., 68, 69
*Pedagogy of Freedom: Ethics, Democracy
   and Civic Courage* (Freire), 73
*Pedagogy of the Oppressed* (Freire), 66
Peregoy, S. F., 40, 53, 55
Perez, B., 2
Perturbation, 32, 179
Piaget, J., 31
Praxis, 78, 157, 179
Problem posing, 77, 136, 150, 179
Problem solving activities
   constructivist curriculum and,
      37, 62, 136
   content areas instructional practices
      and, 56
   critical pedagogy and, 77
   language arts and, 44, 45
Program models
   additive and subtractive, 16–17
   bilingual whole language
      community and, 26
   enrichment and, 25
   ESL, 17–20
   immersion education, 21–24
   mainstream with curriculum
      modifications, 17

native language maintenance
   component and, 20
newcomer programs, 25–26
structured English immersion
   (SEI), 24
submersion programs and, 20–21
TPI, 20, 179–180
Putney, L. G., 33, 34

Questionnaire for Use in
   Classroom-Based Oral History
   Project, 173–175

Reiss, J., 58
Reyes, S. A., 2
Robert's ordinary experiences,
   critical pedagogy and, 70–72
Roe, B., 44
Rolstad, K., 5
Russo, N. M., 4

Saville-Troike, M., 4, 82
Scaffolding
   constructivist curriculum and,
      82, 100, 115, 117, 128
   content areas instructional practices
      and, 9, 53, 54
   culture and, 9
   defined, 8, 178
   language arts and, 44, 45, 49, 51
   social constructivism and, 34
Second language (L2), 5, 178
Second language acquisition/learning.
   *See also* Acquisition, language
   curriculum and, 1, 8, 39
   L1 and, 5
   language arts and, 47, 48
   second language learning vs., 4
SEI (structured English immersion),
   24, 179
Self-contained immersion classes,
   Iraqi students and, 105, 110–132
Self-contained immersion education,
   105, 110, 132
Sequential bilingualism,
   3, 4, 51, 179
Sharon's dinner story, viii–ix
Sheltered instruction
   constructivist curriculum and, 39–40
   content areas instructional
      practices and, 54
   culture and, 9
   defined, 179

immersion education and, 21, 22, 23
  L2 and, 82
  language arts and, 47
Sheltered instruction modifications, 9, 39–40
Simultaneous bilingualism, 3–4, 97, 179
Skoe, E., 4
Slavin, R., 5
Smerdon, B., 28
Smith, S., 44
Social constructivism, 31, 33–35, 36
Social studies activities, 57, 135–165
Structured English immersion
  (SEI), 24, 179
Students, immersion education
  and roles of, 82
Submersion programs
  described, 20–21, 26, 82, 179
  ESL and, 18, 19
  immersion education vs., 21, 81
  mainstream with modification and, 17
Subtractive bilingualism,
  16, 20, 21, 179
Subtractive models, 16–17
Sugarman, J., 22

Target language
  acquisition and, 4
  constructivist curriculum and,
    81–84, 87, 90, 97
  defined, 179
Teachers
  culturally responsive pedagogy
    and, 17, 26
  immersion education, and roles of, 82
  teacher radar, 13, 42, 179
Think Pair Share strategy, 53
Thomas, K., 79
Threshold hypothesis, 6, 179
Tomlinson-Clarke, S., 13
Torres-Guzman, M., 2
TPI (transitional program of bilingual
  instruction), 20, 179–180
Traditional curriculum vs. constructivist
  curriculum, 27–29
Transitional program of bilingual
  instruction (TPI), 20, 179–180
Trina's ordinary experiences,
  critical pedagogy and, 66–70
Tse, L., 11
TWI. *See* Two-way bilingual
  immersion (TWI)
Two-way bilingual immersion (TWI)
  academic content and, 7

constructivist curriculum and, 40
goals of, 84
The Great Second-Grad Bug
  Invasion unit, 83–102, 169
immersion education and, 22
integrated model and, 24
language minority/majority
  students, and effects
  of, 82–83
promotion of bilingualism
  and, 102
schools and, 169

UDL (Universal Design for Learning),
  171–172
Universal Design for Learning (UDL),
  171–172
U.S. Census Bureau, vii
U.S. Department of Education,
  National Center for Education
  Statistics (NCES), vii

Valdez Pierce, L., 59
Van Groenou, M., 5
Velasquez, M., 70, 72, 73
Vocabulary building
  activities, 54–55
Von Glasersfeld, E., 32
Vygotsky, L. S., 9, 33, 117

Weil, M., 48
Western thought paradigm,
  Iraqi students and, 108
White, E. B., 51
Whitmore, K. F., 26
Wiesner, D., 44
Windschitl, M., 31
Wink, J., 33, 34, 74, 77, 78, 136
Wong, P. C. M., 4
Wong, S. L. C., 11
Wong Fillmore, L., xi, 12

Zentella, A. C., 41, 42
Zone of proximal
  development (ZPD)
  assessments and, 59
  cognitive constructivism and, 32
  constructivist curriculum and,
    37, 108, 115, 117, 127, 129
  culture and, 9
  defined, 9, 180
  language arts and, 45
  social constructivism and, 34–35

**CORWIN PRESS**

The Corwin Press logo—a raven striding across an open book—represents the union of courage and learning. Corwin Press is committed to improving education for all learners by publishing books and other professional development resources for those serving the field of PreK–12 education. By providing practical, hands-on materials, Corwin Press continues to carry out the promise of its motto: **"Helping Educators Do Their Work Better."**